MODERN GREECE

WHAT EVERYONE NEEDS TO KNOW®

MODERN GREECE

WHAT EVERYONE NEEDS TO KNOW®

STATHIS N. KALYVAS

OXFORD
UNIVERSITY PRESS

OXFORD
UNIVERSITY PRESS

Oxford University Press is a department of the University of
Oxford. It furthers the University's objective of excellence in research,
scholarship, and education by publishing worldwide.

Oxford New York
Auckland Cape Town Dar es Salaam Hong Kong Karachi
Kuala Lumpur Madrid Melbourne Mexico City Nairobi
New Delhi Shanghai Taipei Toronto

With offices in
Argentina Austria Brazil Chile Czech Republic France Greece
Guatemala Hungary Italy Japan Poland Portugal Singapore
South Korea Switzerland Thailand Turkey Ukraine Vietnam

Oxford is a registered trademark of Oxford University Press
in the UK and certain other countries.

Published in the United States of America by
Oxford University Press
198 Madison Avenue, New York, NY 10016

Cataloging-in-Publication data is on file at the Library of Congress
ISBN 978–0–19–994877–2 (hbk.); 978–0–19–994879–6 (pbk.)

3 5 7 9 8 6 4
Printed in Canada
on acid-free paper

Maybe sometimes—the wrong way is the right way? You can take the wrong path and it still comes out where you want to be? Or, spin it another way, sometimes you can do everything wrong and it still turns out to be right?

Donna Tartt, *The Goldfinch*

CONTENTS

III   Building   37

IV   Turmoil   69

V Takeoff   101

VI   The Great Crisis   153

VII   Future   195

ACKNOWLEDGMENTS

I did not set out to write a history book, much less a comprehensive and detailed one. What I have sought to do instead is produce an essay of historical interpretation. Being Greek, I have been fascinated and puzzled in equal measure by Greece's historical trajectory. I sought to understand where Greece came from, why it evolved the way it did, and how its story speaks to broader themes. Obviously, interpretations require facts, and so this book includes an overview of Greece's modern history, yet always with an eye toward showcasing key processes and drawing general insights, while avoiding too many details, dates, and proper names.

I must confess that I did not imagine I would be writing such a book. But the crisis that hit Greece in 2009, which brought with it a very real possibility of implosion, overshadowed everything else. I wanted to understand why, hence the crisis occupies a significant part of this book. However, this is not a book about the crisis, but one that asks how the crisis fits into Greek history—and how the past helps make sense of the present—and vice-versa.

I am grateful to Oxford University Press's editor Dave McBride for suggesting the idea and for his patience as I was struggling with material that proved more complex than I had expected in the first place. Many people helped me in the course of this endeavor, in ways both direct and indirect, through countless conversations and exhanges. They are too many to name, and I am grateful to all. I wish to single out Dimitris Pipinis for his able research assistance and Alexis Patelis, Manolis Galenianos, Bill Gianopulos, and Angelos Papadimitriou for a close reading of early versions and excellent comments. The Hellenic Studies Program at Yale provided constant motivation. Last, I also wish to acknowledge the opportunity to write a biweekly column in the Greek daily *Kathimerini*, the result of Alexis Papahelas's persuasion skills. Every second Sunday since 2009 I have had the chance, along with an unforgiving deadline, of reflecting, honing, writing, and "test-driving" in a demanding public arena some of the ideas that ended up in this book. My work is all the better for this.

As always, I am deeply indebted to my loved ones for their patience, encouragement, and all the beautiful things they bring to my life.

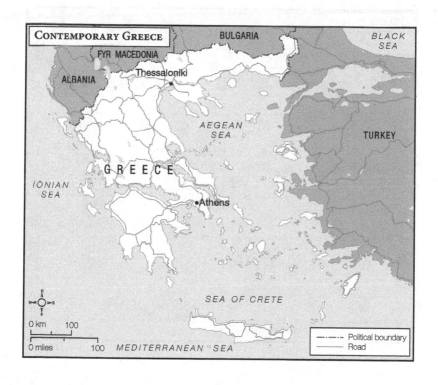

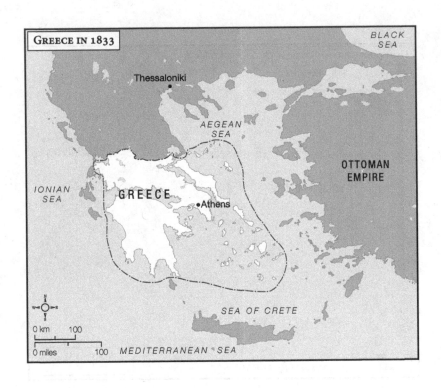

GREECE IN 1833

BLACK SEA

Thessaloniki

AEGEAN SEA

OTTOMAN EMPIRE

IONIAN SEA

GREECE

Athens

N
W—O—E
S

0 km   100

0 miles   100

SEA OF CRETE

MEDITERRANEAN SEA

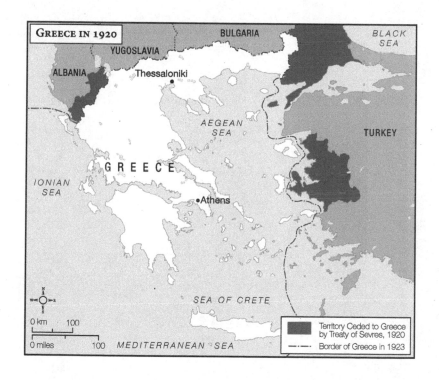

GREECE IN 1920

BULGARIA

BLACK SEA

YUGOSLAVIA

ALBANIA

Thessaloniki

AEGEAN SEA

TURKEY

GREECE

IONIAN SEA

•Athens

SEA OF CRETE

0 km   100

0 miles   100

MEDITERRANEAN SEA

Territory Ceded to Greece by Treaty of Sevres, 1920

Border of Greece in 1923

MODERN GREECE

WHAT EVERYONE NEEDS TO KNOW®

I

WHAT IS GREECE?

What is this book about?

This is an attempt to make sense of the modern history of Greece. Using the term "modern Greece" is common practice in English, implying a sharp contrast between a contemporary society and its ancient antecedent, often called simply "Greece." Greeks, however, do not use this term, calling instead their country by its ancient name *Hellas* and themselves *Hellenes*. As we will see, these contrasting designations of the country and its inhabitants imply important matters of identity and history.

As a Greek, I have always heeded the adage of the historian and author of *Imagining the Balkans* Maria Todorova and have loved Greece without a need to be either proud or ashamed of it. Hence, I have tried to combine an outsider's detached, dispassionate gaze with an insider's insight. As a comparative political scientist, I am also hardwired to search for angles and dimensions that connect the specific to the general. Therefore, this is also a story about broad themes such as nationalism, state building, civil war, autocracy and democracy, polarization, populist politics, and, above all else, the process of modernization.[1]

The book's central theme argues that Greece is an unlikely trailblazer, a very early "late modernizer," whose history foreshadowed key trends in world politics. Greece launched ambitious projects of state building, democratization, and economic development that augured those of many developing nations. Its experience brings into sharp focus the challenges of transplanting Western institutions in non-Western lands and offers a condensed preview of the trials and tribulations of the developing world's quest to achieve modernity, a term alluding to practices and institutions whose adoption is associated with the success of Western Europe in achieving political predominance and economic prosperity.

But Greece is not just a trailblazer. Despite many flaws, its pursuit of modernity has been largely successful. Writing in 1978, William H. McNeill observed, "If satisfaction of human wants and aspirations is taken as the criterion, then the development of Greece across the last thirty years must be viewed as an extraordinary success story. Things that seemed impossible in 1945 have in fact come true for millions of individual Greeks." He went on to conclude, "The metamorphosis of human life that has been taking place is without historic parallel in Greece's past. It has affected the entire population within a single generation."[2]

To describe Greece as a success is bound to raise eyebrows, particularly in the current context. In fact, Greek history is characterized by a stark contradiction. On the one hand, its history is full of major, almost epic, disasters, of which the 2009 crisis is only the latest one. On the other, this is a country that has also succeeded in gaining entry into the exclusive club of the world's most prosperous democracies. Despite the current crisis, it remains the most prosperous country in its region, and its inhabitants continue to enjoy an enviable quality of life by global standards. Unlike most late modernizers, Greece is a successful one.

In endeavoring to resolve this contradiction between failure and success, I have identified a key recurring pattern in the course of Greek history, namely a succession of peculiar boom and bust cycles. These cycles begin with highly ambitious projects and produce in turn disastrous failures, extensive foreign bailouts, and ultimately positive outcomes. Obviously, I am aware of the intrinsic tendency to see patterns where none may exist. Yet, I argue, the evidence is compelling, as I hope this book will demonstrate.

Why Greece now?

In 2010 Greece found that it was no longer able to borrow from financial markets in order to service its huge debt, triggering a global financial crisis. Suddenly, the country commanded the type of outsize attention that was traditionally reserved, at least in more academic quarters, to its ancient counterpart. This time around, most analysts and observers had no interest in Greece's ancient legacy, although they still felt compelled to draw on it in order to come up with half-clever puns, an art perfected by the *Economist* in headlines on its covers: "The Greek Run," "Europe's Achilles' Heel," or the hackneyed "Acropolis Now!"

This tongue-in-cheek approach may have been dubious, but the alarm was very real. Details of the crisis that hit Greece read like a collection of horrible world records. At a cost of over €270 billion, Greece was the recipient of the most expensive financial rescue of a country ever, as well as the largest adjustment program implemented by the International Monetary Fund (IMF) in its entire history. This program, known officially as the "Memorandum of Economic and Financial Policies" (MEFP), was one of the least successful IMF programs in terms of the relationship between its projections and results. In fact, only the bottom one percent of all IMF programs has performed as badly. Moreover, the Greek crisis led to the largest fiscal adjustment and the largest debt write-down in modern history, as well as the first one implemented by a European country since the end of World War II. Greece's crisis threatened to destroy the common European currency and forced the European Union to undertake a painful ongoing reform of its core institutions. "When the history of the eurozone crisis is written," the *Financial Times* pointed out, "the period from late 2011 through 2012 will be remembered as the months that forever changed the European project."[3]

To be sure, Greece was only part of a much broader crisis. Ireland, Portugal, and Cyprus had to be rescued as well. Spain came very close to a similar fate, while Italy and France were threatened by rising interest rates and declining credit ratings. In other words, a large slice of Europe was directly affected in ways that challenged fundamental, established economic and political certainties. The crisis impacted the Eurozone (the eighteen-member European Monetary Union) and threatened the foundations of the European Union. And this was not just a European matter; the emergency was triggered by the 2008 US subprime crisis and subsequent recession, and in turn shook the entire global financial edifice.

Still, Greece was hardly a sideshow. It was the first country to be hit and the one that was probably hit the hardest. Suddenly, political and economic developments there made the world tremble. "This is the epicenter of the world financial crisis," a *Wall Street Journal* reporter told me in Athens during the spring of 2010. He was right. Greece's experience helps bring into sharp focus dynamics and features that are at once specifically its own and also more broadly shared.

Journalists, pundits, and scholars often explain the present by selectively looking into the past. It is tempting to cherry-pick from Greece's history in order to find the causes of its present predicament—and most observers were indeed tempted. Alternatively, and perhaps more productively, it is possible to embed Greece's present into its past in order to make sense of a country that, though saddled with the adjective "modern," found modernity to be an arduous, and sometimes elusive process, yet always an overarching obsession.

This was not the first time that Greece found itself in the midst of a disaster with significant international ramifications. As in the past, this crisis was not a natural disaster befalling an unsuspecting country. Rather, it was the end result of a self-conscious decision to embark on a very ambitious project that eventually overtaxed the country's capacity. In the past, when the dust cleared, Greece almost always found that its net benefit from such ventures exceeded the cost. As a result, each cycle led Greece closer to its goal of becoming a modern European nation. To understand how this happened, we must go back to ancient history.

What is the weight of ancient Greece on the present?

As in most countries, there is a strong temptation among Greeks to stress the uniqueness of their country. The distinctive weight of ancient Greece has reinforced the tendency to assert the superior character of their country and identity. However, the contrast between this tendency toward self-aggrandizement and the shortcomings of reality has stoked a sense of insecurity and a feeling of persecution.[4]

Greece is often regarded as the cradle of Western civilization, the universally admired source of some of the greatest intellectual and artistic achievements of humanity. No wonder, then, that its symbolic weight in the world is so disproportionate to its actual size and influence. But take away this ancient legacy and what is left? Not much, it is often argued besides an allegedly corrupt and mismanaged country that somehow sneaked into the rarified world of Western Europe where it arguably never belonged.

Former president of France Valéry Giscard d'Estaing, generally seen as a good friend of Greece, captured much of the prevailing perception when he remarked in September 2012, "To be perfectly frank, it was a mistake to accept Greece. Greece simply wasn't ready. Greece is basically an Oriental country." The ambiguous location of Greece on the West/non-West spectrum is part of an old trope, one that emerged with its bid for independence at the dawn of the nineteenth century and never abated since. For example, an observer in 1911 described Greeks as "racially and geographically European . . . but also not Western . . . Oriental in a hundred ways," but with "an Orientalism that is not Asiatic, a bridge between the East and the West." Likewise, a traveler reported in 1893, "Within the last thirty years the advancement of the people and development of the resources of the country have been so rapid that we may reasonably feel confident that the Greek nation will become an important factor in Eastern civilization." Seen from a contemporary vantage point, not only is modern Greece definitively unrelated to ancient Greece, it may well be its antithesis.[5]

Even those willing to avoid this sort of orientalist judgment seem unable to find something positive within the long series of unmitigated disasters. Peter Aspden of the *Financial Times* described modern Greek history as a chain of misfortunes; and Roger Cohen of the *New York Times* painted a picture of Greece's "awful past century," replete with economic calamities, military coups, dictatorships, wars, occupations, and civil strife. Greece underperformed, this perspective suggests, simply because it always had. It just could not be expected to do better.[6]

But is this really the case? Although the disasters that befell Greece are all real, the perception of a perennially underperforming country incapable of surpassing itself is much less accurate. Most likely, this perception is an artifact emerging from the contrast between an idealized ancient Greece and its real modern version.

What have Greeks thought about themselves?

Contrasting ancient glory and modern underperformance has always been a common way to interpret Greece for Greeks and non-Greeks alike. It may be impossible to measure up to ancient Greek civilization; nonetheless, when it comes to Greece, the past is never very far from the present. Whether we look at geography and landscape or alphabet and spoken language, the startling signs of continuity between a remote past and the present are both manifest and tantalizing. No wonder then that ancient Greece looms so large in modern Greek minds.

At the core of modern Greek identity lies a powerful belief in the seamless continuity of Greek civilization from antiquity to the present. This belief was central in the ideological ferment that led to the war of independence and the emergence of the modern Greek nation. It was developed and refined during the nineteenth century by Konstantinos Paparrigopoulos in his monumental history of Greece, which linked ancient and modern Greece by moving the Byzantine Empire away from Edward Gibbon's "declining Rome" narrative and recasting it as a full-fledged part of Greek civilization. This crucial intellectual move allowed a blend of two contradictory heritages: pagan antiquity and Orthodox Christianity. Public mass education propagated this belief, which became the core of Greek identity.

Meanwhile, awareness of the distance between the achievements of ancient and modern Greece has bred considerable insecurity among Greeks, contributing to the formation of a persistently defensive posture, particularly when the link between the two is challenged. This was the case most notably when the Austrian writer Jakob Phillip Fallmerayer argued in his 1830 book *Geschichte der Halbinsel Morea während des Mittelalters* (*History of the Morea Peninsula during the Middle Age*), that the inhabitants of modern Greece were not the heirs of ancient Greece but instead were racially descended from Slavic populations who settled there during the sixth and seventh centuries A.D.

Greek identity may be based on a belief in seamless historical continuity between antiquity and present, but the exact meaning of this continuity has been a matter of persistent dispute. The British writer Patrick Leigh Fermor, an astute observer of Greece who spent most of his life there, called it the "Helleno-Romaic" dilemma, pitting the archetypal categories of Hellenes and Romioi against each other. These categories stand in for a cosmopolitan, Western-leaning, modern worldview on the one hand, and an Orthodox, Eastern-leaning, traditionalist sensibility on the other. This enduring antagonism has lurked below the surface, rarely fully articulated or explicitly politicized, but nevertheless essential for understanding Greek politics and society.[7]

Identities are not static. Greek identity has evolved in response to political and social developments. Up until the 1920s, it was built around the pursuit of irredentism and the idea that the Greek state should succeed the Ottoman Empire as a regional superpower combining Ancient Greece's symbolic reach with Byzantium's Orthodox legacy. When this dream was dashed, the country turned inwards and so was its sense of itself, until the 1950s when a feeling of optimism emerged, driven by economic development. Following the collapse of the military regime in 1974, a populist narrative succeeded it, infusing orthodox traditionalism with long-suppressed leftist rhetoric, and grafting the concept of the people onto that of the nation. Initially, this narrative had emerged in the 1940s but receded after the end of the Greek Civil War. In the following decades it was preserved and developed by Greek intellectuals. In an essay published in France in 1953, the historian Nikos Svoronos argued, "the deepest meaning of Modern Greek history can be condensed in an ancient people's painful effort to constitute itself into a modern nation, acquire a consciousness of its special character, and gain its rightful position in the modern world." He also claimed that a distinctive and central part of Greek identity was the Greek people's natural predisposition to resist constant foreign encroachment, a proposition that bestowed a heroic glow on the intrinsic Greek insecurity. What matters, however, is less the veracity of this claim and more the fact that it was incorporated into Greek identity when post-civil war certitudes collapsed along with the authoritarian regime in 1974. This narrative encouraged the spread of the belief that Greece's failures were caused by foreign meddling and that it was enough to remove it in order for the country to achieve greatness.[8]

A more recent transformation began during the prosperous years of the last decade of the twentieth century and the first decade of the twenty-first—when a new, optimistic, extroverted, and European-centered version of Greek identity timidly began to emerge. It found its most striking expression in the opening ceremony of the 2004 Summer Olympic Games in Athens, where ancient and recent history were blended in a brilliant artistic interpretation that confidently stressed present achievements as much, if not more than ancient ones. In contrast, the 2009 crisis produced an explosive blend of nationalist xenophobia, extreme right-wing radicalism and leftist populism that challenged this earlier development.

In what sense is Greece a pioneer?

Claiming Greek uniqueness makes little sense, of course. Recently however, the British historian Mark Mazower put forward an intriguing interpretation of Greek history that stresses its pioneering dimension. "For the past 200 years," he argues, "Greece has been at the forefront of Europe's evolution," where it has "paved the way for Europe's future." His observation captures the surprising tendency of Greece to surface on the global stage much more often than would be expected given its demographic, political, or economic weight. Mazower bases his claim on five chapters of Greek history. First, the Greek War of Independence in the 1820s, which "became an early symbol of escape from the prison house of empire" and introduced a "radically new combination of constitutional democracy and ethnic nationalism" that "spread across the continent, culminating in the First World War." Second, the mass population displacement of the early 1920s, which was the largest organized refugee movement in history up to that point, serving as "a model that the Nazis and others would point to later for displacing peoples in Eastern Europe, the Middle East and India." Third, the resistance to the Nazis during World War II, which was among the earliest and most visible such efforts. Fourth, the Greek Civil War, which became the "frontline of the Cold War." And, fifth, Greece's democratization in 1974, which "prefigured the global democratization wave of the 1980s and 1990s, first in South America and Southeast Asia and then in Eastern Europe."[9]

Mazower is right to point to these pioneering aspects of Greece's history, but it is harder to demonstrate that Greece has been indeed at the forefront of Europe's political evolution. A more convincing claim is that Greece often anticipates the path taken by "late modernizers." It is one of the first non-Western states (for Greece was absolutely not part of Western Europe when it emerged as an independent state), to put itself through the process of Westernization, foreshadowing the massive push toward modernization that took place during the second half of the twentieth century among postcolonial states reaching out for economic development.

The Greek state arose as a self-conscious outpost of European modernity in what may have been an illustrious place in the ancient world but was in the opening of the nineteenth century an obscure, economically backward corner of the Ottoman Empire. Greek nationalism was among the earliest to emerge on the periphery of Europe, setting the stage for the emergence of nation-states in Southeastern Europe. The War of Independence, in the 1820s, mobilized public opinion in Western Europe, motivated many Europeans to join the fight on Greece's side, and inspired what would be later termed "humanitarian interventions." Gradually, a modern state structure was erected, providing its diverse population with a cohesive identity. Greece was also instrumental in promoting irredentism in the Balkans and played a key part in the Balkan Wars of 1912–1913, which many historians consider to be the opening shot of World War I. It paid a steep price for its ambition, having to resettle a huge wave of uprooted refugees mainly from Asia Minor in 1922–1923, a humanitarian disaster prefiguring similar ones that took place in Europe following the end of World War II, in the Middle East after the creation of the State of Israel, and in the Indian subcontinent after its partition. The Greek Civil War presaged the "proxy wars" of the Cold War and triggered active US involvement in global affairs through the Truman Doctrine, signaling America's changing international role and its transformation into a superpower. Greece's postwar economic takeoff was a striking demonstration of a country's capacity to lift itself out of poverty. The democratic transition of 1974 announced the velvet revolutions of the democratic "Third Wave," spurring legal innovation in human rights prosecutions and transitional justice. Greece spearheaded the enlargement of European integration for countries outside the core of Europe, a process that helped transform the European Common Market into today's expansive European Union. Greece went on to adopt the common European currency early on, and initially profited before stumbling badly. The 2009 crisis rippled through Europe and the world, forcing a painful and ongoing process of reform within the European Union.

In short, Greece became involved in political and social developments that eventually played out on a much bigger scale. Its history, therefore, provides insights that are much broader than what one would have normally expected.

What is Greece's lesser-known record of achievements?

Grafting Western liberal and democratic institutions on an Ottoman agrarian society was bound to be challenging. It was indeed a process peppered with many failures, which were typically followed by expressions of consternation and dismay from foreign observers. Like Giscard d'Estaing, they were often surprised when Greece failed to behave the way a proper Western state should. However, positing such an a opposition between West and East misses the point, which is that becoming Western has been Greece's supreme aspiration. This is indeed a great irony: throughout its history, there is nothing that modern Greece has aspired to more passionately than becoming modern.

By placing Greece resolutely in the East, many writers (such as Samuel Huntington, for instance) have overlooked Greece's trajectory from East to West. In doing so they have projected the country's origins onto its present. A more accurate analysis would point to the fact that Greece's record of failures is matched by an equally remarkable, if much less known, string of significant achievements.

In fact, Greece has frequently innovated, overcoming disasters and performing above expectations. It has a consistent record of punching above its weight. It was the first "new" nation to emerge out of the Ottoman Empire; and it spearheaded an early democratic revolution, ushering in a long stretch of stable parliamentary rule. Military coups did take place, but the country experienced only three relatively short breaks in democratic governance from 1864 to the present: 1922–1929, 1936–1945, and 1967–1974. Despite difficulties, democracy was sustained by an egalitarian social structure, itself the outcome of a remarkably comprehensive and successful land reform. Greece was alone among its Balkan neighbors to escape communism. Its economic takeoff in the 1950s was so impressive that it became known as the "Greek economic miracle." The 1974 transition to democracy set an example of how to peacefully exit autocracy and prosecute its leaders. Despite its current problems, Greece is a prosperous democracy, arguably the most successful post-Ottoman state.

There is perhaps no greater sign of achievement than the fact that, for all its shortcomings, Greece was seen at the dawn of the twenty-first century as a "normal" West European state. This perception may have been challenged by the 2009 crisis, but the country's global position has not significantly changed, as shown by several metrics. To cite just two, Greece placed 34th in the Economist Intelligence Unit's ranking of countries where it would be best to be born in 2013, and 35th globally in the Social Progress Index. Not bad at all, given how poor its initial prospects were.[10]

And yet, despite this remarkable trajectory, Greece has been constantly associated primarily with failure, underperformance, unfulfilled expectations, and backwardness. A well-known book published by a Greek sociologist in 1978 bears the suggestive title *Modern Greece, Facets of Underdevelopment*. Even before the 2009 crisis, Greeks had a hard time thinking of themselves as prosperous Europeans and tended to spontaneously reject this characterization almost as if it were insulting to them.[11]

How to reconcile disasters and achievements?

How can a country stumble from disaster to disaster only to find itself propelled so high in the end? The answer highlights the close association between failure and achievement. Throughout Greek history, ambitious cosmopolitan elites launched a series of grand modernizing projects that inevitably clashed with the underlying reality, overtaxing the country's human and material resources. These ambitious projects initially produced booms, but eventually (and somewhat inevitably) ended up in busts. For a number of reasons, including their trailblazing aspect and Greece's ancient legacy, these busts almost always elicited international attention and triggered an international response, usually in the form of a major foreign intervention. These interventions mitigated the fallout from the bust, while preserving many of the gains that had accrued during the boom. This sort of resolution, in turn, facilitated the transition to the next boom-bust cycle following a similar pattern. Seen from this perspective, the 2009 crisis is but the latest episode in a string of such cycles—the seventh in the country's history.

Overall then, the modern history of Greece is both general in terms of the processes it foreshadows and serves to illustrate, and specific in its capacity to achieve positive outcomes out of ambitious and often disastrous projects. In short, Greece is a case of an early, highly ambitious, creative, incomplete, and imperfect—but overall quite successful—effort by an underendowed upstart to catch up with the most advanced nations.

II

EMERGENCE

How did modern Greece come into being?

Most people see modern Greece as a successor state of ancient Greece and the last chapter in a long history going back three thousand years. Both geographic location and linguistic continuity imply a close association between modern and ancient Greece, with the Roman, Byzantine, and Ottoman eras providing the links. From this perspective, the emergence of the modern Greek state in the early nineteenth century appears almost as a natural process: a nation emerged, thrived, was conquered, and survived centuries of servitude to stage a historic comeback. This sounds compelling but, as is often the case, reality is more nuanced.

For all its shared features, the ancient Greek world was not a unified or homogeneous political and social system and it evolved in complex ways during late antiquity. The Byzantine Empire emerged from Rome, from where it drew its organization and legitimacy. Its culture was derived from Christianity, language from Greece, and power from its wealthy Anatolian and Syrian hinterlands. The Byzantine nobility, officialdom, and intellectual elite viewed themselves primarily as Roman and Christian and its relations to Hellenism was always ambivalent. During these centuries, Greece was a frequently contested, politically fragmented, and backward imperial province, while

Greek civilization was associated with paganism, which was rejected and reviled; Greek monuments were ignored, vandalized, or looted, and Greek temples typically were turned into Christian churches. But the Greek language survived because it had spread to the East following Alexander's conquests, thus becoming the lingua franca of a vast region. Only during their terminal decline, did the Byzantines come closer to Greece and Hellenism, geographically and philosophically.[1]

The centuries between, on one end, the fall of the Greek city-states to the Roman Empire and, on the other, the rise of the modern Greek state were anything but uniform and linear. A variety of political systems, social arrangements, and cultural regimes emerged, fell, and cross-fertilized. In short, a historical survey of the area of the world presently constituting the territory of modern Greece uncovers more discontinuities than continuities, compelling us to treat the emergence of the modern Greek nation-state less as the inexorable outcome of powerful, timeless forces and more as a historically contingent process worth exploring in its own right. In this perspective, the ancient past is not so much a direct link to the present but rather a source of symbolic capital to be discovered and deployed.

Crafting a new state in the name of a nation has been one of the most popular political causes of the modern era. In turn, new states are usually born by seceding from older ones. Nationalism has been typically a violent process, requiring the mobilization of substantial material and ideological resources before any fighting can begin. The key political actors in this process are nationalist movements, which emerge out of decentralized networks of individuals who generate and disseminate ideas and coordinate actions.

What was the Greek nationalist movement?

The Greek nationalist movement appeared at the end of the eighteenth century and beginning of the nineteenth century, most notably in several cities of Western, Central, and Eastern

Europe. Its emergence was part of an emerging global trend that followed on the heels of such movements in North and South America and foreshadowed the rise of similar movements in Europe, in the Balkans, and, following the end of World War II, across the entire world.

Like all nationalisms, the Greek version is a modern phenomenon. In spite of shared cultural traits, ancient Greeks owed their fundamental political loyalty to their city-state, or *polis*, rather than to some unitary Greek state, while Byzantine emperors did not see themselves as the heirs to ancient Athens or Sparta. When the Ottomans conquered Constantinople in 1453 and put a formal end to the long-lived and, by that time, moribund Byzantine Empire, the southern end of the Balkan Peninsula comprising present-day Greece had evolved into a politically fragmented region, ruled by various Byzantine and Frankish rulers, with the Venetians playing an increasingly prominent role on the coastal areas and islands. It was the Ottomans who unified this region politically by placing it under their control.

A perception of the Balkan Peninsula as being populated by separate ethnic groups, which were differentiated primarily by their language and connected through tradition, political institutions, and historical memory to well-defined, preexisting medieval states, precedes the formation of modern Balkan nation-states. However, this perception was not dominant, intellectually or politically; it competed against the existing social organization of the Ottoman Empire, which favored religious affiliation over ethnic or linguistic identity, organizing everyday social relations in a way that benefited religious institutions (a practice that eventually became formalized as the *Millet* system). Hence, the head of the Christian Orthodox Church, the Ecumenical Patriarchate of Constantinople, was able to exercise significant influence over the *Millet-I Rum* (lit., the Roman *Millet*), that is, the Orthodox Christian population of the Ottoman Empire. As a result, this population also came to be perceived as a single group despite its underlying differences.

Although local rebellions were frequent throughout the Empire among both Muslim and non-Muslim populations, they were not led or inspired by national movements aiming to create independent nation-states. The emergence of a Greek nationalist movement at the end of the eighteenth century was a ground-breaking development, embodying novel ideas that originated in the French Revolution and spread through the Napoleonic Wars. The intellectual process that spawned Greek nationalism later became known as the Greek Enlightenment. Although this process varied widely depending on time and place, it was initially focused on the promotion of scientific rationalism and political liberalism. Gradually, several thinkers began to formulate a radical idea: the creation of a new state that would represent the aspirations of the Greek nation.

In short, this was a truly revolutionary development, initially restricted to tiny elites who articulated, debated, and disseminated these ideas mainly in Western and Central Europe and Russia—in cities like Vienna, Trieste, Venice, Padua, Livorno, or Mariupol. Like many other nationalisms later on, Greek nationalism largely emerged far away from the geographic area that would eventually become Greece. Indeed, the conspirators who began planning a secessionist uprising to create such a state were three merchants who lived in the Russian town of Odessa on the Black Sea: Emmanouil Xanthos, Nikolaos Skoufas, and Athanassios Tsakalof. What would later become modern Greece was at the time a backward and isolated province of the Ottoman Empire with few towns, far removed from all this intellectual ferment.

Where did Greek nationalism come from?

Greek nationalism emerged from the interaction of three distinct but interlinked social actors: the Christian Orthodox Church, a group of Ottoman Christian elites known as Phanariots, and Greek-speaking merchants and intellectuals living across the European Ottoman Empire and in various European countries.

Because the Orthodox Church played a pivotal role in the Ottoman Empire, its liturgical and administrative language was important; inherited from the Byzantine era, this language was Greek. The Church ran several educational institutions to train its personnel, thus providing a rare venue of social mobility for the Orthodox Christians of the Balkans. As a result, educated Christians from diverse ethnic backgrounds became fluent in Greek and acquired an intellectual outlook that drew heavily on cultural symbols embedded within the Greek language. Thus, an intellectual class emerged, gradually identifying with Greece. This process explains why Greek nationalism was such an early phenomenon in the Balkans.

Although the Church helped create the conditions that gave rise to Greek nationalism (and many of its clerical and lay staff became Greek nationalists), it did not endorse it. In fact the Patriarchate of Constantinople was openly hostile to nationalist ideas. It was opposed to the ideology of the Western Enlightenment, which promoted secularism, posing a threat to religious authority and threatening the Patriarchate's prominence within the Ottoman Empire and its control over the Christian Orthodox flock. Only later, toward the end of the nineteenth century, and following the formation of national churches in the Balkans, did a partial realignment of interests occur between the nationalist goals of the Greek state and the Greek-dominated Patriarchate.[2]

Taking their name from the Istanbul Phanar quarter, site of the Christian Orthodox Patriarchate, the Phanariots were a Greek-speaking elite from diverse ethnic backgrounds, employed in the higher rungs of the Ottoman administrative bureaucracy. Their influence peaked during the eighteenth century, when prominent Phanariot families were granted the right to govern the two Danubian principalities of Moldavia and Vlachia, in present-day Romania, where they spurred the emergence of a thriving Greek-speaking intellectual milieu.

Although the Phanariots were open to new ideas coming from the West, they were also generally reluctant to adopt them openly, being conservative and loyal to their Ottoman overlords from whom they received their privileges. Nevertheless, a number of Phanariots eventually joined the ranks of the Greek nationalist movement and played a key role in the Greek rebellion, such as the brothers Alexandros and Dimitrios Ypsilantis and Alexandros Mavrokordatos. Others, however, such as Stephanos Vogorides, chose to demarcate themselves from the Greek national project, remaining loyal to the Ottoman Empire.[3]

The Orthodox Church and the Phanariot elites sowed the ground from which Greek nationalism sprang, but they were too conservative to take the initiative. Instead, this role was played by Greek-educated merchants and intellectuals, whose rise in the late eighteenth century led to the creation of a vast commercial network spanning Western, Central, and Eastern Europe. By the end of the eighteenth century, these merchants controlled a significant part of commerce in the Ottoman Empire. Behind this rise were global economic changes, but also the opening of new trade routes following the Russo-Turkish and Napoleonic wars. Travel in Europe and intellectual curiosity triggered a startling breakthrough as these merchants and intellectuals discovered that their Greek linguistic identity connected them to a glorious ancient civilization, which was older than Christianity and widely admired in the most advanced nations of the day and among the most progressive people. In other words, they discovered that they possessed an unmatched symbolic capital. At the same time, they were appalled by the contrast between the modern European nations and what they saw as a backward Ottoman Empire. They also resented their second-rate social status vis-à-vis Ottoman officials as well as the Phanariots and Orthodox high clergy.

Most merchants eschewed the leap to the nationalist project, but they helped create material conditions for the emergence of an intellectual class that was independent of the Orthodox Church and attracted by the most progressive and liberal ideas of the day. These intellectuals were often the merchants' children. They typically studied in Western Europe and proved highly enthusiastic and intellectually prolific. For instance, they published seven times as many books during the last quarter of the eighteenth century as were published during the first one. They also began to agitate. Initially, their energy was directed less against the Ottoman authorities and more in opposition to the conservative hierarchy of the Orthodox Church and local Christian elites. Needless to say, the great majority of the population, illiterate Christian peasants toiling mainly under Muslim overlords, was unaware of these developments and indifferent to them.[4]

Who were the nationalists?

Perhaps the best way to gain an understanding of Greek nationalism is to take a brief look at a few early key figures of the Greek Enlightenment. Consider three of them: Iosipos Moisiodax (1725–1800), Rhigas Feraios (1757–1798), and Adamantios Korais (1748–1833). Their education was Greek, their ethnic origins were diverse, their social background was bourgeois, their culture was diasporic, and their vision was cosmopolitan. The first one was an early intellectual force; the second was an early revolutionary activist; and the third put forward the most elaborate and ambitious version of a liberal Greek nationalism.

Moisiodax was born in the village of Cernavoda on the south bank of the Danube, in the Dobruja region of present-day southeast Romania. He came from a family of Hellenized Vlach merchants and studied in the Italian city of Padua. He traveled throughout Central Europe, translated and published several books, promoted new ideas, and became embroiled in frequent disputes with local Christian elites. His considerable intellectual energy was a key factor in the development of the

Greek Enlightenment. Rhigas Feraios (known primarily as Rhigas), a teacher from Thessaly in Central Greece, was also from a merchant background. He spent his formative years in Wallachia, where he worked in the Phanariot court and was inspired by the French Revolution. After extensive travels he settled in Vienna, where he published a Greek newspaper; he envisioned a new state that would be ethnically plural but culturally Greek. The title of one of his pamphlets was indicative of his vision: *New Political Constitution of the Inhabitants of Rumeli, Asia Minor, the Archipelago, Moldavia and Wallachia*. He quickly began to agitate in favor of a Balkan uprising. In the end, he was arrested by the Austrian authorities, handed over to the Ottomans, and executed in Belgrade.[5]

Both Moisiodax and Rhigas exemplify the marked Balkan dimension of the early Greek nationalist vision. Like them, Korais was a cosmopolitan thinker, most comfortable in global intellectual debates. An heir to a merchant family, he was born in Smyrna (present-day Izmir) in Asia Minor and spent most of his life in Paris, after passing through Amsterdam and Montpellier. His political thought was shaped by the experience of the French Revolution, and he was influenced by the ideas of Thomas Jefferson, with whom he corresponded. He wrote extensively, promoting liberal ideas, and gained considerable influence in Greece. His formal articulation of Greek nationalism was published in 1803 (*Mémoire sur l'état actuel de la civilization dans la Grèce* or *Memorandum on the Present State of Civilization in Greece*) and became its most influential statement. There, Korais argued that the inhabitants of contemporary Greece were the descendants of the ancient Greeks and that it was by virtue of this realization that they would be transformed from a people into a nation.[6]

Unlike early non-Greek nationalists in the Balkans who gravitated toward Russia, Greek nationalist thinkers immediately and forcefully turned their gaze toward Western Europe. This was a radical break with the past when Western Europe was perceived as either unknown, alien, or potentially hostile given the long history of animosity and conflict between the Catholic and Orthodox churches. The sacking of Constantinople by the crusaders in 1204 had been a traumatic event for the Christian Orthodox.

In a nutshell, the Greek national project was extraordinarily innovative: early to emerge, oriented toward the West, unabashedly intellectual, diasporic in character, and above all else highly ambitious. These features set the stage for the emergence of the Greek state.

How did they rebel?

The Greek War of Independence, known in Greece as the "Greek Revolution," is remarkable in many ways. It was the first successful nationalist insurgency in the lands of the Ottoman Empire; the earliest of the national revolutions of Europe to be fully successful in terms of establishing an internationally recognized, lasting polity; and the first major successful war of independence by a subject population against an imperial power since the American Revolution of 1776. Greece became the first post-Ottoman state and the first new European nation-state to win full sovereignty and international recognition in the nineteenth century. Equally remarkable is the fact that the Greek war was so much in sync with Europe's early-nineteenth-century liberal moment that its secessionist and nationalist dimension is often overlooked in favor of its anti-absolutist claims. The Greek War of Independence also led to the rise of a novel humanitarian agenda and marked the first modern international humanitarian intervention.[7]

Many Greek nationalists believed that all Ottoman Christians were Greek or potentially Greek, while others began to conceive of the Balkan Peninsula as divided along ethnic rather than religious lines and offered a narrower foundation for Greek nationalism. Perhaps the earliest formulation of the narrower version can be found in the writings of Dimitrios Katartzis from Bucharest, who put forward in the

1780s the notion of a Greek nation defined as "a collectivity clearly delineated by its language and its cultural heritage." To be sure, cultural heritage was a very broad concept that could be a remarkably flexible political tool.

However, narrowing the reach of Greek nationalism was less the outcome of an intellectual quest and more a reflection of the actual constraints of geopolitical reality. When the time for a nationalist uprising came, it turned out that it could only be sustained militarily in the mountains of the southernmost tip of the Balkans, the Morea (now known as the Peloponnese) and the Roumeli (today called *Sterea Ellada*, a loose translation of "Continental Greece"). This was as much a reflection of the geographical distribution of nationalist sentiment as an expression of the material conditions required for a rebellion to break out.[8]

Indeed, translating wishes and ideas into actions was far from obvious. The three merchants from Odessa formed in 1814 a secret society inspired by freemason groups that proliferated at the time. They called it *Philiki Etairia* ("Friendly Society"). The society had initially limited success in recruiting members, but eventually word spread. Its membership provides an informative social profile of early Greek nationalism. Most members were merchants, followed by professionals, local notables, clergy, and military men. Most joined in the Romanian Principalities and in cities of southwestern Russia. Socially, its members occupied an intermediate position between the illiterate peasantry and the more established wealthy Christian elites, the higher clergy, and the Phanariots. The society never evolved into a well-structured organization because it lacked both a centralized command and a clear plan, and it descended into irrelevance immediately after the rebellion began. Nevertheless, it succeeded in its objective because it set up a network that brought people together in a political context characterized by the retreat of the Ottoman Empire. Although the view that the Empire was entering a state of inevitable decline is now dismissed by scholars, it is true that it was weakened by successive wars against Russia. In attempting to face this challenge, it implemented policies that strengthened central rule over the provinces but caused substantial local acrimony and turmoil.[9]

In keeping with the Balkan vision of many Greek nationalists, the Greek War of Independence began in lands that are today part of Romania. In early March 1821, Alexandros Ypsilantis, a senior officer in the Russian army and the son of a Phanariot ex-governor of Wallachia, crossed the Pruth River separating Russia from the Ottoman Empire into Moldavia, an area that was under the nominal control of the Ottomans. Ypsilantis and his small band of volunteers hoped to be joined by local insurgents, but these hopes failed to materialize, making his defeat a foregone conclusion. Furthermore Russia, which Ypsilantis proclaimed would come to his assistance, did not move. While this part of the uprising ended in utter failure, the insurgency proved much more successful in the extreme southern end of the Balkan Peninsula.

Who rebelled?

The Morea and Roumeli featured a military class, which was part of the *armatolik-klephtic* system that emerged in areas where adverse geographical conditions prevented the establishment of full Ottoman control. These were essentially mountainous areas with populations tending poor, scarce land. The geographic and economic conditions there favored brigandage or "primitive rebellion" and the emergence of "specialists of violence" called *klephts*. To counter them and provide some degree of security and protection to the local population, the Ottomans fostered the creation of the *armatoloi*, local militias that acted as guards of outlying fortresses and frontier passes. Although in theory, the *armatoloi* were supposed to act as a counter to the *klephts*, in reality the dividing line between the two was less clear, since opportunism led many *klephts* to become *armatoloi* and vice versa.[10]

These military bands formed the backbone of the revolutionary army, led by local notables in the Morea and by independent chieftains in Roumeli. Of course, these were not the only places in the Balkans featuring this type of military class, which was common in many mountainous areas and whose members were often known as *hajduci*. The difference here was that several local notables and band chieftains, particularly in the Morea, had been recruited into the Friendly Society through their connections to diasporic merchants and shipowners. In fact, the Morea provided close to 40 percent of the society's recruits.

Their initial motivations for joining the uprising were multiple and ambiguous, though at least some saw the rebellion, originally at least, in local or regional terms, rather than as part of a radical, nationalist enterprise aiming to create a new state. The prospect of acquiring the lands of their Ottoman overlords was also a significant factor. Politically, the notables and military chieftains who joined the insurgency appear to have been among those who had been losing out in struggles against their local competitors during the years preceding the war. For them, the war also offered a unique opportunity to challenge these competitors.

Predictably, coordination with the assorted merchants, intellectuals, and Phanariots proved to be extremely hard given the cultural gap that separated them, and often led to violent internecine conflict. As for the foot soldiers, they were primarily loyal to their chieftains through local and kinship ties, rather than commitment to the larger nationalist cause. Insofar as nationalism was a motivation, it more likely was induced by the war itself. As elsewhere, war forged Greeks out of peasants.[11]

How did they fight?

What kind of war was it? It consisted of a combination of a few pitched battles, many ambushes and skirmishes, and several sieges of forts and fortified towns. The ruggedness of the insurgents and their knowledge of the terrain constituted their main military advantage, counterbalanced by strong local loyalties and a corresponding suspicion of any nonlocal authority, which often led to disputes over territory as well as frequent feuding among various bands of insurgents. Mass atrocities punctuated the war, largely because siege warfare, traditionally associated with atrocity, was a key feature of the fighting. Perhaps the worst massacre carried out by the insurgents was the one in September 1821 that followed the conquest of the town of Tripolitsa in the Peloponnese. On the Ottoman side, the massacre of the Christian population of Chios became famous after it inspired the French painter Eugène Delacroix to produce his famous *Scène des massacres de Scio* in 1824, which had an effect on European publics that was not very different from Picasso's *Guernica* a century later.

In retrospect, the rebellion could appear carefully planned—even inevitable. Such a reading, however, would be incorrect. In fact, when the Greek rebellion erupted, it was a bit of a sideshow to another military clash, which the Ottomans saw as much more threatening to their rule: the attempt by Ali, the pasha of Joannina, who ruled a large area comprising contemporary Northwest Greece and Southwest Albania, to gain autonomy from the sultan. As a result, the Ottomans turned their attention to Ali and eventually defeated him. By diverting the Ottomans during a critical time, but also by mobilizing many important band chieftains who would go on to join the Greek rebellion afterward, Ali's failed bid inadvertently helped the Greek national cause get off the ground and gain momentum.[12]

What was the outcome?

The war went through two broad phases. The first, between 1821 and 1824, saw a string of successes by the rebels who conquered several important fortresses; transformed an extensive merchant fleet into a powerful navy that disrupted Ottoman communications in the Aegean Sea; and defeated several efforts by the Ottomans to suppress them, including a major campaign led by Mahmud Pasha Dramali in 1822. The failure of the Ottoman campaigns of 1822 and 1823 to suppress the insurgents made more likely—in the eyes of the European powers—the possibility that the Greek uprising would succeed, thus encouraging a shift in their initially negative attitude vis-à-vis the rebellion.

However, early successes were followed by stalemates, along with several episodes of internecine conflict, pitting regional chieftains against each other and splitting the rebels based on complex cleavages and personal politics. Eventually, the Ottomans contracted out the counterinsurgency effort to Egypt's ambitious overlord, Mehmet Ali. His son, Ibrahim Pasha, landed in the Peloponnese with a French-trained army in 1825, launching a devastating scorched-earth counterinsurgency campaign that almost brought the rebellion to an end.

In the meantime, however, a series of international developments took place in the rebels' favor, including their financing by the City of London; the international recognition of belligerent status for the rebels; the Russian memorandum of 1824, which envisioned the partition of Greece into three principalities enjoying a status similar to the provinces of Moldavia and Wallachia; and, most importantly, the Treaty of London, signed on July 6, 1827 by Russia, France, and England, which provided for the establishment of Greece as an autonomous (though tributary) state under Turkish suzerainty and called for imposing a negotiated solution to the conflict on the Ottomans.

After the Ottomans turned down their demands, the three powers dispatched a combined fleet to Greece, where it engaged and destroyed the Turkish and Egyptian fleet in the Bay of Navarino in the Peloponnese. This battle effectively terminated Ibrahim's counterinsurgency campaign and, along with the Russo-Turkish war of 1828–1829, led to a process of protracted negotiations culminating in the London Protocol of 1830 and the Treaty of Constantinople, signed on May 7, 1832 between the Ottomans and the Great Powers. This treaty defined the boundaries of the Greek kingdom, whose crown was offered by the powers to a young Bavarian prince, Otto, the second son of King Ludwig I of Bavaria.

How was the war internationalized?

As the previous section makes clear, for all the significance of the military operations on the ground, the war was eventually settled on the international diplomatic scene. The internationalization of the conflict was due to two key features. First was the power balance between two expanding great powers, Britain and Russia. The British sought to counteract the rise of Russian influence in the Eastern Mediterranean and saw a newly formed Greek state as a buffer to Russia's ambitions. The Russians, on the other hand, saw the emergence of a new Christian Orthodox state as a potential ally. Second was the Greek nationalists' ability to turn what was a doomed local uprising into a global event. It is indeed striking how the status of the Greek struggle attained a highly privileged international status in comparison to other uprisings of the time. For example, the Serb rebellions in 1804 and 1815 failed to produce international interest and recognition. Largely as a result, the Serbs were able to obtain a sovereign state only in 1878. Together, these two features explain the ultimate success of the rebels.[13]

How did the Greek rebellion attain global status? When the news of the uprising broke out, it was met with a wave of enthusiasm in European liberal circles as well as great apprehension by the conservative European powers of the time. The end of the Napoleonic wars had given way to a conservative system of collective hegemony, known as the Concert of Europe, which was led and personified by the Austrian Foreign Minister Klemens von Metternich, whose hostility to liberal revolutions was well known. As a result, the rebels had to play their hand with considerable skill—and they did. They framed the conflict in a way that ended up appealing to almost everyone in Europe. In a way that prefigured twentieth-century insurgencies, they deployed a variety of symbols, effectively appealing to multiple constituencies: romantics, liberals, and conservatives.

At the dawn of the nineteenth century, many educated Europeans saw Greece not as the obscure, impoverished, and backward province of the Ottoman Empire it was, but as the birthplace of the most important ancient civilization, whose values shaped and defined modern Europe. The Romantic Movement fed this notion and nurtured it. Interest in all things classical gave rise to a generalized perception of historical continuity between past and present, and when travelers reported negatively on the present condition of the Greeks, this was typically blamed on Ottoman backwardness. It was, therefore, natural for European public opinion to greet the demand for a modern Greek nation with enthusiasm and excitement. The rebels were seen as the descendants of the civilization to which the West owed its values—and now they rose from the ashes! "We are all Greeks," intoned the British poet Percy Bysshe Shelley, in a verse drama written in response to the outbreak of the Greek insurrection. Greek nationalists played up the connection between ancient and modern Greece very skillfully and laced their proclamations with references to the renaissance of Greece.[14]

But it wasn't just the classical legacy that the Greek rebellion played into. The leaders of the Greek revolt formulated their claims and demands in a way that showcased liberal values. They told the world that they were fighting for liberty and national rights against tyranny, and for civilization against barbarity. In 1822 they adopted a constitution so liberal that it generated widespread excitement among progressive circles in Europe; indeed, this constitution was drafted primarily with this audience in mind.[15]

The combined appeal to romantics and liberals gave rise to the Philhellenic movement, whose activities ranged from public petitions and financial contributions to volunteering to fight in the Greek war. "Greek Committees" were set up across Europe, where they raised subscriptions for new recruits, coordinated expeditions of volunteers, sent money and supplies to Greece, organized relief for Greek refugees, and applied pressure on governments in favor of the Greek cause. As many as 1,200 individuals came to Greece to join the fighting and many perished there, including one of the biggest stars of the time: the English poet Lord Byron, a leading figure of the Romantic Movement. His death in the Greek city of Messolonghi, in 1824, shocked England.[16]

Being pragmatic, the Greeks were gradually able to tone down the wildest liberal fantasies. They proceeded to adopt a revised constitution that was more conservative in tone and deployed a series of religious symbols, including the Christian idea of resurrection. Chief among these symbols was the cross, which became the flag of the rebellion. The emphasis on the cleavage between Christianity and Islam overlapped with the dichotomy between progress and backwardness. This favored the Greeks, given the widely established negative perception of the Ottoman Empire in Europe, which was seen as a barbarous, primitive, and degenerate entity. And this dimension clearly appealed to conservatives. Lastly, the Greeks played well at the game of Great Power politics and wisely chose to tie their project to Britain rather than Russia, by explicitly appealing for its intervention.[17]

How did the rebellion spur the rise of humanitarian intervention?

Because it became interlaced with the themes of human suffering, massacre, and atrocity, the war helped spur an incipient humanitarian agenda—both in terms of mobilizing public opinion and as a way to organize and justify a military intervention against the Ottoman counterinsurgency campaign. European diplomats were genuinely concerned about human rights abuses, and this concern shows up in their private and official correspondence. British Foreign Secretary Viscount Castlereagh, for instance, explicitly warned the Ottoman authorities about the consequences of these abuses. George Canning, the next British Foreign Secretary, asked the following in a letter: "Can it be necessary to suggest the advantage to humanity of bringing within the regulated limits of civilised war, a contest which was marked on its outset, on both sides, with disgusting barbarities?" Admiral Edward Codrington, the commander of the British fleet in Navarino, wrote to his wife, "This Ibrahim, who boasted to us his humanity and complained of being called in the newspapers the 'Sanguinary Ibrahim,' is ravaging the whole country; and Hamilton, whom I sent to drive back his army near Kalamata, tells me that some of the poor houseless wretches in the country which he has desolated are living upon boiled grass!"

Thus, despite its realpolitik concerns, the British foreign policy vis-à-vis Greece, including its military intervention, was at least partly motivated by moral concerns. Navarino marked the first modern humanitarian intervention, and the Greek War of Independence provided fertile ground for debates about the conditions and modalities of this type of intervention. This is a striking aspect of the rebellion that anticipates many debates on humanitarian intervention that took place during the twentieth century.[18]

What explains the love-hate relationship between the West and Greece?

For all the advantages it provided, the internationalization of the Greek rebellion had a flip side, helping set the stage for what would become an enduring love-hate relationship between the West and Greece, based on both shared admiration and mutual resentment.

On one hand, many Westerners saw the Greek national project with sympathy and helped to bring it to fruition. For many of them, modern Greece was a dream come true, a fantastic resurrection of a magnificent ancient world that had been left for dead. At the same time, however, they were appalled by the unreliability, infighting, corruption, and fickleness of the Greeks. They were also annoyed by what they believed was an arrogant belief held by them, namely—that their nations owed them undying gratitude because of the legacy of classical Greece.

On the other hand, most members of the Greek intellectual elite who helped conceive and execute the modern Greek project saw themselves as fully European; they had studied and lived in European countries and fully took part in European intellectual debates. Yet, they resented the arrogance and sense of superiority they often discerned in the European gaze and couldn't help but realize that they were often used as pawns in a game of Great Power politics. The "more European" (or "modernizers") among them were also aware of the fact that the country they had dedicated themselves to, did not really satisfy the criteria of European modernity they held so dear and that its people often saw them as foreigners or "Franks." All this generated an intense feeling of insecurity and inferiority.

As for the "less European" among the Greeks (the "traditionalists"), who were actually the majority, they felt little community with the Westerners, who often berated them as "Christian Turks" and resented their constant presence and meddling. Thus, both modernizers and traditionalists were, for their own different reasons, ambivalent about their relation to Western Europe, while at the same time being dependent on it—an attitude that endures to the present.

Likewise, a most sensitive issue in the relationship between Westerners and Greeks was the link between ancient and modern Greece. Every attempt to challenge this relationship— most famously by the Austrian writer Jakob Philipp Fallmerayer, who suggested in 1830 that modern Greeks were the descendants of Slavic peoples—caused an intense emotional reaction in Greece. The link between ancient and modern Greece remains a sensitive issue in Greece today, as it is simultaneously a cornerstone of Greek national identity and an expression of the nation's pronounced insecurity.[19]

Obviously, this mix of admiration and resentment is a key feature of the relationship between colonizers and the colonized. However, the Greek case is unusual in two respects. To begin with, the particular salience of classical Greece gave this relationship an edge that is rather unique, in the sense that the inferior party to the relationship (Greece) could claim ownership to the feature coveted by the superior one (the West). Furthermore, the Europeans were not the colonizers of Greece; rather, it was the Ottomans who had been its imperial overlords. In short, the Greeks had to manage a rather complicated relationship.

This relationship is crucial for understanding how Greece interacts with the West—and vice versa. Most Greeks see Western Europe (and the United States) as unwelcome meddling foreigners, even though they have largely profited from their interventions. Conversely, Europeans (and Americans) are exasperated that Greeks have failed to see those benefits, even though their interventionism has been driven primarily by their own self-interest and has been imposed over the Greeks—their discourse about the importance of ancient Greek civilization notwithstanding. Nevertheless, despite this animosity, Greece never seriously considered abandoning the West, and the West never gave up on Greece.

It is worth pointing here to the key elements of what will form a recurring pattern as we move forward. First, what began as a wild venture launched by a few merchants and intellectuals, scattered not just in Greece but also in present-day Romania, Russia, and various European cities, ended with the emergence of the first new state in nineteenth-century Europe. Second, the boldness of these pioneers' vision was matched by a favorable local and international conjuncture, which in the end trumped the shortcomings of the project and its various, almost fatal, setbacks. In a pattern that would be repeated in the future, ambition, good risk management, and chance combined to produce a successful outcome, despite many errors and failures. Third, in the emergence of modern Greece as an independent state we can discern several processes that would later emerge on a global scale, from nationalist mobilization and secessionist insurgency to humanitarian intervention and the fraught relationship between interveners and locals.

III

BUILDING

How was the new state built?

Becoming independent was the easy part. The leaders of the new state faced a daunting task. They sought to create a modern European state in a rather primitive region of the world, inhabited by an illiterate population of subsistence farmers who were preyed upon by disgruntled warlords, demobilized fighters, and assorted brigands—a situation common to many post-conflict settings. The country lay in ruins and the population, smaller by 20 percent since the outbreak of the war, was dispossessed and exhausted. Worse, the most dynamic sectors of Greek commerce, entrepreneurialism, and intellectual activity remained outside the Greek state. An impossible task was made even harder by the foreign debt that Greece had accrued during the war.[1]

First to take on this formidable task was a former foreign minister of the Russian czar, Ioannis Kapodistrias, selected as Greece's governor by the leaders of the rebellion. Kapodistrias set foot for the first time in mainland Greece in 1827. After taking over from the remaining Ottoman troops, he undertook a program of administrative organization that, naturally, undermined the authority of the military chieftains who had fought in the war. They reacted by launching several rebellions against him. In the end, Kapodistrias was assassinated in 1831 by members of the Mavromichalis clan, whose base was the Mani region in the Southern Peloponnese. A combination of banditry (including piracy in the Aegean Sea) and generalized anarchy ensued. Thus, the Greek state was born as a failed state.

Kapodistrias had always been intended as an interim leader. Following his assassination, the newly designated King Otto came to Greece accompanied by a contingent of Bavarian advisers and a Bavarian military detachment that proceeded to suppress local rebellions and establish the authority of the new state. Greece thus became an absolutist monarchy; but because Otto was only eighteen years old at the time, power was entrusted to a "troika" of Bavarian regents whose charge was to create the new state from scratch. Their list of tasks included administration, taxation, the status of religion and the church, education, justice, city planning, and architecture. The regency also invested heavily in symbols, especially Greece's connection to antiquity. It immediately created an archeological museum, along with various agencies tasked with archeological research and excavation. Most importantly, it selected Athens as the site of the new state's capital, drew an ambitious city plan, and proceeded to build a multitude of grand official buildings featuring a style of architecture (dubbed "neoclassical") that reproduced ancient Greek motifs. Luckily, a proposal to build the new royal palace on the Acropolis was eventually bypassed; the palace was built instead on a hill nearby, overlooking an imposing public square. It now houses the Greek Parliament.[2]

Since the backbone of any modern state is its administration, setting one up became the overarching goal for Greece's new rulers, who also sought to consolidate their authority vis-à-vis a multitude of powerful local elites. To accomplish this task, the Bavarian regency brought in administrative specialists to fill positions in the newly created, highly centralized administration. This process carried obvious colonial overtones, and the resentment it generated was reinforced by the fact that the regency depended on the active collaboration of *heterochton* intellectuals, that is, educated Greeks who came from across the Ottoman Empire, Western Europe, and Russia to participate in the rebellion and, later, to contribute to the state-building enterprise. Their presence caused considerable resentment among the generally less educated and unsophisticated *autochton* Greeks—those native to the liberated territory who expected to be in charge of the process.

The dissension between *heterochton* and *autochton* Greeks was one of the earliest cleavages in Greek politics, and would prove a lasting one. The prize was substantial: public administration jobs became a key political resource since they provided livelihood, prestige, and social mobility in an economy providing few opportunities. Thus, the creation of a modern bureaucracy quickly devolved into a spoils system, undermining the initial goals of the regency, which sought to impart efficacy and impartiality. Of course, European observers saw Greece's new public administration as little more than a slender layer of European veneer disguising an "oriental" reality.[3]

Overall, this was a messy effort that generated constant friction between the Bavarian and *heterochton* state-builders on the one hand and local notables and former warlords on the other. Various policies, such as the imposition of fixed municipal boundaries on a territory that had been organized in a much more informal and fluid way, the disarming of military bands, or the implementation of a more extractive taxation system, kept feeding local rebellions during the 1830s and 1840s that were usually repressed by force. State building interfered with, and upended long-rooted practices, and its benefits failed to materialize quickly or clearly enough. As a result, the regency's reputation sank, a process that became encapsulated in the term used to describe it ever since: *Vavarokratia,* or Bavarian rule/occupation, a term echoing with *Turkokratia,* used to describe Ottoman rule. Most Greeks today have come to see this period in a very negative light as little more than thinly disguised colonialism, the trading of one foreign rule for another one.[4]

However, such a negative perception should not distract us from recognizing the extensive amount of groundwork that was accomplished during a very limited time. For example, the introduction of a completely novel Western legal system altered Greece in profound ways. The commercial law of 1835 upended the way the economy operated by doing away with both Ottoman law and traditional practices. A new regular army was slowly built, and the regency completely recast the role of the Orthodox Church by establishing a new Church of Greece, subordinate to the Greek government rather than the Ecumenical Patriarchate of Constantinople (which remained dominated by Ottoman Greeks). And in spite of its absolutist nature, the regime was eventually able to co-opt the majority of local notables, which made it perhaps less effective compared to other, more top-down Balkan states, but certainly more flexible.[5]

Altogether, this period saw the establishment of the foundations of a European-style state in a place that had been ruled up to then by a non-European empire. This was hardly a minor achievement, as the contemporary checkered experience of postcolonial state-building suggests. Hence, rather than seeing these efforts as pathetically inadequate, we should recognize them instead as the painful and messy initiation of nothing less than an formidable enterprise.

How did nation building succeed?

The companion process of modern state-building, nation building, was much more seamless. When seen from the vantage point of contemporary Greece, this may appear as natural or inevitable. However, the postcolonial experience hints at the enormous difficulties entailed by the construction of a highly cohesive nation-state rooted in a powerful sense of national identity.

Two key institutions that are crucial to nation building are mass schooling and mass conscription. Mass schooling aimed to homogenize a fragmented country and impart a common identity on a fragmented and often isolated peasant population. Reflecting contemporary European ideas about education, it followed a model based on centralization; compulsory public and secular education; selective secondary and university education; and a highly formalistic canon that emphasized classics, Greek language, and Greek history. The founding of the University of Athens, in 1837, was the pinnacle of this effort. A key issue that emerged was the standardization of the Greek language. Vernacular Greek was fragmented along several different dialects and coexisted with a highly formal and archaic "high Greek" used by the Orthodox Church. The resulting "linguistic question" became a highly divisive and politicized issue, pitting supporters of high Greek against those promoting a less formal but equally artificial demotic version, and generating considerable conflict for decades before being definitively resolved in favor of the demotic in 1977.[6]

In 1834 Greece was one of the first states to introduce compulsory primary education. Despite limited financial resources and a lack of qualified teachers, primary and secondary education expanded rapidly during the nineteenth century. As a result, Greece achieved relatively low levels of illiteracy compared to other Balkan, Eastern European, and Iberian countries. For example, only one out of four Greek males over the age of ten who immigrated to the United States between 1900 and 1914 was illiterate, compared to one out of two Italian immigrants. Enrollment in secondary education was also high. Greece enrolled 5,000 secondary school students in 1855, while France (with a population twenty times larger) had only four times more secondary school students. At the turn of the nineteenth century, Greece could boast the highest proportion of university students among its population across Europe—even higher when factoring in the significant number of Greeks attending universities abroad. Two additional features of higher education are also worth mentioning. Students from lower economic strata were significantly represented in higher education, and the distribution of students across academic disciplines was highly skewed toward the humanities and law to the detriment of sciences and engineering. The oversupply of law school graduates helps explain the rise of a legalistic mindset that came to dominate both the operation of state administration and the articulation of political debates.[7]

The creation of a modern regular army and the introduction of mass conscription (aimed at both forging a strong national identity and providing the new state with a credible instrument of force) proved much more contentious than mass education. These measures threatened the military class that had formed the backbone of the revolutionary army. The Bavarian regency disbanded the irregular bands in 1833 and issued a military conscription law in 1837, but the measure met with official corruption and draft evasion. As a result, the state was faced with constant brigandage and frequent local revolts. As a result, it had to resort to the traditional Ottoman practice of playing one local leader against another. A few decades later, the formation of a regular army based on the European model and the elimination of warlords was achieved, but brigandage would remain a problem for much longer. The Greek state would also encourage in the years to come the formation of irregular bands in border areas, as a way to carry out its foreign policy aims vis-à-vis the Ottoman Empire and other Balkan states.[8]

A crucial step toward nation building was the Church settlement of 1833, which created an independent Orthodox Church of Greece, thus severing its links with the Ecumenical Patriarchate of Constantinople (the latter recognized it only in 1850). By essentially placing religion in its service, the Greek state gained a powerful instrument in forging a national identity. The association of church and state, cemented by the official narrative of the Greek War of Independence, made the Orthodox faith a constituent part of Greek identity, very much like Catholicism became associated with Polish or Irish national identity, while also preempting the emergence of a confessional cleavage in politics of the type experienced by

France or Spain. It is telling that not even the communist insurgents of the 1940s dared turn against the Orthodox Church, so central had it become to Greek identity. This coextensiveness of national identity and Orthodoxy came at a cost for the Church, namely the gradual decline of religious sentiment. Insofar as the Church became a national and state institution, it was able to fulfill its purely religious functions at a much less adequate level.[9]

Overall, through mass schooling, mass conscription, and the imposition of state control on religion, the new state was able to acquire some powerful policy instruments and impart a cohesive national identity on a disparate population of illiterate peasants scattered in hundreds of isolated mountain villages. This was clearly a very significant achievement.

An additional and powerful driver of nation building was irredentism: the idea that the overarching mission of the Greek state was its territorial expansion, aimed at bringing all the Greek population within its borders. This goal became known as the *Great Idea*.

What was the Great Idea?

The emergence of an independent Greece was a significant achievement, but it hardly satisfied the leaders of the new state, who felt that they had liberated only a small, indeed a "microscopic," part of what they considered to be a much larger nation. As one of them put it, the new state was nothing more than the "kingdom of Athens and Piraeus." Furthermore, the Greek elites believed that this state contained the worst section of Greece, its "least educated and poorest part." Hence, the perception was that the new state was provisional, a mere placeholder for the much better and bigger state to come. First formulated by the politician Ioannis Kolettis in 1844 in the midst of the intense political conflict between *autochton* and *heterochthon* Greeks, the Great Idea turned into an all-consuming central mission for the new state.[10]

The "Great Idea" was a fancy name for what was in essence an irredentist project, based on two key beliefs: first, that the state should become coterminous with the much larger nation; and second, that the "unredeemed" Greeks expected and desired to be absorbed by the Greek state. Besides being a vehicle for territorial aspirations, the Great Idea served many additional functions: it acted as a legitimizing device for the struggling Greek state, provided the key justification for the need to shore-up state capacity, and was used as a unifying and mobilizing ideology that spurred social and political cohesion. The Great Idea became the central ideological expression of the new state, its true raison d'être. It is no exaggeration to say that without taking into account the Great Idea, it is impossible to make sense of Greek politics for the entire century that follows the new state's establishment. In that respect, Greece was no different from the emerging Balkan states that were about to pursue equally vigorous irredentist policies based on their own grand narratives of historical continuity with old civilizations and empires. The key difference between Greece and the other Balkan states was that Greece was the pioneer, holding the formidable twin advantage of its privileged link to both the Greek-dominated Ecumenical Patriarchate and to ancient Greece.[11]

Of course, there were several drawbacks to the powerful hold that the Great Idea had on the imagination of the Greeks. Given very limited state resources, this project kept generating a constant stream of hard policy dilemmas. Most notably, it produced inflated military expenditures, which accounted for about 30 to 40 percent of Greece's total budget. This effectively turned Greece into one of the world's highest-defense-spending countries, diverting resources away from badly needed domestic projects.

Who were the unredeemed Greeks?

In its maximal version, the Great Idea implied the recreation of the Byzantine Empire, with a restored Constantinople as the capital of a Greek state composed of a Hellenized Orthodox population. Beyond this, a multiplicity of versions circulated, depending on both the ambition of those promoting them and the prevailing international balance of power. A few Greek nationalists clung to the thesis that all Ottoman Christians were potentially Greek, but as rival Balkan states emerged, this idea could no longer be sustained. However, defining the actual boundaries of a "realized" Greek state was not easy.

Greek-speaking populations were scattered across the Ottoman Empire, intermixed with a variety of religious and ethnic groups, often in urban centers and the coastline rather than in well-defined contiguous areas. Moreover, considerable groups of non-Greek-speakers inside and outside Greece began developing a strong sense of a Greek national identity and loyalty to the Greek state, including speakers of Albanian, Slavic, Vlach, and Turkish. The hellenization of these Christian populations, both inside and outside Greece, was the result of the Greek state's efforts and its vigorous literacy campaign, based on an extensive program of teacher training and the creation of Greek schools across the Ottoman lands. Increasingly, however, Greece faced competition from neighboring Balkan states that sought, with equal vigor, to instill their own national identities on the mass of illiterate Christian peasants.[12]

For many Ottoman Christians the twin questions of national identity and state loyalty were far from settled, especially in the wake of various Ottoman reforms such as the Tanzimat, which sought to integrate non-Muslims into the Empire by promoting legal equality, extending civil liberties, and granting political participation rights. Navigating between the opportunities offered by a possible integration within the Empire and the attraction of identifying with rising (and competing) nationalisms outside of it was a treacherous road. This was particularly the case for elite Ottoman Christians who chose to remain in the Empire after Greece broke free, and continued serving it loyally from the "edge of the center." These processes were complicated by the fact that the nineteenth century was a period of considerable migration, with Ottoman subjects flocking to Greece (the *heterochtons*), but also tens of thousands of newly Greek citizens migrating to the Ottoman Empire—especially Istanbul and the Asia Minor coast—in search of better economic opportunities. For all these reasons, defining who the unredeemed Greeks were and what they wanted soon became an issue fraught with considerable, and increasingly violent, conflict.[13]

What were the consequences of irredentist foreign policy?

The pursuit of territorial expansion led Greece repeatedly toward an adventurist belligerency, which was only made worse by its military weakness. During the Crimean War (1853–1856), King Otto supported the efforts of irregular bands staging raids on the north side of its border with the Ottoman Empire, in the region of Thessaly. Ignoring French and English wishes, Greece threatened to declare war against the Ottoman Empire, which eventually prompted the occupation of Piraeus by French and English forces and forced Otto into a humiliating declaration of neutrality. During the nineteenth century, repeated rebellions in Crete brought Greece to the verge of a military confrontation with Turkey, to which it eventually succumbed in 1897 with disastrous consequences given its military weakness.

However, despite its mishaps, Greece ended up extricating itself from these adventures, not only with minimal damage but also sometimes with considerable gains. Indeed, by aligning itself with the Great Powers in opportune times, Greece was able to expand territorially without firing a shot, first by acquiring the Ionian Islands from Britain in 1864 and then by annexing the agriculturally rich region of Thessaly in 1881.[14]

Greece's military weakness meant that foreign policy success hinged on a proper alignment with the interests of the Great Powers. Overall, Greece's foreign policy during this period followed a pattern that would recur up to the present. Sometimes Greece made ill-prepared and risky moves that eventually led to humiliating defeat, which was typically blamed on the Great Powers. In other instances, however, Greek decision-makers read international alignments correctly and were able to derive considerable gains, which they were eager to ascribe to their own prowess.

Nevertheless, Greece's biggest (and inevitable) setback during this period did not come by way of the Ottomans; rather, it was the loss of its ability to claim the representation of all Christian Ottomans. After nationalist movements emerged elsewhere in the Balkans, they began making competing claims on the identities and loyalties of the Ottoman Christian populations. The new Balkan states adopted irredentist and expansionary programs that mirrored Greece's Great Idea and clashed with it. Nowhere was this clash more intense than in Macedonia.

What was the Macedonian conflict?

The fate of Macedonia mobilized the energies of all Balkan states at the turn of the century. This Ottoman province, a mosaic of linguistic and religious groups, became ground zero for the irredentist goals of Serbia, Romania, and especially Greece and Bulgaria. Because the Macedonian conflict was tied to the fate of the Ottoman Empire, it also became an issue with broad international ramifications, directly engaging the Great Powers and their increasingly conflicting aims about what they perceived to be the Ottoman endgame, known as the "Eastern Question."

In its very essence, this was a conflict between the emergent Balkan states over the loyalties (willingly offered or coerced) of Macedonia's Christian population. Bulgaria emerged as a threat to both Serbia and Greece when the Russo-Turkish War of 1877–1878 concluded with the Treaty of San Stefano in 1878, which created a Bulgarian state encompassing almost all of Macedonia. This new entity, perceived to be a Russian client state, caused a forceful British reaction that led to the treaty's revision in the Congress of Berlin, limiting the size of Bulgaria and returning Macedonia to the Ottomans.

However, this did not prevent Macedonia from becoming the new hotly contested ground.[15]

Macedonia did not fit neatly into the competing Balkan nationalist narratives. Speaking a variety of local languages and largely illiterate, the rural population's loyalties were primarily tied to religion and locality rather than national categories associated with various Balkan states. A Greek activist, for example, observed about the local peasantry: "Whenever I asked them, what they were—*Romaioi* [i.e., Greeks] or *Voulgaroi* [Bulgarians], they stared at me incomprehensibly. Asking each other what my words meant, crossing themselves, they would answer me naively: 'Well, we're Christians—what do you mean, *Romaioi* or *Voulgaroi*?'" National identities, in other words, had yet to fully emerge and take hold of people's consciousness.[16]

This hardly prevented the Balkan states from claiming the population as exclusively theirs. Initially they did so by diplomatic means, attempting to sway European public opinion by producing lavishly detailed ethnographic maps that were widely circulated and publicized. Later on, they tried to shape, as it were, these ethnographic maps on the ground by opening hundreds of local schools to make Greeks, Bulgarians, Serbs, or Romanians out of the local Christian peasantry. In fact, they supplied these groups with a mix of incentives and threats to ensure they sent their children to the schools, a process that triggered multiple local clashes. In fact, the conflict assumed two dimensions. While it was a factional conflict at the local level, articulated around religious and national claims but expressing all kinds of local cleavages, it also escalated into a violent guerrilla-type conflict between irregular military bands linked to the Balkan states.[17]

The conflict began as a struggle between competing local political factions arrayed around a religious division or "schism" within the Orthodox Church, reflecting the clashing political aims of Greece and Bulgaria (the substantial Muslim population of the region remained largely a spectator to this conflict). The schism took place in 1870, pitting the pro-Bulgarian Exarchate against the pro-Greek Ecumenical Patriarchate. It cut within communities and even families, giving rise to a vicious local factional conflict waged under the labels of Patriarchists versus Exarchists, often "translated" by outside observers as a clash between Greeks and Bulgarians.

Of course, knowledgeable observers knew better: they realized that national identities were the prize to be won rather than the cause of the conflict. The fight was, in other words, about political choices to be made rather than identities determined by birth. The *Daily Express* correspondent Frederick Moore, for instance, noted in 1903 the bizarre phenomenon of three brothers belonging to three different ethnic factions and, therefore, adopting different national identities. Although emerging national identities were associated with the competing Balkan states (Greek, Bulgarian, Serbian, or Romanian), a new identity also began to emerge at the margins, associated with a new Macedonian nation.

Initially, individual choices were driven by a combination of factors such as location, community disputes, guerrilla band threats, and material incentives. For example, conversion to the Exarchate meant relief from the heavy (and often arbitrary) taxation imposed by Patriarchist bishops; Bulgarian and Romanian schools were free or even occasionally subsidized. Eventually though, and especially as they were reinforced by violence, these initial choices began to consolidate, gradually morphing into strongly held national loyalties referring back to allegedly ancient identities. This causal loop provided the foundations for nationalist histories that saw the conflict as the outcome of a struggle between clearly delineated and preexisting ethnonational groups, a discourse that remains hegemonic throughout the region today.[18]

The local factional conflict acquired its intense edge only because it was encouraged and amplified by a bloody conflict, waged by armed guerrilla bands organized and financed primarily by Greece and Bulgaria. These bands were largely composed of military officers and volunteers from these two countries, although they quickly recruited locals as well. They not only fought against each other but also exercised tremendous pressure on the civilian population in order to extract from it exclusive national identifications. Despite the atrocities and destruction, the conflict failed to resolve the fate of Macedonia, although the Greek side managed to check the growth of Bulgaria's Macedonian ambitions. That fate would be determined a few years later, largely in Greece's favor, during the Balkan Wars. The conflict would simmer, however, and reemerge during the two world wars and the Greek Civil War (see below). Altogether, this was a traumatic conflict that intertwined land and identity in complex ways, amid violence and mass displacement.

Although it is fair to say that the conflict effectively ended by the late 1940s, its dim echoes resurfaced after the collapse of the Soviet Union, taking the form of a diplomatic quarrel over the name of the suddenly independent former Yugoslav Republic of Macedonia. Greece was opposed to the use of the name "Macedonia" by another state entity, arguing that it signaled territorial claims over its northern territories, also known as Macedonia. Many international observers were baffled by Greece's seemingly bizarre insistence over that name and challenged Greece's claim that it could ever be threatened by this new, weak Balkan state. The traumatic history of the Macedonian conflict, however, helps provide some context for Greece's concerns while highlighting their psychological dimension.

How did democracy come to Greece?

Like most of its European contemporaries, the Greek state began life under a regime of absolute monarchy. Therefore, it is surprising to observe how quickly and smoothly democratic institutions were introduced and adopted in Greece. To be sure, these institutions did not emerge under ideal conditions. Greece lacked a well-functioning state, a sizable bourgeois class, a tradition of aristocratic representative institutions, an industrial working class, a strong liberal intellectual milieu, and a vigorous urban culture—all factors associated with the rise of democracy in nineteenth-century Europe. However, it did enjoy an important advantage, one that has been linked to the rise of democratic regimes a relatively egalitarian social structure associated to the absence of a large landowning class.[19]

Greece's first postindependence constitution was drafted following a military coup that took place in September 1843, one that was planned and executed by military units in Athens, in conjunction with political factions that had been marginalized by King Otto's absolutist rule. The dire financial situation of the treasury played an important role in instigating the revolt; the trigger was Otto's decision to reduce military spending, which was typically consuming more than half of the annual budget. The 1844 constitution, modeled after the French constitution of 1830, fell short of parliamentary rule, but it did introduce the first parliamentary institutions in Greece, including an assembly whose members were to be directly elected triennially by the people and a senate whose members were chosen by the king and had life tenure. An important law, which was voted immediately afterward, introduced a nearly universal male franchise. Voting rights were granted to all males above twenty-five who were citizens and could demonstrate that they either owned property or had a profession or trade in the area in which they were registered. In practice, this provision excluded only a very small proportion of the adult male population, mainly servants and apprentices.

And so it was that in 1847, a year before a wave of European revolutions led to franchise extensions in the continent, that Greece became one of the very few countries in the world with near-universal male suffrage. France did the same in 1875, Belgium in 1893, Norway in 1898, Austria in 1907, Sweden in 1909, and the United Kingdom in 1918. In 1875 Greece's surprisingly broad franchise was accompanied by introduction of a parliamentary principle that called for the king to give the government formation mandate to the leader of the party commanding a parliamentary majority. Thus was accomplished a remarkable political transformation.[20]

Three factors explain this surprising outcome. First, Greece was born without a landed aristocracy. The best lands had belonged to the Ottomans, and after being expropriated, they were eventually handed out to landless peasants. Hence, there was an absence of landed elites facing the threat of expropriation brought by the extension of democratic franchise. This explains why there was no opposition to the introduction of democratic institutions, but it doesn't explain why they were introduced in the first place. The second factor, which goes in the direction of such an explanation, is the absence of a dominant, cohesive elite faction that could impose an authoritarian solution. The presence of evenly balanced elite factions, all with privileged access to the rural population, turned democratic institutions into a good system of adjudicating their competition while checking the power of the king, the most powerful actor up to that point. Lastly, as we will see below, the actual practice of democracy diverged significantly from its ideal, suggesting a system that could easily be manipulated and even subverted, initially through fraud and violence and eventually through the practice of clientelism.[21]

How did the new democratic institutions operate?

Inevitably, Greece's new democratic institutions were shaped by the social context from which they emerged, thus suffering from several distortions. The first one was the widespread use of electoral violence and fraud, particularly during the first twenty years of their operation between 1844 and 1864. While the use of violence diminished and essentially vanished after 1877, electoral fraud affected most elections during this period. In addition, incumbents used their access to state resources in order to reduce the level of political competition. For example, the minister of war could distribute medals or use the army to intimidate voters. Likewise, the minister of justice could pardon brigands or promise them immunity from prosecution. Not surprisingly, only one incumbent prime minister suffered defeat in elections during that period. The second distortion was institutional. The constitution did not include adequate controls on the executive power of the king and allowed him to appoint minority governments, while creating a senate whose members were appointed by the king. The third, and most enduring distortion was clientelism.[22]

Recall that the initial attempt at state building sought to create a centralized authority as a way to break the power of local elites. Although local elites lost considerable power, they did not melt away and the establishment of democratic institutions reinforced their power. During the Ottoman period, peasants had relied on local notables in their dealings with Ottoman authorities. Once the democratic revolution took place, these notables reconstituted themselves in the context of political parties that were able to offer considerable benefits to their clients—such as improving the terms for repayment of personal debts, delivering free medical and legal services, and providing employment in the public administration. As a result, citizenship was channeled through kinship networks and mobilized by political parties via local brokers. Thus, clientelism became an enduring characteristic of Greek politics up to the present—though by no means the only or even dominant one, as is sometimes asserted.[23]

The use of violence and fraud gradually declined, and the institutional distortions were lifted after a military revolt forced Otto to abdicate in 1862, ushering in a new royal dynasty hailing from Denmark. The new king took the name George I and the new constitution, modeled this time after the Belgian and Danish constitutions, abolished the senate and completed the expansion of the franchise. More significantly, it limited the powers of the king, although it still allowed him the right to dissolve the parliament and appoint ministers, which meant that he could still rule through a minority or extraparliamentary ministries. The construction of the democratic process was completed by a set of ambitious reforms introduced by Prime Minister Harilaos Trikoupis, aiming to improve the political system by producing stable and more legitimate governments with no interference by the crown. His main achievement was the introduction of the parliamentary principle in 1875; he also bolstered the role of political parties vis-à-vis local political brokers, by increasing the size of the electoral districts and reducing the number of deputies elected. Overall, and in spite of the challenges, the democratization of political institutions was a pioneering accomplishment that shaped Greek politics and society in profound ways.[24]

How did Greece become a nation of small farmers?

Democratic institutions naturally increased the political weight of the small peasantry, in turn ensuring the success of more extensive land redistribution policies. It is impossible to understand the democratization of Greece without taking into account land reform. By nationalizing the great bulk of the lands that had belonged to Ottoman landowners, the Greek state stymied the emergence of a native landed aristocracy. The Treaty of Constantinople had protected the landed property rights of Ottoman individuals and institutions, but in practice Greek governments tolerated transactions and practices that were detrimental to these rights. Eventually, Greece nationalized these lands as a temporary measure, but it took almost half a century before the first extensive land redistribution took place in 1871. The delay had multiple causes: political indecisiveness, the absence of effective protection of property rights, the difficulty of devising a solution that could satisfy multiple and often conflicting interests, and the use of public lands as a guarantee for foreign loans. At the same time, the pressure for additional revenue increased the incentives of a radical land reform, since the sale of public lands was expected to increase state revenues, both through the sale of property titles and an increase in agricultural production. As a result of this reform and of subsequent measures, Greece became a society of small peasant proprietors. Most peasants

benefited, as did the urban population, although the fragmen-
tation of landholdings failed to boost agricultural efficiency
and productivity as had been expected.[25]

Later on, when Greece annexed the land-rich region of
Thessaly in 1881, it inherited for the first time an incipient
agrarian conflict. Contrary to "Old Greece" (the original territory of the Greek state), Thessaly was dominated by large
landed estates that were cultivated by landless sharecroppers.
Although the individuals who usually bought these holdings
from the departing Ottomans represented a potentially high-
powered group, they could not prevail over the power of a government that depended on the vote of small farmers. As a result,
they failed to become an influential political lobby. In 1913 the
annexation of Macedonia, an area rich in land, gave new impetus to reform, and a second major land reform was announced
in 1917. Ultimately, the influx of more than a million refugees in
1922–1923 (see below) settled the issue once and for all.

This time land reform took on really massive proportions:
it expropriated 1,724 large estates and settled 130,000 landless
families. It is worth noting that this reform was achieved via a
provision suspending the constitutional clause protecting private property, a process amounting to expropriation, perhaps
the most revolutionary action in modern Greek history. When
the 1928 census took place, 88 percent of all rural households
owned the land they cultivated. By 1938, the Greek state had
redistributed about 40 percent of all arable land in Greece,
creating some 310,000 small family farms, a revolutionary
achievement that took place without the kind of bloody agrarian conflict so common elsewhere. Land redistribution and
democratization reinforced each other and shaped the social
and political character of Greece down to the present.[26]

The remarkable success of land reform in Greece holds a
significant lesson: in spite of its slow pace and disorganized
method, the Greek state was eventually able to deliver when
the need came in a way that is impressive in light of the
global experience. This was no doubt due to some initially

favorable conditions, but the combined impact of democratic institutions and state capacity is also worth stressing since both tend to be overlooked.

Was Greece a failed state?

Overall, how did Greece perform during the nineteenth century? For most European observers, and also many Greeks, Greece was a clear instance of failure. The state was seen as barely functioning, the economy fared poorly, and the country seemed stuck somewhere between its grandiose aspirations and a miserable reality. The Greek state was often seen in Western Europe as a hopeless effort—a failed state, in contemporary parlance. Greece's slow but nevertheless real achievements went underreported or ignored, while highly visible blunders received top media coverage and generated widespread consternation, along with not infrequent calls for military intervention to fix the country.

Several incidents cemented Greece's awful international reputation during that period, and the bottom was reached after a disastrous military defeat in 1897. The Don Pacifico Affair in 1850 and the Dilessi murders in 1870 are two representative incidents of the era in that both received widespread international attention, caused the eruption of significant diplomatic hassles, and confirmed Greece's negative reputation in the West, while reinforcing Greece's sense of humiliation and dependence on the Great Powers.

David Pacifico was a Portuguese Jew, a trader, and the Portuguese consul in Athens. Because he was born in Gibraltar, he also was a British subject. In 1847, he became the target of an anti-Semitic mob that ransacked his home while the police stood by. After failing to obtain compensation from Greece, he appealed to the British government amid considerable media attention. Eventually, the British responded to his plea, sending their Mediterranean Fleet to Piraeus in 1850, with an ultimatum that threatened drastic action if Pacifico's claims were not met. King Otto refused, the dispute escalated, and the British imposed a naval blockade that lasted two months. The affair ended when the Greek government agreed to compensate Pacifico, but in the meantime it also caused a big political crisis in Britain, leading the House of Lords to censure the British government. The entire commotion caused widespread consternation along with considerable damage to Greece's reputation.[27]

Twenty years later, another incident reinforced the perception of Greece as a failed state. In 1870 three English noblemen and an Italian aristocrat were abducted by Greek brigands while visiting Marathon, just outside Athens. Brigandage was a persistent problem in Greece, partly because the brigands themselves were closely involved with politicians. The abduction brought international attention to Greece. The four victims were held for ransom, but after the negotiation process failed, they were killed by their captors. When this happened, the British press erupted with indignation, criticizing not just the Greek state's inability to police its territory but also the relationship between Greek politicians and brigands. A passionate debate erupted in Britain about Greece's failure to become a proper modern state, and it was accused of not keeping up with European standards of public order. Several commentators, including members of the Liberal government, the Foreign Office, and the Conservative opposition, called for an armed intervention in Greece in order to restore order.[28]

The view of Greece as a failed state culminated in the military disaster of 1897, known in Greece as "the Black '97" and widely seen as the worst hour of Greece since its independence—This was the first war between Greece and the Ottoman Empire since Greece had become an independent state. It was triggered by a revolt on the island of Crete, which was then an Ottoman province, and it resulted in a complete military defeat for Greece, highlighting all the shortcomings of the Greek state: the army was not a fighting force but part of the political machine, the officers were almost all political appointees, and the rank-and-file were unequipped and poorly trained. Anyone could purchase their way out of the conscription system, there was hardly a trace of discipline, reserves were nonexistent, and there were significant shortages of weapons. Even a plan for military operations was lacking. Of course, all these shortcomings were hidden from public view, and Greek public opinion was seized by a highly emotional rhetoric. When the defeat came, it caused perplexity, anxiety, and anger. The feeling of humiliation was only strengthened by the government's desperate call for assistance from the Great Powers. Their positive response, triggered by their concern about the eventual fate of the Ottoman Empire, blunted much of the impact of the defeat. In the end, Greece was forced to cede only minor border areas, although it had to pay heavy reparations.[29]

So, was Greece a failed state, as these episodes suggest? Compared to the high expectations the emergence of Greece had generated among both Europeans and Greeks, Greece was indeed a failure; it was hardly the thriving replica of Western Europe in the Eastern Mediterranean (or the Levant, as this region was often called) that had been originally envisioned, let alone the worthy successor of ancient Greece. But, as we saw, this is only one side of the whole picture. That both Europeans and Greeks thought this new state to be destined for greatness speaks volumes. In a motif to be frequently repeated since, the country's performance was not judged against a realistic benchmark. The bar was set so high that failure became the only possible perception.

What was the state of the economy?

Greece's defeat in 1897 was not the only disaster to befall the country. It followed on the footsteps of a massive sovereign default. Both combined to send the country into international financial receivership.

We saw that the Greek state emerged in an underpopulated, economically backward region of the world, bereft of productive agricultural land or natural resources. As a result, the state of the economy during the nineteenth century remained precarious. The state played a central role in the economy, which is why Athens developed into the most prominent city in Greece.

The economy of the Southern Balkans was deteriorating even before the War of Independence and the widespread destruction it caused. In the absence of adequate investment in infrastructure, large swaths of otherwise fertile ground either remained uncultivated or were turned into swamplands. Lowland communities were affected by malaria, which in its turn reinforced the tendency of the population to relocate to higher altitudes in order to avoid Ottoman exactions such as the poll tax (*jizya*) that had to be paid by all non-Muslim males. The flight to the mountains was accelerated by the sharp decline of Ottoman power after the seventeenth century. The weakening of central authority, combined with chronic inflation, made the peasants more vulnerable to the whims of local officials and tax farmers on which the Ottomans had come to rely increasingly for fiscal purposes. The latter usually bought the right to taxation for a limited number of years in exchange for the obligation to raise a fixed amount for the central authorities, and so had strong incentives to extract as much as possible. As a result, long-running concerns related to agricultural production, such as investment in land and equipment, were increasingly neglected in what became a vicious cycle.[30]

The Bavarian regency focused its energies on land registration, but repeated attempts to implement a cadastral survey (a process that surveys and registers land) failed due to the lack of funds and technical expertise. In fact a full cadastral survey of Greece remains incomplete to this day. Effective land policy was seriously impeded by the absence of both a land registry and an organized state system for tax collection. As a result, the government had to rely on local officials for tax farming, which not only invited endless abuses but also allowed collusion between tenants and tax farmers for the purpose of altering property rights on land. Low administrative capacity, low land productivity, chronic lack of capital, and widespread banditry meant that investment in basic agricultural infrastructure remained below the level required for an appreciable increase in agricultural productivity to occur. Combined with the insecurity of property rights on land, this led the wealthier classes to abstain from investing any surplus in agriculture, preferring instead to either engage in real estate speculation or trade or take up positions in public administration.[31]

The extent to which economic activity revolved around the state is discerned in the growth of public administration, which, though not exceptional by comparative standards, became a dominant economic sector. During Otto's tenure, state bureaucracy came to employ almost one-fourth of the nonagricultural active population and served as a means to "absorb the unemployed, satisfy the dissident, reward heroes of the revolution and accommodate the loyal followers of the Crown and of the ruling political cliques." By 1907, the number of civil servants per 10,000 of population was roughly seven times higher than in Britain, a feature that Greece shared with other Balkan states. As a result, the Greek state diverted a substantial part of its meager revenues to provide employment rather than invest in infrastructure, which might have raised the competitiveness of the country's economy. At the same time, a demographic explosion was taking place. The economy was failing to absorb the available labor, and surplus labor was channeled to immigration.[32]

During the forty-year period between 1880 and 1920, 370,000 Greeks (almost one-seventh of the total population of the country) settled in the United States. Overall, this led to a loss of about 40 percent of Greece's adult population during the late nineteenth and early twentieth centuries. The potential contribution of Greeks living abroad to the

Greek economy is evident in the amount of wealth that prominent members of the Greek diaspora had accumulated and the size of migrant remittances to Greece. In fact, during the mid-nineteenth century, the wealth of the richest Greeks abroad appears to have exceeded the entire Greek Gross Domestic Product (GDP). As for remittances to Greece, they were equivalent to about half of the country's trade deficit and one-third of its exports. The size of migration and, remittances, and the fact that during the Balkan wars 57,000 migrants returned to Greece to fight as volunteers provide evidence for both the willingness of Greeks to migrate in order to escape the lack of prospects in Greece and their determination not to sever ties with their homeland.[33]

What led to successive defaults?

Greece was born in a state of economic default and international receivership. The 1832 treaty establishing the Greek state "explicitly obliged the Greek government to meet its debt payments each year before expending income for any other purpose, and gave the [great European] powers the right to insist upon compliance." Greece's recurring failure to repay its loans, and the economic implications of this failure, became a permanent feature of Greek political, economic, and social life. In fact, the country would end up spending half the years between independence and 2006 in a state of default/rescheduling of its debts. It is quite telling that the International Financial Commission set up after the 1893 default remained in operation until 1978![34]

In 1824–1825, seeking to finance its rebellion, the rebel Greek government sold bonds valued at £2.8 million in Britain. To make them attractive, each £100 bond was priced in the range of £55.5–59, making the real capital raised closer to £1.5 million. Of that sum, only about £540,000 made it to Greece, the rest having been spent on various fees.

The disastrous course of the war meant that Greece had to default by 1827. As a result, the country lost its access to foreign capital markets, while various committees of bondholders were formed to claim their dues. It took fifty-two years for a settlement to be finally reached with regards to these loans—in 1878. In spite of this, the Great Powers found themselves in a situation where they had to finance the new state in order to make it viable—and use this as a lever to shape Greece's foreign policy. In the wake of the 1832 treaty, the country received a loan of 60 million francs guaranteed by the Great Powers for purposes of reconstruction. However, once again repaying these loans in a consistent manner proved elusive. Between 1832 and 1843, when a new rescheduling agreement was reached, the country met its obligations only between 1840 and 1843. Greece simply couldn't raise enough revenue to service its obligations in a satisfactory way, leading to the ballooning of the debt, which reached 156 percent of the country's GDP in 1843. However, at least until the Crimean War, Greece managed to avoid meeting its loan obligations without direct intervention by the Great Powers, which used the issue as a way to pressure the Greek government on foreign policy issues. The renewal of foreign pressures for a settlement of the guaranteed loan of 1832 came mainly as a reaction to Greek involvement on the side of Russia, during the Crimean War. As a result of those pressures, a new settlement, the second one vis-a-vis this loan, was reached in 1860. This provided that one-third of the custom revenues of the port of Syros would be allocated to servicing the debt, finally settling the question of the 1832 loan.[35]

By 1878, when Greece managed to either convert or settle its debts to return to the foreign capital markets, the country had already defaulted on or rescheduled its debt three times (1826, 1843, and 1860). The 1878 agreement essentially gave the country a clean slate, as at the time debt payments amounted to only one-fifteenth of annual government receipts. Following this, the country embarked on a period of increased foreign borrowing to fund its growing defense and public infrastructure budget, as well as the needs of its expansive public administration (and the associated costs of political patronage). The heavy reliance on foreign loans quickly led to a new ballooning of the public debt, which increased from 331 million drachmas in 1882 to 823 million in 1893. It was then that Greece defaulted, a result of both its growing debt and the sharp fall in the price of currants, the main export of Greece during this period. The policies of Prime Minister Theodoros Deliyiannis didn't help either. Here was an archetypal old-style politician who relied on external debt to finance the country's budget, while neglecting revenue from taxation. Between 1885 and 1898 the drachma suffered from constant devaluations. Following Greece's defeat in the 1897 war, a regime of foreign financial control was imposed on Greece by the Great Powers, so that it could satisfy Turkey's demands for war reparations as well as settle its outstanding debts.[36]

How did Greece build an infrastructure?

Greece's state of fiscal affairs may convey a sense that the Greek economy was stagnant and that things never changed, an assessment that would be far from the truth. Nothing perhaps better conveys the state of infrastructure in Greece than the fact that it had not a single railway before 1869, the year when Athens and Piraeus were joined by a little local line (now Line One of the Athens Metro). However, the last two decades of the nineteenth century witnessed a sea change in this respect, one that is associated with Harilaos Trikoupis.

Trikoupis was the scion of an elite Phanariot family. He was the son of Spyridon Trikoupis, the author of an authoritative history of the Greek War of Independence. He studied in Paris following a brief diplomatic career in London, then returned to Greece where he entered politics on a progressive political platform. He headed several governments between 1880 and 1895, during which he implemented an ambitious modernization program that included political and economic reforms. In parallel with his political reforms, Trikoupis initiated a highly ambitious program of improvement in public infrastructure, particularly the creation of a communications and transportation network that ensured the integration of the national market and boosted economic activity. To achieve this goal, his administrations sharply increased the share of public expenditure allocated for works of infrastructure, including the road and railroad network, from an average of 1.2 percent in 1833–1872 to 18 percent in 1890–1891. The road network expanded from 1,359 km to 5,221 km and the railroad network from 19 km to 1,300 km between 1882 and 1890. In order to finance this ambitious infrastructure program, Trikoupis had to borrow heavily from financial markets and introduced several unpopular measures aimed at increasing government revenues. The latter included an increase in custom duties on luxury imported items and the creation of state monopolies on several goods.[37]

The positive effects of Trikoupis's program aside, he ultimately paid a high political price because of both the reaction of vested interests led by old-style politicians and the fiscal and electoral implications of an infrastructure program that was based on extensive borrowing. Nevertheless, Trikoupis's project laid the foundations for the modernization of the Greek state and the territorial expansion that took place at the beginning of the twentieth century.[38]

How did Greece double up its territory?

The 1908 Young Turk Revolution froze the Macedonian conflict, which had escalated after 1897. Its eventual resolution, however, had to wait for the two Balkan wars (1912–1913). The First Balkan War saw the defeat of the Ottomans by a coalition of Balkan states (Serbia, Montenegro, Romania, Bulgaria, and Greece), while the Second Balkan War was a crushing defeat for Bulgaria at the hands of its former allies as well as by the Ottomans. Macedonia was carved into three parts, with the most sizable one, including its crown jewel, the city of Salonika, going to Greece.

To understand how Greece managed to emerge victorious from the Balkan wars after having suffered a stinging defeat in 1897, it is necessary to explain how the Greek state was able to up its game. The story begins with Trikoupis's modernization drive in the 1880s, continues with the financial discipline introduced by the regime of international financial control in the late 1890s, follows with a series of economic and political reforms that took place at the turn of the century, and is capped by a brief military revolt in Athens, in 1909, which triggered a decisive political change.

Like the previous revolts of 1843 and 1862, the 1909 coup was organized by a group of officers, the Military League, which forced a change in government. The leaders of the coup demanded, among other things, reforms in administration, justice, education, and the military. Although motivated by narrow professional concerns, this coup would capture the demands of a rising urban middle class for more effective governance. It was the third time that a military coup led to a major institutional shift.[39]

The 1909 revolt set in motion events that paved the way for the entrance of Eleftherios Venizelos onto the country's political stage. Venizelos, a charismatic politician hailing from the island of Crete, is a towering political figure in Greek history. He founded a new political party, the Liberals, and became prime minister for the first time after winning the elections of 1910. He then embarked on a program of radical reforms that included a liberal revision of the 1864 Constitution; the abolition of the spoils system in civil service (which now had to recruit its members through an examination system); the establishment of a ministry of agriculture; the breakdown of the large estates that dominated Thessaly; the recognition of trade unions; and the provision of employers' liability, sickness, and old age pensions. In addition to reforms aimed at upgrading the army's operational capabilities through a sharp increase in military spending, Venizelos created specialized military schools and called upon foreign missions to improve the quality of training provided. The results of these reforms became clear in the improved performance of the Greek military during the Balkan wars. In short, the combination of Venizelos's strategic vision and reformist drive transformed the country—a transformation, however, that stood on top of Trikoupis's reforms.[40]

Venizelos proved particularly skilled in matters of foreign policy. He was able to steer Greece toward an alliance with its erstwhile Balkan competitors, while keeping the country closely aligned to Great Britain. In a series of secret talks he held with the British Prime Minister Lloyd George in 1912–1913, he hatched the idea of an Anglo-Greek alliance, according to which Greece was to become the main power in the Eastern Mediterranean, replace the Ottoman Empire, and be the pillar of Britain's policies in this area. Of course, Venizelos's "Ionian vision" was an ambitious and optimistic project that disregarded important geopolitical and demographic obstacles, but it provided the impetus of Greece's territorial expansion.[41]

And so it was that Greece, widely seen as a failed venture just a few years before turned into an ambitious and self-confident regional power, nothing less than the potential beacon of European modernity in the Levant. When World War I ended in 1918, Greece bore little relation to the country that had emerged out of the Treaty of London almost a century before. But, as had been the case in the past, it had embarked on a new boom-bust cycle.

How was Greece transformed?

At the end of the nineteenth century, Greece had looked like a failed state: militarily defeated, bankrupt, and under international financial supervision. The hopes that had been generated by the Greek uprising a few decades back seemed all but dead. Twenty years after 1897 the situation was dramatically different. A reorganized and seemingly efficient country was able to reassert itself, emerge victorious from a series of challenging wars, double up its territory, and claim a prominent international role in Southeast Europe. What explains this remarkable turnaround?

It has always been tempting to see Greek institutions as a deceptive facade, below which hides an inalterable Balkan or Oriental reality. In this view, almost everything in Greece—state, nation, political institutions—is a cover, a sham. What matters instead are deep, unchanging beliefs and practices. This view conveniently resurfaces whenever a major Greek failure calls for an explanation. Needless to say, this approach is not particularly helpful.

The fact is that during the nineteenth century the foundations of a modern European state had been established, and the new entity was slowly maturing. Setbacks were causing adaptation. Sovereign default and military defeat spurred the emergence of new political actors. The regime of international financial control imposed on Greece stabilized the drachma and led to the reorganization of the Greek economy. In turn, fiscal discipline brought benefits: Greek banks expanded, the economy grew, and the country urbanized. Trikoupis's investments in infrastructure helped transform Greece.[42]

The trajectory of independent Greece during the nineteenth century replicates many of the features that marked the War of Independence: ambitious projects (state building, economic modernization); an incapacity to execute them properly, culminating in defeat and disaster; and humiliating foreign interventions that nevertheless proved ultimately beneficial to Greece, preserving many of the gains that had been achieved while minimizing losses. Greece's trajectory also illustrates the contrast between the initial optimism of early state-builders and their subsequent disappointments, as well as the difficulty of implanting Western institutions on new soil—typical experiences in many post–World War II postcolonial nations.

IV

TURMOIL

What was the National Schism?

Following a pattern similar to the past, Greece's triumph in the Balkan Wars would eventually turn into a disaster. Despite (or, perhaps, because of) his intense reformist drive, Eleftherios Venizelos became a polarizing political figure, contributing to the emergence of the "National Schism," Greece's deepest political fissure. The trigger was Greece's participation in World War I.

On one side stood Venizelos, who advocated Greece's entry in the war in support of the Entente, the alliance of Great Britain, France, and Russia. He had received assurances from Great Britain about substantial territorial concessions on the coast of Asia Minor, in case the Entente emerged victorious from the war. He believed that irrespective of the outcome of the war, Great Britain would, by virtue of its naval supremacy, remain the major power in the Mediterranean—hence Greece had to be close to Britain. He also thought that the interests of the Central Powers were more closely aligned with Bulgaria and Turkey, both of which had territorial claims on Greece. Thus Greece had little to gain by adopting a positive stance toward the Central Powers and everything to gain by joining the Entente. For Venizelos, therefore, World War I provided Greece with a truly unique opportunity. On the other side stood King Constantine, George I's son, who was close to Germany. He believed that Greece had little to gain by getting involved in the conflict and that neutrality was the less risky proposition, especially in light of his belief about the invincibility of Germany.[1]

These contradictory views led to a clash and from there to an unprecedented domestic crisis that divided the country into two irreconcilable political camps, a legacy that would endure for decades to come. At times, the National Schism even took the form of an open, though low-intensity, civil conflict.[2]

The clash between Constantine and Venizelos over Greece's position in the war led to the latter's resignation in March 1915. Elections were called in June and Venizelos won, but the dispute was not resolved; new elections were then called in December, which the Venizelists boycotted, thus leading to an outsize royalist victory. After the surrender of a number of Greek border forts and the abandonment of Eastern Macedonia to the Central Powers, Venizelos decided to assume the leadership of the National Defense, a military coup initiated in Salonica in 1916 by a group of Venizelist officers. A provisional government was formed in that city and the country effectively split in two: Northern Greece (the so-called New Lands, which had been incorporated into Greece after the Balkan Wars), controlled by Venizelos's provisional government; and Southern Greece ("Old Greece"), controlled by the royalist Athens government. The two governments undertook extensive purges of their political opponents, thus escalating the intensity of the conflict. At the same time, the National Defense entered the war by joining the Entente, which launched a decisive action against the Athens government, eventually forcing the abdication of the king in favor of his second son Alexander. By then, however, the conflict had spawned a deep political fracture between the supporters of Venizelos and Constantine, adding to other geographical, social, and cultural cleavages. In turn, this fracture gradually evolved to encompass the question of whether Greece should be a monarchy or a republic, with most Venizelists eventually becoming Republicans.[3]

The National Schism affected the country in important ways. In the short run, it made it much more difficult for the country to wage an effective war on the side of the Entente and eventually undermined its dreams of territorial expansion. In the long run, its legacy shaped politics for decades to come by defining the character of the Greek party system, forging the political identities of Greeks, and politicizing the military. Most importantly, it infused politics with a degree of intensity never seen before, reinforced by successive reciprocal purges of public administration and the military. The flip side of the polarization of Greek politics was the emergence of mass politics and the creation of a national political sphere that extended beyond local politics. Politics became much more coherent. For better or worse, Greek politics became modern via the National Schism.

What happened in the aftermath of World War I?

The victory of the Entente in World War I meant Venizelos was vindicated. His risk taking was rewarded with impressive territorial gains. It now appeared as if a maximal version of the Great Idea was about to become true.

In 1919 a Greek military contingent landed in the city of Smyrna/Izmir on the Aegean shore of Asia Minor. A year later, the Treaty of Sèvres formalized the Greek presence in Asia Minor by awarding Greece the administration of Smyrna and the surrounding region, inhabited by a mixed Christian and Muslim population. The region's ultimate fate was to be decided five years later. Territorial gains included Thrace (in Northeastern Greece, between the Black and Aegean seas) and the Aegean Islands. Thus emerged the "Greece of the two continents and five seas." This was an impressive achievement, but an unstable one. The French and the Italians were unhappy about the treaty provisions and had their own ambitious plans to carve up the Ottoman Empire. Indicative of French views was the opinion of Prime Minister Raymond Poincaré, who announced that "the Treaty would prove to be as fragile as the porcelain vases made in the famous Sèvres factory [in the town] where the treaty had been signed." Unfortunately for Greece, Poincaré's prediction proved accurate. The arrival of Greek troops on the Asia Minor shore sparked a wave of inter-communal violence between Christians and Muslims and served as a trigger for the emergence of Turkish nationalism. Under the leadership of Mustafa Kemal (later to be known as Atatürk), a former officer of the Ottoman army, a Turkish armed resistance movement emerged, turning against both the remnants of the Empire and the Greek army, as well as the Anatolian Christian population that was seen as its support base. A disaster of unimaginable proportions was about to befall Greece.[4]

What was the Anatolian disaster?

When elections took place in 1920, Venizelos was soundly defeated despite his foreign policy triumph. This outcome was due in large part to the population's fatigue after eight consecutive years of war; it was also a backlash against the Entente's constant meddling into Greek politics and a reaction against the extensive purges that had been implemented by the victorious Venizelists. Moreover, the large minority populations of the New Lands (Muslims, Slavophones, and Jews) voted overwhelmingly in favor of royalist candidates. The royalist victory was followed by the triumphal return of King Constantine, made possible by the accidental death of King Alexander, which led to the shutdown of allied financial support for Greece. Nevertheless, Venizelos's successors reck-lessly decided to launch a major offensive deep into Asia Minor with the objective of seizing Kemal's main base Ankara, which they did in July 1921. From the outset, the success of the Greek expedition was up against significant challenges. The Greek presence had strengthened Turkish resistance, while Turkish military strength was underestimated. The operation also faced significant logistical challenges. Furthermore, Greece's allies were divided over their intentions about the future of Turkey. The Greek military expedition failed, and in the summer of 1922, its retreat quickly turned into a rout. In September, the Greek headquarters in Smyrna were evacuated and a day later the Turkish army entered the city, launching a massacre of the city's Christian population and setting the city's Christian sections ablaze. Thousands met a terrible death on the quays of Smyrna in full view of an international fleet anchored just outside its port.[5]

The Anatolian debacle—the "Asia Minor Catastrophe," as it became known in Greece, or the "Turkish War of Independence," as it is called in Turkey—spelled the end of Greece's expansionist dreams, and allowed the remnants of the Ottoman Empire to be reborn as Turkey. Almost one century after the emergence of the Greek nation-state, a Turkish nation-state emerged from the combined ashes of the Great Idea and the Ottoman Empire. The Greek War of Independence had come full circle.

The defeat precipitated significant political changes in Greece. In Athens, it was blamed on the royalist politicians running the country and on Greece's allies who failed to support them. With the return of Greece's defeated army in 1922, a military coup led by Colonel Plastiras overthrew the royalist government, forced King Constantine to abdicate in favor of his son George, and, more importantly, led to the court-martial and execution of six prominent royalist leaders who were held responsible for the defeat, thus rubbing salt into the open wound of the National Schism. A new treaty, by which Greece conceded to Turkey all its gains in Asia Minor as well as Eastern Thrace and the islands of Imvros and Tenedos, concluded this episode, though not its humanitarian consequences. Most importantly, the population issue was settled by a bilateral treaty between Greece and Turkey, which provided for a massive and compulsory population transfer between the two countries that became known as the "population exchange." Approximately 1,300,000 Christians (close to one-fifth of the population of Greece) were forced out of their homes and arrived in Greece, while 585,000 Muslims left Greece for Turkey. Exceptionally, the Christians of Istanbul were allowed to stay on, as were the Muslims of Western Thrace. A centuries-old Christian presence in Asia Minor ended. A subsequent agreement signed between Greece and Bulgaria also led to a similar exchange between those identifying with Greece and Bulgaria, although the numbers involved there were much smaller.[6]

For Greece, the population exchange was the deeply ironic and tragic flip side of the Great Idea: since Greece had failed to extend its borders so as to include all the Greeks of the Ottoman Empire, it was those Greeks who had to leave their homes and move inside the boundaries of the Greek state. Once more, an ambitious project ended with disaster, as the Balkan Wars' territorial "boom" was succeeded by the Anatolian "bust." But, once more as well, the tragic dimension of this development carried a much less known redeeming aspect.

What was the impact of the population exchange?

The population exchange was a deeply traumatic experience for those who experienced it directly, as well as for those who felt its impact in more indirect ways. Much less known, however, are three redeeming features of this disaster that make its aftermath equally remarkable. First, the population exchange was probably less painful compared to the realistic alternatives. Second, the resettlement and integration of this enormous displaced population was largely and unexpectedly successful. Third, the refugees proved a boon for Greece.

The massive dimension of the population exchange, its compulsory nature, and the use of religion as the criterion by which the populations to be "moved" were selected became hotly debated issues. Lord Curzon, the British foreign secretary, described the compulsory exchange of population as "a thoroughly bad and vicious solution, for which the world would pay a heavy penalty for a hundred years to come." Yet, the realistic alternatives were no better. Given the suspicion cast on minority populations associated with the irredentist projects of neighboring states, it was possible to expect the worst. After all, the Armenian genocide was a very recent occurrence in the same region. In fact, the fate of the populations that were exempted from the exchange suggests that it is unlikely that minority populations would have avoided hardship or displacement in the absence of the exchange agreement.[7]

To reflect on this counterfactual, consider four actual examples. The Greek Orthodox community of Istanbul, which had been exempted from the exchange, was ultimately forced to flee after anti-Greek riots broke out in 1955. The small Muslim Cham population of the Epirus region in Greece, which had also been exempted from the population exchange on account of its Albanian ethnic identity, became enmeshed in collaboration with the Nazis during Greece's occupation and, in 1944, was subsequently violently displaced to Albania. The bulk of the Slavophone population of Greek Macedonia that had survived the Balkan Wars and the population exchange with Bulgaria also got caught in the maelstrom of World War II and largely ended up displaced after the Greek Civil War. The exception was the Muslim population of Western Thrace in Greece, which survives to this day, but had to endure a regime of intense surveillance and discrimination that ended only recently.

The terrible humanitarian fallout notwithstanding, it is true that the emergence of ethnically homogeneous nation-states through this kind of demographic engineering, undoubtedly a troubling development in many respects, did contribute to a substantial reduction of interstate conflict in the region.

Following the population exchange, relations between Greece and Turkey were normalized, only to deteriorate again during the 1950s because of the Cyprus conflict. As a British colony at the time of the population exchange, Cyprus had not been included in the exchange agreement and remained ethnically mixed, making possible the eruption of extensive interethnic violence.[8]

The arrival of more than a million refugees (accounting for about 20 percent of Greece's population) was a tremendous challenge for the Greek state. Although Greece had accommodated refugees in the past, this was a massive influx that took place in the aftermath of a devastating military defeat, with the country financially exhausted after almost a decade of continuous war. Coping with the financial demands of this effort, while lacking the administrative capacity necessary for dealing effectively with a project of such magnitude, appeared to guarantee a humanitarian disaster of epic proportions. However, the national effort sparked by the disaster and the assistance provided to Greece by the League of Nations, and especially the Refugee Settlement Commission, made all the difference in the end, ensuring that the resettlement succeeded faster than anyone had thought possible. According to George Mavrogordatos, the resettlement of the refugees stands out as the Greek state's greatest peacetime achievement.[9]

Clearly, there is no denying that this was a very traumatic process with several negative social and political consequences. Although most refugees resettled in rural areas, many others formed an impoverished urban proletariat on the outskirts of Athens and Piraeus. In the countryside, the refugees often clashed with the native population, which responded to their arrival with a variety of discriminatory practices. The bulk of the refugees settled in Macedonia, where they constituted over 50 percent of the population. Local land conflicts there reinforced ethnic polarization between refugees and natives, giving rise to conflicts that would explode into violence during the civil war. Indeed, many of these clashes would be eventually camouflaged or repurposed under a variety of political labels, such as resistance versus collaboration or nationalist right versus communist left. The population exchange also completely reshaped Greek politics. The great majority of refugees became ardent Republicans, having blamed the royalists for the Anatolian disaster and their own terrible fate. Their demographic weight turned them into political kingmakers and upset traditional patron-client relationships, facilitating the advent of a more ideological type of politics by superimposing the royalist-Republican cleavage onto a more explicit right-left axis.[10]

It is equally true, however, that the refugees infused Greece with considerable energy and drive. Their integration was facilitated by the prevalence of social norms among them that stressed hard work and family solidarity. During the 1970s, an ethnographer was surprised to find that a poor refugee neighborhood on the outskirts of Piraeus did not look like the slum she had expected to find but instead was a prosperous and socially functional neighborhood. Furthermore, the settlement of many refugees in Macedonia contributed to the ethnic homogenization of this region, undermining the credibility of revisionist claims by Greece's Balkan neighbors and injecting a measure of stability in this troubled area. Lastly, the refugee crisis provided the impetus for much-needed investment in public infrastructure and spurred economic growth.[11]

The Greek military defeat in Anatolia was blamed on the royalists under whose watch it had taken place. In the ensuing backlash, the monarchy was abolished and Greece became a republic in 1924. Politics continued to play out as an intense confrontation between two clearly delineated and hostile camps, Republicans and royalists, representing two distinct political and social coalitions. The royalists' coalition included segments of the bourgeoisie and the urban petty bourgeoisie linked to the state, the small farmers of Old Greece, and various ethnic minorities, such as the Slavophones of Macedonia. This coalition resisted modernization and defended local and economic particularisms.

The Republican coalition was composed of the entrepreneurial bourgeoisie, the inhabitants of the New Lands, and Anatolian refugees; it stressed the need for modernization and reform, relying on Venizelos's charisma.[12]

Both coalitions relied on the support of factions within the military, which became thoroughly divided across partisan lines. Although the Greek military had intervened in Greek politics in the past (recall the interventions of 1844, 1862, and 1909), it had done so briefly and in the name of the general interest. It had also quickly handed back power to politicians and had encouraged the immediate implementation of important political reforms. This type of intervention ceased after the Anatolian disaster. Now, the military became factionalized— so much so that it was possible to talk of civilian and military branches of the Republican and royalist camps. Permanent infighting and frequent coups poisoned political and military life, as constant politicking mixed political preferences with opportunistic careerism. A failed military coup organized by the Republicans in 1935 almost triggered a real civil war, leading to a vast purge of Republican officers from the military and the restoration of the monarchy under King George II. In some instances, coup leaders turned into political chieftains. The symbiotic relationship between civilian and military politics was best captured by a statement of general Georgios Kondylis, who pointed out that "the politicians could not hold power without the officers, while the latter could not preserve and promote their own interests unless they attached themselves to a party." As a result, the military lost much of the prestige and sacrificed much of the professionalism that it had gained through its performance in the Balkan Wars.[13]

To conclude, the Anatolian disaster turned the question of Greece's fundamental institutions (monarchy versus republic) into a matter of intense political contention, deepened the polarization of Greek politics, and led to a sharp politicization and factionalization of the Greek military. The arrival of over a million refugees in Greece changed the country and transformed its demography. The challenge of absorbing this huge population of impoverished and traumatized people was colossal, but Greece met it head-on in what turned out to be one of the greatest peaceful achievements of the Greek state. On top of all else, by bringing the Great Idea to a definitive end, the Anatolian disaster redirected Greece's energies and aspirations within rather than outside its borders. Lastly, a little-known but important consequence of the disaster was the implementation of a highly ambitious modernization effort that altered the nature of the Greek state in fundamental ways.

What was the impact of the Great Depression?

In the economic history of Greece, the period between 1928 and 1932 stands outs as a time during which the modernization drive gained substantial momentum. Under the premiership of Venizelos, the Greek government implemented a forceful "developmentalist" program that continued where Trikoupis's program had stopped, turning the state into a much more forceful and proactive economic actor. The creation, for instance, of the Agricultural Bank of Greece in 1929 was a key element in the modernization of agriculture. The achievements brought by these measures were substantial, but their promise was only partially fulfilled because Greece was hit by an economic tempest unleashed by the 1929 US stock market crash and the Great Depression. Despite this, Greece managed to orchestrate a surprisingly effective response to it, one largely based on economic autarky and the stimulation of the domestic market.[14]

The country abandoned the gold standard, depreciated its currency in 1932, and defaulted on its obligations. These measures led to a speedy recovery in both agricultural and industrial production. In fact, only the Soviet Union and Japan registered higher industrial growth rates after 1932. These results were achieved in four ways. First, the increase in the relative price of imports compared to nontraded goods and exports boosted domestic agriculture and industry. Second, the decrease in real wages, itself the result of the sluggish response of nominal wages to price increases, further allowed domestic industry to expand. Third, Greece's Central Bank stepped up by introducing a set of economic measures that were better adapted to the needs of the Greek economy. Finally, the default that accompanied abandonment of the gold standard and devaluation allowed the country to free up resources for use in the domestic economy. Of course, there was a flip side to these economic measures: they encouraged the development of an inefficient, ill-equipped, and eventually uncompetitive manufacturing sector and led to the creation of domestic monopolies, which further stifled innovation and modernization in the manufacturing sector.[15]

There is no denying that for all its relative success in dealing with the fallout from the Great Depression, Greece did experience challenging social conditions. Spurred by the twin global ideological trends of the time, fascism and communism, social unrest led to sustained political turmoil.

How did communism emerge in Greece?

When the Socialist Workers Party of Greece was founded in Salonica in 1918, the urban working class was tiny, in the image of the country's minuscule industrial base. The party became affiliated with the Comintern in 1920 and accepted the full communist program in 1924, renaming itself the Communist Party of Greece (its Greek acronym is KKE). The KKE posed a threat to the Republican camp by appealing to a part of its social base. In response, the Venizelist government of the time passed the *Idionym* Law of 1929, penalizing "attempts to develop, implement or propagate ideas that aimed at violently overthrowing the established social order or detaching part of the state's territory." A major wave of repression followed and many communist cadres found themselves imprisoned. Nevertheless, by 1936, the KKE had gained a small but well-disciplined following with a membership of roughly 15,000, as the party made inroads among urban Anatolian refugees.[16]

The Communist Party's appeal was severely circumscribed by the country's political culture and its social structure, including the extensive political identification with two
established political camps, the pervasiveness of clientelistic
"retail" politics, the prevalence of small property, and widespread suspicion of modern, impersonal, bureaucratic struc-
tures. Despite these constraints, however, the party forged
ahead, riding on the global wave of communism's appeal and
exploiting a tradition of popular sympathy for Russia. A key
moment came when the party was reorganized under the
tutelage of the Soviet Union and a new Soviet-trained secretary general, Nikos Zahariadis, who took over the party and
turned it into a well-run Bolshevik organization.

What was the Metaxas regime?

The turbulent interwar period concluded with Greece becoming an authoritarian regime that relied on the kind of fascist symbols that had become popular during this period in
Europe, under the command of an ex-general and prominent
royalist politician, Ioannis Metaxas.

Although its electoral appeal had remained small, the KKE
took full advantage of the Great Depression. It succeeded
in building up a national network of cadres and became a
kingmaker when the 1936 elections produced a hung parliament. The ensuing political stalemate between royalists and
Venizelists convinced the king to call on Metaxas. On August 4,
1936, Metaxas suspended the operation of the parliament and
declared martial law and a state of emergency.

The new regime invested heavily in mass mobilization; it set
up mass organizations for various segments of Greek society,
with a special emphasis on the youth; and introduced a vigorous,
state-led process of economic and social reforms. This process
of authoritarian modernization was accompanied by a harsh
and effective repression of the Communist Party, which was
effectively obliterated. In Macedonia, the regime undertook a

policy of forced linguistic homogenization of the Slavophone minority, which backfired during the Civil War. At the same time, the regime made sustained efforts to acquire the loyalty of the population by, among other steps, settling favorably the farmers' loans.

Perhaps the Metaxas regime was a fitting end to a stormy period of Greek history, yet the turmoil was far from over. The 1940s would be dominated by foreign invasion and war, followed by a deeply traumatic civil war. Along with the 1920s, it is perhaps the worse decade in the history of Greece.

How did Greece enter World War II?

The Metaxas regime did everything it could to keep the country out of the looming world war. In spite of his obvious ideological attraction to European fascism, Metaxas was at heart a traditional politician rather than a radical leader. With a clear-headed understanding of geopolitical realities, he realized that Greece's interests aligned best with Great Britain. In addition, he did not harbor revisionist territorial claims against Greece's neighbors and was particularly wary of Italy's territorial ambitions that threatened Greece directly, especially after Mussolini's takeover of Albania in 1939. When the war erupted in Poland, he made strenuous efforts to keep the country neutral, including downplaying some very open displays of Italian aggression. However, when Italy requested Greece's unconditional surrender on October 28, 1940, he flatly refused to comply. His stance was later celebrated as Ochi ("No") Day and is now one of Greece's two national holidays (the other one, on March 25, celebrates the War of Independence).[17]

Italy invaded Greece from Albania expecting a short and easy campaign. To its surprise the Greek army, having anticipated the invasion, fought back with courage, determination, and effectiveness. Taking advantage of a solid preparation and a knowledge of the mountainous terrain of Northwestern Greece, it exploited the poor state of the Italian military, drew moral force from the defense of the homeland, contained the invasion, and quickly forced the Italians to retreat into Albania. The military success emboldened the Greek side, but eventually the war turned into a stalemate, forcing Hitler's hand and leading him to launch a Balkan blitzkrieg in April 1941. Despite the arrival of a British expeditionary force in March 1941, Greek defenses collapsed and the Germans entered Athens soon after. King George II and the Greek government fled to Crete, which they had to abandon after the Germans captured the island. They eventually ended up in Egypt, setting up a Greek government in exile.

The occupation that followed was arbitrary, violent, and destructive. Italy, Germany, and Bulgaria divided Greece into three zones of occupation, with the Italians reserving the largest chunk for themselves. The occupation caused enormous hardship and was particularly notable for a deadly famine. Armed resistance was rather slow to emerge, especially when compared to Yugoslavia. As elsewhere in occupied Europe, it was accompanied by savage reprisals and eventually a bitter, fratricidal civil war. How did a nation that had mobilized successfully to fend off a foreign invasion turn so quickly against itself?

Like many other instances of foreign occupation and colonization, the occupation of Greece sowed the seeds of division and conflict among the occupied population by activatng preexisting political cleavages and creating new ones on top, while infusing both with an unprecedented level of violence.

What was the Greek Civil War?

The Greek Civil War was an armed conflict pitting a coalition of conservatives and liberals against the communists. The war began during the occupation and mutated into one of the earliest Cold War "proxy wars" following the end of World War II. Its proximate cause can be found in the forces unleashed by the invasion and occupation of the country, but it was also an expression of deeper social and political fractures within Greek society and a reflection of the great international faultines of the time.

Like most civil wars, the Greek one was a complex and composite phenomenon that can be better understood when properly disaggregated. It is possible to distinguish four distinct phases. The first one took place during the occupation period (1941–1944) and consisted of two distinct but interrelated wars. One pitted the forces of a communist-led resistance organization, the National Liberation Front (EAM) and its armed wing, the National Popular Liberation Army (ELAS), against various noncommunist resistance groups, while the other one was a clash between EAM and various Greek collaborationist militias. This phase mixed resistance and civil war and ended with the German withdrawal from Greece in September–November 1944. The second phase took place after the liberation, in December 1944 and January 1945, when the communists withdrew from the British-backed national unity government and launched an armed uprising against it, which ended with their defeat after a vigorous British intervention. The third phase, in 1945–1946, saw the failure of various attempts to shore up a new political order; leftist supporters were hunted down by right-wing militias, while, later on, leftist guerrilla groups attacked gendarmerie stations and right-wing supporters in a climate of rising insecurity and violence. The fourth and final phase began in February 1946, when the communists decided to launch an all-out guerrilla insurgency against the government. The war peaked after 1947 and ended with a military defeat of the communists in 1949. Some historians designate this last phase as *the* Greek Civil War, but the war forms a longer sequence of intermittent armed conflict that begins in 1943 and ends in 1949.[18]

How did foreign occupation morph into civil war?

When the occupation began, the new authorities seized public and private stocks of food, apparel, medical supplies, military material, means of transport, and fuel and made the newly formed collaborationist Greek government responsible for paying the costs of occupation, causing hyperinflation and, eventually, economic disintegration. The collapse of supply routes within Greece and the British blockade of Greece produced a terrible famine, causing deaths in the tens of thousands during the winter of 1941–1942. The famine was deadliest in food-deficit areas, most particularly in many cities and islands. In spite of the grievances caused by the defeat, the famine, and the humiliation that many Greeks felt from being ruled by Italy (which they had defeated on the battlefield), resistance was rather slow to emerge, especially when compared to Yugoslavia. Initially, it was primarily unarmed, consisting mostly of spontaneous individual acts of hosting, protecting, and helping to evacuate British military personnel stranded in Greece. Soon, small clandestine intelligence cells that had been set up by the British before their withdrawal from Greece began to collect information and organize sabotage actions. A few early and isolated instances of attacks against German and Bulgarian troops in Northern Greece were quickly subdued through mass reprisals that effectively deterred armed resistance.[19]

Things began to shift in mid- to late 1942. The occupiers' presence was thin on the ground, particularly in Greece's mountainous hinterland, which was hard to access and control in the first place. There, order and security collapsed, and banditry became the scourge of villagers left to fend for themselves. When the first guerrilla bands emerged, they were warmly welcomed in these villages because they restored order and suppressed banditry, while their frequent references to the heroes of the Greek War of Independence resonated deeply. These bands came in two broad kinds: they were sometimes led by Greek army officers, both royalist and Republican, and sometimes by communist cadres. The British Special Operations Executive (SOE) actively encouraged the emergence of both types through financing and arms supplies, a part of Churchill's ambitious strategy to encourage guerrilla warfare in German-occupied areas and, thus, "set Europe ablaze."

The combination of British support, thin control on the ground by the occupation forces, strong patriotic feelings, and the old tradition of brigandage encouraged the growth of these guerrilla bands. Despite a vigorous British attempt to combine nationalist and communist bands into a single effective fighting force, the two sides clashed in a series of battles across the country during the fall of 1942 and winter of 1943. The communists emerged victorious, liquidating or co-opting most of their opponents and effectively establishing their control over the mountainous countryside. Although these clashes were accompanied by limited violence, they alienated a significant portion of the population and encouraged the fusion of the Greek officer corps, which was still reeling from its Republican-Royalist fracture. Many officers had clandestinely left Greece to participate in the creation of a new Greek army in exile based in the Middle East, but most remained in Greece and were looking for ways to act. Realizing that the communists were emerging as a new threat led the British to reconsider their support, but it was now too late. British concerns only grew more intense when the Greek armed forces in exile almost self-destructed following a string of communist mutinies. In the autumn of 1943, Italy capitulated and the Italian occupation forces in Greece disintegrated. The communists took advantage of this and extended their control over the greatest part of rural Greece, to the great consternation of their anticommunist foes. The attempt by the Germans to check the communist expansion through a campaign of mass reprisals and indiscriminate violence proved at best counterproductive, while causing enormous devastation and human loss in the countryside.[20]

What explains the transformation of the Communist Party?

The Communist Party took full advantage of the occupation to engineer a remarkable transformation, from a small and marginal party prior to the war to a powerful, armed political organization during the occupation.

The KKE relied on clandestine organizational know-how honed through years of repression. It was able to deploy a small, but highly disciplined and frequently ruthless, centralized network of political cadres. It fostered (and benefited from) the radicalization of the population caused by the occupation, embraced a strategy of revolutionary guerrilla warfare that took advantage of Greece's rough terrain, its rugged poeasant population and a tradition of irregular fighting going back to the Greek War of Independence, adopted a broad patriotic and nationalist political platform rather than a narrow revolutionary and communist one, exploited the collapse of traditional political parties and their extensive local networks, and rode the wave of Soviet prestige following the battle of Stalingrad.

Once in control of an area, the communists would set up an extensive governance structure that included a local administration, a court system, a taxation system, an extensive surveillance apparatus, and a dense network of mass organizations for various constituencies including young people and women. Although they were often initially popular, the ruthless and violent practices of communist cadres, their frequent lack of familiarity with peasant culture and insensitivity to local norms, as well as their policy of suppressing all dissenting opinions and their tendency to undertake military actions that triggered indiscriminate German reprisals often undermined their initial popularity, caused polarization, and contributed to the unification of their fractious rivals. However, the non-communist guerrillas lacked the discipline and centralization of their rivals they also did not understand the importance of setting-up grassroots political organizations in the countryside and were generally much less effective compared to the communists. And after having been chased away from the countryside, they had no means of regaining access.

The situation in the cities, especially Athens, was different. There, the communists relied initially on a political strategy based on mass mobilization, particularly of the poor and marginalized population of the Athenian suburbs. Eventually, this social movement strategy was coupled with a campaign of urban warfare against various competing resistance and collaborationist groups that led to a rise in violence and polarization.

In short, taking skillful advantage of the conditions created by the occupation, the communists were able to transform themselves, via EAM and ELAS, from a marginal party into a redoubtable armed actor that ruled the countryside, commanded a large army, and led an ebulient mass social movement in Athens. Power was well within their reach.

What explains the paradox of late and mass collaboration in Greece?

Having been pushed out of the resistance, many of KKE's rivals initiated a massive anticommunist countermobilization that found its most powerful expression in the formation of a variety of militias armed by the occupation authorities, a process that took explosive proportions in the summer of 1944.

Up until early 1943, the occupation authorities had been reluctant to raise collaborationist militias. They did not feel that the resistance threatened them and did not trust their Greek collaborators who were isolated and unpopular. However, things changed after the communist-led resistance took control of the countryside, particularly after Italy's capitulation in 1943. The Greek collaborationist government under Ioannis Rallis was growing alarmed by EAM's expansion and saw in anticommunism a unique opportunity to capture the social support it lacked.

Thus, the escalating resentment caused by the communist resistance met both the growing counterinsurgency needs of the German authorities and the collaborationist government's quest for legitimation. This process resulted in the formation and explosive growth of various collaborationist militias. The most prominent among them were the Security Battalions, initially formed in Athens, in April 1943, which really took off in 1944 by expanding in the countryside. Eventually, the number of men that served in various collaborationist militias came to be comparable to the size of ELAS, which is estimated to have mobilized between 30,000 and 35,000 fighters. These militias were based in provincial towns and villages of the plain, from where they launched bloody counterinsurgency campaigns against the communist-controlled mountain villages.[21]

Until recently, the magnitude of armed collaboration had not really been fully appreciated; it is puzzling in light of the absence of a grassroots, mass fascist movement in Greece and the loathing that the occupation regime inspired in the population at large. The puzzle only becomes greater when one considers that the collaborationist militias were composed of volunteers and the upsurge of collaborationist mobilization took place in the spring and summer of 1944, when it was clear to everyone that the German war fortunes had been upended.

Explaining this puzzle calls for an examination of both top-down and bottom-up processes. At the elite level (traditional politicians, officers, etc.) collaboration was often seen as a last-ditch effort to prevent a communist takeover, a relatively small price to pay in order to steer Greece's postwar path away from a Soviet takeover, especially after the elimination of nationalist resistance bands. At the mass level, there existed a variety of motivations for joining the militias, ranging from coercion, opportunism, and resentment against the communists all the way to conflicts between villages and feuds between families.

As a result, what began as resistance against occupation eventually morphed into a full-fledged civil war, pitting Greeks against Greeks, less concerned about the occupation itself and more about the future of postwar Greece. The descent into civil war was characterized by increasing radicalization and polarization, as violence deepened the gap that separated the two rival camps. The conflict was replete with massacres of civilians by both sides, and the end of the occupation came to be seen increasingly less as the hoped for deliverance and more as a prelude to a decisive clash between the two sides that would settle the question of who would rule Greece.[22]

How did liberation give way to more civil war?

The combined effects of occupation and civil war left the country deeply traumatized. The material destruction was enormous; thousands of villages had been destroyed during counterinsurgency operations. Thousands of lives had been lost, either in the famine or because of German reprisals and Greek-on-Greek fighting and killing. The Germans also decimated Greece's Jewish population, including Salonica's sizable community, which was almost entirely destroyed. Altogether, between 300,000 to 500,000 people lost their lives, out of a population of about seven million.[23]

Immediately after the Germans left Greece in September and October 1944, ELAS attacked and defeated the demoralized collaborationist militias, often sealing their victories with wholesale massacres of members and sympathizers. A communist takeover looked imminent. And yet, it did not happen. The KKE refrained from taking over Athens under the terms of an agreement it signed with the Greek government in exile, orchestrated by the British. Following this agreement, the KKE was to participate in a new National Unity government that included a majority of politicians from the old political parties, while the monarchy question would be settled in a referendum. The KKE had reluctantly signed this agreement, under pressure from the Soviet Union, whose leader Joseph Stalin had reached an understanding with Winston Churchill according to which Greece would continue to be in the British sphere of influence. However, the political fate of Greece was not yet settled.

Although the communists were now part of a broad government of National Unity headed by the Republican politician

George Papandreou, the tension between the two camps was palpable. The countryside was still ruled by the KKE, which was busy installing the foundations of a people's republic. In Athens, street violence was a daily occurrence in the face of intense polarization and mistrust. The communists resented the fact that political power, which they had conquered during the occupation, was slipping out of their hands, while their rivals were convinced that the communists were getting ready to install a leftist dictatorship.

In early December, the issue of the demobilization of ELAS and the formation of a new national army led to an open confrontation. On one hand, Papandreou, along with the British, demanded a swift ELAS demobilization, with a limited place for its fighters in the new national army. On the other hand, the KKE was reluctant to let its army go since its power depended on its armed might. The two sides could not be reconciled and the clash was inevitable. There is a lot of speculation about the stance of the Soviet Union given the understanding it had reached with the British. It seems that the Soviets sent out ambiguous signals which the Greek communists were happy to interpret as a call for action.[24]

After leaving the National Unity government, the communists prepared for armed action. They called for a demonstration in Athens and a general strike. The government forbade the demonstration which eventually took place and turned bloody on December 3, 1944, following which the KKE launched a full-scale military attack against the government and eventually the British as well. The 33-day urban clash became subsequently known as the Battle of Athens or the "December events" (*Dekemvriana*). The fighting was intense, causing widespread material destruction in Athens, which had been largely spared during the war. It also spread to other areas, such as Epirus and Macedonia, where ELAS attacked and destroyed the few nationalist resistance groups that had survived the occupation. Civilians bore the brunt of the fighting as both collateral damage and direct targets. However, the widespread massacres perpetrated by communist death squads and the systematic abduction of thousands of civilian hostages stood out and caused a majority of Greek public opinion to turn away from them.[25]

Winston Churchill understood that the Battle of Athens would decide the postwar fate of Greece. Determined not to allow Greece to fall to the communists, he gave the matter his undivided attention. Accompanied by Foreign Minister Anthony Eden, he even visited Athens on Christmas Day in 1944, with the battle raging all around him. With the world war still in full swing, Churchill committed substantial British troops to the battle, thus tipping its balance. The Battle of Athens turned out to be one of the very first shots of the Cold War, fired before World War II was over.

With their position untenable in Athens, the communists were forced to retreat and eventually sue for peace. Because they still controlled the rest of the country and had important resources left at their disposal, a compromise settlement emerged: the Varkiza Treaty, signed in that Athens coastal suburb on February 15, 1945. The treaty provided for the demobilization of ELAS, an amnesty for "political crimes," and both parliamentary elections and a referendum on the monarchy. Though this agreement outlined a peaceful end to fighting and anticipated normal democratic politics, both sides immediately violated it. The government allowed the persecution of KKE sympathizers mainly by right-wing paramilitary bands, while the communists chose not to surrender their best arms as a way to keep their future options open. In retrospect, it is difficult to see how this treaty could have ushered in an era of peaceful politics. The fratricidal violence during the occupation and the Battle of Athens had opened deep wounds, and the cries of vengeance could be heard high and loud. What is more, both sides were uncertain about their rival's commitment to peace and thus unwilling to fully commit to democratic politics.

How did the Civil War restart and end?

The period following the Varkiza Treaty was a time of constant brinkmanship. Political parties competed in the electoral arena to win public support for the forthcoming elections; the KKE, for instance, held giant rallies and recruitment drives, and so did the reconstituted traditional parties. At the same time, however, they both tested each other's intentions and resolve by engaging in violent politics. Dozens of right-wing paramilitary bands emerged throughout the country, harassing the supporters of the left with the tacit (and frequently explicit) support of the local authorities. Hundreds of alleged communist supporters were intimidated, beaten up, and often assassinated; thousands were arrested and tried, charged with crimes that had taken place during the occupation. In contrast, thousands of former collaborationist militiamen, often involved in similar if not worse crimes, escaped punishment only to keep tormenting their rivals. In response, the KKE encouraged the creation of so-called self-defense guerrilla bands that gradually engaged in the harassment of their tormentors and their families. Several thousand KKE cadres were evacuated to Yugoslavia, where they reassembled in training camps and engaged in intense political and military preparation. The communist leadership, feeling robbed of a victory it had thought certain, and inspired by the emergence of communist regimes throughout the Balkans, began to lobby the Soviet Union, asking for its support in a renewed bid for power.[26]

This period of brinkmanship ended when the Greek communists decided to boycott the first postwar parliamentary elections, held in March 1946. Following several small-scale engagements between communist guerrilla bands and the gendarmerie, the KKE established the Democratic Army of Greece (DSE) in December 1946 and launched a full-scale insurgency against the Athens government. By then, the KKE was able to obtain the full (though less than open) backing of the Soviet Union and its satellites, especially Yugoslavia. Their involvement was officially ratified in August 1947 at Bled, Slovenia, where the governments of Yugoslavia, Bulgaria, and Albania pledged to fully back the insurgency with massive aid. The insurgency got off to a promising start, as the Greek gendarmerie and army proved to be poorly trained. The conflict was concentrated in Northern Greece, where the insurgents were able to take advantage of large safe havens in Albania, Yugoslavia, and Bulgaria. However, when the communists failed to capture the mountainous town of Konitsa and install a provisional government, the war entered into an attrition phase, with the government unable to defeat the insurgency and the insurgents unable to claim any substantial territorial gains.

In the meantime, the United States was following the situation in Greece with growing concern. In February 1947, the US Undersecretary of State Dean Acheson outlined in Congress an early version of the domino theory, arguing that a communist victory in Greece would give the USSR the chance to get a foothold on three continents, rendering Africa, the Middle East, and Europe vulnerable to Soviet influence. Acheson helped persuade Congress to endorse the Truman Doctrine, which fleshed out the strategy of Soviet containment, opening the gates to massive US support of the Greek government. Now, Greece became the frontline of the Cold War.[27]

Despite the massive influx of US assistance, Athens was unable to win a quick and decisive victory, because each time the insurgents were defeated on the battlefield, they were able to retreat to their safe havens in Yugoslavia and Albania, where they could regroup and launch new incursions in Greece. They also set up heavily fortified bases in Greece's northwest mountains, alongside Greece's borders with Yugoslavia and Albania. On its side, the Greek government targeted these bases for massive conventional attacks that led to considerable human losses; it also implemented a policy of civilian relocation, moving thousands of peasants from their mountainous villages to the cities and plains, thus depriving the insurgents of access to new recruits. In desperation, the communists resorted to mass abductions of men, women, and children as a way to replace their escalating casualties, which made them even more unpopular, while degrading their military effectiveness. Toward the end of the war, probably more communist sympathizers were fighting in the government army, where they had been drafted, than in KKE's Democratic Army, which was increasingly composed of forcibly recruited peasants.[28]

The Civil War ended because of a shift in international politics. To be sure, the communists were socially and politically isolated: they had no political allies, they were operating in depopulated rural areas, and they had a hard time recruiting fighters. What is more, their dependence on Yugoslavia's assistance led them to adopt a highly unpopular position in favor of an independent Macedonia that would include Greece's northern province. Furthermore, their decision to transport thousands of children away from their villages and resettle them across the Soviet block countries was stigmatized by the government and met the public's disapproval. In spite of all this however, the KKE could have kept fighting given its access to safe havens outside of Greece and the assistance it was receiving from Greece's northern neighbors.

It was then, however, that the fallout between Yugoslavia's leader Josip Broz Tito and Stalin took place, forcing the KKE to pick sides. After the Greek communists chose to align themselves with Stalin, they lost access to their Yugoslav safe haven, which forced them to cease hostilities and admit defeat. Thus, the Civil War ended with a decisive military outcome. The Communist Party, along with the remains of its army, cadres, and their family members, as well as a few peasant communities that had supported it, fled to the countries of the Soviet bloc. Although it retained a measure of influence within Greece, the party itself remained outlawed until 1974.

What was the legacy of the Civil War?

The Civil War can be interpreted in several ways. It is an example of how things can go terribly wrong when order collapses; how the unfinished business of national integration can feed civil strife; how easily the patriotic willingness to resist foreign occupation can be transformed into fratricidal violence; how national and international priorities may clash with each other; and how political and social realities may turn out to be incredibly fluid in a context of worldwide turmoil.

The ability of the Greek Communist Party to transform itself from marginal to dominant political player can also be seen as another instance of the Greek aspiration toward modernity. Greek communists put forward a model of communist modernization built around a disciplined party that attempted, often with notable success, to transcend local and personalistic loyalties. The model was of course wrong, but the project was homegrown and ambitious and attracted considerable, if dwindling, support.

The Civil War caused enormous human and material damage to the country. Like in all civil wars, the damage was also psychological and moral. The realization that neighbors could turn against each other was traumatic. Because a great deal of this violence took place in small rural communities or urban neighborhoods, survivors often continued to live together. Once the conflict ended, however, most overt physical violence stopped and life resumed. The price for this state of affairs was intense resentment. Real or distorted experiences of victimization during the Civil War became the foundation of reconstituted political identities that were transmitted down to the following generations, often shaping political attitudes for decades to come.[29]

Politically, the Civil War caused the marginalization of the communist left. The Greek communist diaspora spread across the countries of the Soviet bloc, from Prague to Tashkent. In Greece, the KKE was outlawed and its members were forced to operate clandestinely. Widespread surveillance was carried out by Greek security services, and suspected communists could be arrested and imprisoned or deported without trial—although death sentences were commuted with the end of the conflict. On the social front, the end of the Civil War led to the political exclusion of a significant minority. In contrast to most other countries, the left in Greece became associated with the Communist Party, an association driven by the twin experiences of resistance and civil war. To be sure, many (perhaps most) ex-ELAS fighters or EAM sympathizers had not been (and never became) communists. They could be persecuted all the same, however, and were socially stigmatized.

What was the nature of the postwar political order?

The postwar political order was ambiguous, mixing democratic and exclusionary features. Unlike many other countries emerging from a bloody civil war during that period, Greece did not become an authoritarian dictatorship, but was rather an anticommunist or Cold War democracy. There was much more freedom in post–Civil War Greece than in, say, Franco's Spain or Tito's Yugoslavia. Furthermore, despite the limitations on personal freedoms bequeathed by the civil war, Greece was a functioning parliamentary regime. Indeed, the left could compete politically and did so quite effectively. The United Democratic Left (EDA), a party whose control by the KKE was an open secret, proved quite successful, winning as much as 25 percent of the vote in the 1958 elections.

More importantly, the left was able to thrive in the cultural sphere and thus shape public attitudes in an indirect yet durable fashion. Composed of a broad constellation of newspapers, magazines, and publishing houses, and represented by some of Greece's top artists in a variety of fields from poetry and painting to music, this cultural presence gave the left a degree of prestige and influence that transcended its actual public support and political weight. The composer

Mikis Theodorakis, perhaps the most famous of these artists, incorporated thinly veiled political themes into his widely popular music that spoke in touching ways of the communist experience during the Civil War. As a result, communism acquired an aura of nobility, transfused with a romanticized sense of pure commitment and unconditional suffering. This is how communist influence came to exceed actual political support for the communist cause.

As the Civil War faded into the past, politics began a slow process of normalization. Political discrimination was gradually relaxed and the number of political prisoners dwindled, as most were released. At the same time, Greece's powerful and omnipresent extended-family networks played an important role in mitigating the effects of political and social exclusion. It was thus not unusual for leftists to be able to obtain public jobs, from which they were officially excluded, through the political contacts of their extended family.

If there was a single positive legacy in the tragedy of the Civil War, it was surely Greece's escape from the fate that befell its northern neighbors, who came under Soviet dominion. To be sure, Greece became a client state of the United States. But by remaining anchored in the West, it was able to benefit from the Marshall Plan and the growth of Western European economies, eventually achieving an unprecedented breakthrough in economic development that placed it far ahead of all its Balkan neighbors.

All in all, there are two ways to make sense of the thirty turbulent years between 1920 and 1950. One way is to see this period as a mind-boggling succession of wars, military coups, and assorted political and economic calamities. The alternative is to try to connect the dots between the ambitious project of territorial expansion, ending with the Anatolian disaster, and the ambitious reform and modernization push in 1928–1932, ending in occupation and civil war. Despite the calamities of occupation and civil war, Greece managed to avoid what could have been the most consequential and long-term disaster of all, namely a communist transformation. Through a combination of wise alliances, foreign intervention, and plain luck, Greece stood on the brink of realizing the dream that had eluded it so far: the leap toward economic development.

V

TAKEOFF

What was the state of Greece in the aftermath of the Civil War?

Greece entered the 1950s in a state of total disarray. It had undergone uninterrupted conflict for nine years and experienced multiple calamities since 1920. In fact, the incidence of war, occupation, civil strife, famine, mass population displacement, political turbulence, and economic depression had been non-stop for close to forty years.

There was an additional, less visible, dimension as well. Greece had experienced anemic growth rates since its appearance on the world stage. With the exception of two short periods in the nineteenth century (1850s and 1880s) and one in the twentieth century (1920s), the Greek economy was characterized by low growth due to a variety of causes including the debt burden accumulated from loans raised to finance the War of Independence; the cost of pursuing irredentist goals, fighting wars, and absorbing refugees; the small size of the country; its geographic location on the periphery of Europe; and the absence of natural resources.[1]

This dire situation was aggravated by governance problems, described in stark terms by Paul A. Porter, the head of a US mission charged with reporting on the state of Greece. Summarizing his report in an article published on September 20, 1947, Porter observed that Greece was a country mired in "hopelessness, discouragement, and lack of faith in the future." The people, he noted, were paralyzed by uncertainty and fear, the economy was ruined, and, despite the end of the war, economic activity was not picking up. "Businessmen will not invest, shopkeepers will not lay in supplies, peasants will not repair their houses." The immediate reason for this state of affairs, Porter wrote, was the civil war. "You can't devote your full energies to repairing docks, building bridges and maintaining roads when you are likely to be shot in the back any moment." He also pointed to a number of deeper structural deficiencies:

> The civil service is overexpanded, underpaid and demoralized. The low salaries have been augmented by a completely baffling system of extra allowances by which a few civil servants probably get as much as four times their base pay. At the same time the bulk of them do not get a living wage. Many of them are forced to supplement their government pay by taking outside jobs.... The result is complete disorganization. I have never seen an administrative structure which, for sheer incompetence and ineffectiveness, was so appalling. The civil service simply cannot be relied upon to carry out the simplest functions of government—the collection of taxes, the enforcement of economic regulations, the repair of roads.

On top of an inefficient and overstretched civil service, undermined by practices of political patronage, lay a myopic economic oligarchy, "a small mercantile and banking cabal determined above all to protect its financial prerogatives, at whatever expense to the economic health of the country." Porter concluded that the US mission was daunting, but so were the stakes. "Today an almost forgotten American mission has got to perform a miracle—or fail in its job. The miracle is to save Greece from economic disintegration and the inroads of communism." Yet, Porter concluded optimistically, "I think

Americans have enough resourcefulness and perseverance to lick the problem."[2]

Porter turned out to be right. Greece was about to embark on an incredible economic boom that transformed it from a perennially poor rural country into an expansive urban service economy with a large middle class and an dazzling per capita GDP growth. Between the mid-fifties and the late seventies Greece's rate of economic growth averaged close to 7 percent annually, while inflation was kept below 2 percent. In many ways, Greece's achievement parallels that of postwar Germany and Japan; but unlike them, Greece had not been an industrialized country prior to the war. In the words of the historian William H. McNeill, this was a true metamorphosis. How was this remarkable outcome achieved?[3]

How did Greece take off?

Three factors explain what has been rightly termed the "Greek economic miracle." The first, most immediate one was political and military: bringing the civil war to a successful end. This was accomplished by 1949, and it is hard to understate its significance. Civil wars tend to last a long time, and such an eventuality would have certainly undermined any development effort. It is also important to underline the significance of the government's victory, as a communist-led Greece would have hardly diverged from the trajectory of its Balkan neighbors. Second was the implementation of a number of critical policies that set the economy on a new path. And third was the ability of Greek society to respond to these policies with remarkable speed and flexibility.

When the civil war ended in 1949, Greece was unable to produce any significant tax income or generate any exports, and its currency inspired no confidence in anyone—in fact, the currency of choice in Greece at the time was the British gold pound. Being part of the Western world, Greece was able to benefit from the Marshall Plan, a massive economic recovery program enacted to counter the threat of communist expansion in Europe. The plan was adopted with the signing of the Greek-American Economic Cooperation Agreement on July 2, 1948, while the civil war was still raging. It was to be implemented in a backward rural economy that had been destroyed by the war.

Between 1945 and 1950, Greece received more than $2 billion in aid, an amount higher than the sum of all the foreign loans it had received during the entire 1821–1930 period. The Marshall Plan contributed between 10 percent and 15 percent of Greek GDP in 1948–1950. During the four years of the plan (1948–1952), 90.6 percent of the balance of payments deficit was financed by foreign funds, chiefly Marshall Plan funds. Considerable investment in infrastructure took place, and by 1955 electricity generated in Greece was 5.7 times as great as in 1939. All in all, US economic assistance was crucial in rebuilding the country's productive capacity by injecting liquidity into the economy; providing for the immediate consumption needs of the population; and allowing the financing of imports, trade balance deficits, and budget deficits. Ultimately, the Marshall Plan laid the foundations of the postwar Greek economy.[4]

Nevertheless and despite its size, the plan's success was far from a foregone conclusion. Its implementation met with several obstacles, including the shortsightedness of Greek politicians, the inefficiency of the bureaucracy, and the inexperience of American planners. As McNeill wryly observed, "Irritable condemnation of the inefficiency and corruption of Greek politicians and civil servants was a poor substitute for thinking through the defects of the original American blueprint, which had naively assumed that Greek society was essentially the same as United States society, and needed only a few pointers in order to duplicate the American New Deal."[5]

In the end, however, the plan turned out to be a success. This was due in no small part to the flexibility and adaptability of Greek society, including the peasantry. McNeill describes how "when a new technique, a new crop, new seeds, or some other novelty could be shown to pay off on an individual family basis, Greek peasants were not slow to accept the innovation, and proved apt pupils in learning whatever new procedures or skills were required." Likewise, innumerable small-scale individual enterprises seized upon the new possibilities and made the most of them in the cities. "The efficiency with which the Greek nuclear family could pursue gain," concludes McNeill, "by combination of hard work, shrewd exploitation of market opportunities, and rigorous saving for the future, lay behind the Greek economic miracle."[6]

By 1951, production in Greece had returned to prewar levels. It was the combination of the restoration of economic activity and the anticipation of the end of US assistance that led to a series of successful monetary stabilization measures that were introduced in 1953 and supervised by Economy Minister Spyros Markczinis—along with various liberalization measures including the removal of several barriers to imports and exports, as well as the introduction of guarantees for foreign investment— that helped the Greek economy leap forward. Along with tight fiscal management, the massive devaluation of the drachma, in particular, proved highly effective, leading to the containment of inflation, the restoration of confidence in the Greek currency, and the shoring-up of bank deposits. This launched a virtuous cycle, as banks were able to inject further liquidity into the economy, fueling a rise in exports, while funds began to flow into Greece from both immigrant remittances and shipping, financing the trade balance deficit. At the same time, the state continued to invest in infrastructure and channel private capital into investment. As a result, the average yearly growth achieved by the economy between 1953 and 1960 reached 4.4 percent.[7]

By the end of the 1950s the economy had been restored and stabilized. What happened next was a real takeoff, reaching previously unseen levels. Between 1961 and 1973, Greece achieved an average growth rate of 7.4 percent, placing the country among the top achievers globally. This was made possible through a combination of political stability;

monetary stabilization (based on a peg of the drachma to the dollar, which led to more confidence in the Greek currency); macroeconomic stability (inflation was kept below 4 percent between 1957 and 1972, and government budgets were balanced or near-balanced); the opening up to international trade (thus taking advantage of the country's growing connection with the booming economies of Western Europe, as Greece had become an associate of the European Economic Community in June 1961); massive investment in both infrastructure (especially electrification, as well as a huge construction boom in Athens); industry (the share of investment to GDP averaged 26.2 percent during the 1960s and 1970s, leading to substantial gains in productivity); and the adoption of a developmentalist approach in economic management, with the state playing a guiding role in the economy and facilitating credit access to both industry and agriculture. A new industrial sector emerged, accounting for 25 percent of GDP in 1961 and reaching 33 percent in 1973, while large gains in productivity were made in agriculture. Higher education was expanded, the country was urbanized, and an emerging middle class boosted domestic demand, thus lifting domestic industries. After 1961 and for about a decade, massive migration took place both internally, from villages to cities, and externally toward Western Europe and especially West Germany, thus generating a flow of labor remittances and absorbing the surplus labor force. In sum, during the 1960s the country was transformed economically and socially and Greece was effectively "modernized."[8]

While recognizing this huge achievement, it is also necessary to point out that modernization remained an incomplete and ongoing project—unsurprisingly perhaps, since it is, almost by definition, always an open-ended process. Nevertheless, by the early 1970s, the proportion of the labor force employed in agriculture remained large; the industrial sector was dominated by small firms specializing in import substitution, with a focus on domestic demand rather than export-oriented growth; and many of the values and norms prevailing among the urban middle class harked back to the rural world from which it had just emerged.

In the end, the inability to shift Greek industry away from the domestic market and toward a focus on exports proved to be the most consequential shortcoming. At the same time, the absence of a professionalized bureaucracy contributed to the neglect of some critical aspects of the developmentalist approach. Greece privileged monetary stabilization over a coherent long-term plan for industrial development. The combination of protectionism and easy availability of credit for the emerging domestic-oriented industrial sector made the Greek industrial sector prone to high indebtedness levels and low competitiveness. These factors also created powerful interest groups who resisted changes toward export orientation because they were risky and could threaten their profits. This is why, when the limitations of developmentalism became apparent the Greek industrial sector failed to take the necessary leap toward export-oriented growth. And when protections began to be lifted, it suffered a huge blow.[9]

What caused the 1967 military coup?

Greece's economy may have been booming, but its politics was not faring as well. For sure, the end of the 1950s saw a political thaw with the gradual liberalization of politics. After many failed efforts, the Venizelist camp managed to unite under a new umbrella party, the Center Union, headed by veteran politician George Papandreou. Quickly, this party emerged as the voice of the newly urbanized Greeks who were clamoring for freedoms to match their newfound economic might.

Politics during the 1950s had been dominated by the royalist right, under the umbrella of ERE (National Radical Union). The first half of the 1960s saw a reversal, with the Center Union winning elections and beginning to challenge some elements of the post–Civil War status quo. ERE won the 1961 elections, but the extensive use of electoral fraud caused a rift between the two rival sides. The Center Union won in 1963 and triumphed in the subsequent 1964 elections, but a conflict erupted the following year around the issue of who controlled the military. Prime Minister George Papandreou had asked his defense minister to sack the army's chief of staff, but he refused to do so and resigned instead. When Papandreou decided to take over the defense portfolio, he faced King Constantine's objection and was forced to resign, which sparked a severe political crisis known as the July events (*Iouliana*), replete with demonstrations and riots. The crisis was further stoked by the inflammatory rhetoric of Andreas Papandreou, George's son and an emerging firebrand politician. The king contributed to the escalating political turbulence by encouraging the defection from their party of a large number of Center Union parliamentarians and the formation of a new government based on a coalition of the right and the defectors from the Center Union. This created a justified feeling that democratic institutions were being tampered with and that both the king and the military were operating above the law, which sparked additional unrest.[10]

Thus, the early sixties were a period characterized by political turmoil and street agitation, a potent mix that gave Greece a Latin American flavor best captured in Costa-Gavras's famous 1969 film Z, a thinly veiled fictionalization of the 1963 assassination of the leftist politician Grigoris Lambrakis by extreme-right thugs with the complicity of police elements. Everyone was ready for change and when elections were called for May 1967, they were widely expected to lead to a Center Union victory. They never took place.

The April 1967 military coup brings into sharp focus the obstacles to democratization faced by the country. Although the coup was widely perceived as having been masterminded by the United States, this interpretation is not supported by evidence. The coup could be seen instead as an attempt by the military to preserve its privileged institutional position in the face of mounting challenges from civil society. In this sense, it was an expression of the military's particularistic interests.

More specifically, the coup was an attempt by a class of junior officers, primarily colonels, to address grievances related to dim professional prospects. Recent research, however, has nuanced this view by showing that the military was, at least since the early 1950s, under the control of the political leadership. It was the political crisis of the 1963–1967 period that led to the loosening of political control over the military and created an opening for a group of staunchly anticommunist and antiparliamentarian officers to seize power. In short, the coup was less a legacy of the Civil War and more the result of failure by the political elite to reach a consensus over how to manage the incipient democratization process.[11]

The coup was executed flawlessly on April 21, 1967. The plotters proclaimed martial law, banned political parties, shut down the parliament, and arrested all prominent politicians. They swiftly formed a government with the initial support of the king (who would flee Greece a few months later, after engineering a failed countercoup) and got down to running the country. The United States did not instigate the coup, but quickly extended unconditional support to the military regime. And this was how the Greek economic miracle morphed into a political nightmare.

What was the military regime like?

The military regime—or junta, as it was typically known in Greece following Latin American practice—initially benefited from the positive economic outlook of the late 1960s. The Greek economy continued to grow, although the rate of growth declined compared to the previous decade and inflation inched up. The government, eager to win popular support, proceeded to raise the country's public debt by adopting populist measures such as the forgiveness of farmers' debts. It is obviously impossible to know the extent to which Greek society supported the regime, but the absence of major acts

of resistance and the overall good shape of the economy suggest that many people generally consented, passively if not
actively. Of course, the regime was keen to deploy coercion
in a highly selective fashion, targeting both well-known leftists and actual dissidents and submitting them to a regime of
imprisonment, internal exile, and often torture.

An American journalist provided a cogent assessment of
the situation in July 1972:

> Business is booming, standards of living are rising.
> Most of the people are economically satisfied and politi-
> cally apathetic. The old privileged class is being suc-
> ceeded by a new and larger one coming mostly from
> the countryside—the officer corps and their business
> protégés. They may not be particularly astute, but for
> the moment the Greeks are tired of political astuteness.
> The situation may last for some time, but it will not last
> forever. The Greek is a political animal who sooner or
> later will grow bored with his exclusion from politics.
> The present silence is unnatural. The colonels will even-
> tually have to adapt or quit.[12]

Indeed, when the global recession of 1973 hit the Greek
economy, ending twenty years of uninterrupted growth,
society began to agitate for change. The regime was not helped
by the fact that the country itself had changed considerably
since 1967, with the steady growth of an urban middle class.
Sensing these trends, the colonels launched a process of controlled liberalization. A referendum aimed at abolishing the
monarchy was organized, and the regime began to approach
politicians with a view toward implementing a managed
transition. A new government was formed in October 1973
under Spyros Markezinis, the architect of the 1953 monetary
stabilization plan. Its mandate was to organize elections the
following February and initiate a gradual process of gradual
democratization under the tutelage of the regime.

This process ended in abject failure in November 1973, when students of the prestigious Athens Polytechnic School staged a series of protests culminating in the occupation of their school. The protests were initially motivated by student demands, but they were also inspired by the global explosion of youth culture in the late 1960s and in some ways can be seen as a delayed echo of the May 1968 events in Paris. The location of the Polytechnic School in downtown Athens provided very quickly a focal point for the open expression of generalized opposition to the regime and demands for democratization. Feeling threatened, the regime responded in a heavy-handed way, first through police action and eventually by bringing in the army in the streets of Athens and imposing martial law. The crackdown worked, but it triggered a series of developments that ultimately led to the collapse of the regime. A group of regime hardliners took advantage of the student uprising to stage a coup, bring the government down, and end the liberalization process. However, in their quest to legitimize their rule, they committed an enormous blunder, embarking on a foreign military adventure that ended in disaster. In July 1974 they helped stage a military coup against the government of Cyprus, an action that triggered an immediate Turkish invasion of the island. The regime's inability to counter this invasion militarily led to a new coup, the collapse of the regime, and the restoration of democracy.

Seen in retrospect, the military regime stands out as a political parenthesis. Begun as an attempt to obstruct the gradual democratization of Greece following the end of the Civil War, it ended with propelling the country toward it. Postwar economic development had radically transformed Greek society, and the regime was out of line with both local social trends and broader developments in Western Europe.

Before turning to an examination of the transition to democracy, it is necessary to take a look at the Cyprus question, and the broader Greco-Turkish rivalry, which contributed to the regime's downfall.

Is there a never-ending Greco-Turkish rivalry?

The rivalry between Greece and Turkey is one of the most enduring clichés—both inside and outside of Greece. It is often the first thing to come up in a casual conversation and as is usually the case, the distance between reality and cliché is not trivial.

In contrast to what many people believe, it is not true that the conflict between Greeks and Turks is unrelenting and permanent, going back all the way to the Byzantine era. In fact, the Turks were one among many groups that clashed with the Byzantines, and relations between them went through various phases, peaceful as well as violent. Moving closer to the contemporary period, it is important to stress that rivalry requires a measure of symmetry. The two countries fought several wars during the nineteenth and twentieth centuries, but Greece was hardly the Ottoman Empire's unique concern. The Ottomans faced a multitude of external and internal challenges, and the Russian threat loomed large. Rivalry can also be a misleading term to describe the complex relations among the citizens of the newly independent Greek state, Ottoman Christians, Muslims, and the authorities of the Ottoman Empire. During the nineteenth century, Ottoman Greeks were able to thrive economically and culturally, while Greek citizens migrated to the Ottoman Empire in search of better economic opportunities. Even after the formulation of the Great Idea, Greece ranked low on the security agenda of the Ottoman Empire, which was much more preoccupied with the threats posed by Austria-Hungary and Russia. Moreover, during the Macedonian conflict, Greeks were much more concerned, almost obsessed, with another rival. Indeed, Greece's most acute rivalry during the second half of the nineteenth century and the first half of the twentieth century was not with Turkey, but with Bulgaria. The two countries locked horns over Macedonia and fought two bloody wars between 1913 and 1918, while Bulgaria also occupied a substantial part of Greek Macedonia during World War II, where it undertook a program of ethnic cleansing.[13]

The Greco-Turkish rivalry truly intensified after the First Balkan War. Turkish nationalism replaced both the old imperial Ottoman ideology and the Young Turk movement, which for some time had envisaged the creation of a multiethnic, democratic, quasi-federal state that presumed the active participation of Ottoman Greeks. Events in the following years exacerbated relations between the two states. Both World War I and the Greek-Turkish War of 1919–1922, with its accompanying atrocities and population dislocation, further inflamed relations. The birth of modern Turkey in 1922 created an unusual situation, whereby both Greece and Turkey emerged as nation-states through a struggle of liberation against the other one. Even more surprising is the fact that following this traumatic experience, the two countries enjoyed relatively peaceful relations for almost three decades, between the late 1920s and mid-1950s. It is only with the emergence of the Cyprus issue that relations deteriorated again. They were made worse by a conflict over the Aegean Sea and remained at a low point until 1999, when a thaw between the two countries took place that has lasted until the present. In short, the Greco-Turkish rivalry as currently understood is largely a reflection of the early twentieth century and applies more recently to a rather limited period from the mid-1950s to the late 1990s.[14]

What is the Cyprus issue about?

Unlike most Ottoman European territories that were incorporated into a variety of successor nation-states, Cyprus passed under British colonial rule in 1878. It was an ethnically mixed island, whose population included roughly 80 percent Greek Cypriots and 20 percent Turkish Cypriots. The colonial status of Cyprus meant that its ultimate fate could be contested, and thus it became a flashpoint between Greece and Turkey. The initiative was taken by the Greek Cypriots with an early insurrection against the British colonial regime in 1931, the result of the fusion of economic grievances with Greek irredentism, expressed as a demand for union (*Enosis*) with Greece.[15]

As in many other instances, ethnic conflict in Cyprus was related to conflict within the two communities. On the Greek side, the prospect of an immediate union with Greece was naturally unpalatable for Cypriot communists, members of the powerful local communist party AKEL (Anorthotiko Komma Ergazomenou Laou—Progressive Party of Working People). This situation gave an advantage to the nationalist right for, by pushing the *Enosis* agenda, it had the opportunity to marginalize the Cypriot communists. At the same time, the reliance of Greek governments on British support complicated Athens' position toward the question of *Enosis*. The decolonization wave that began in the 1950s gave a boost to the nationalist cause in Cyprus, and the declining global influence of Britain combined with Greece's growing association with the United States to give the Greek government much more freedom vis-à-vis Great Britain with respect to the Cyprus issue.[16]

It was around this time that the nationalist right, assisted by volunteers from Greece, launched a guerrilla insurgency against the colonial authorities, thus provoking a violent British reaction. Greece took the issue to the United Nations in 1954 as a way of internationalizing it. In reaction to this development, Britain brought the previously neutral Turkish Cypriots as well as Turkey into the dispute, thus triggering a violent clash between Greek and Turkish Cypriots that escalated quickly. In Istanbul, a pogrom was launched against the city's Greek population causing its mass departure for Greece.

Apart from its consequences for Greek-Turkish relations, Cyprus became a constant source of instability in Greek politics. Greek governments had to hew to a delicate balance between the interests of their Western allies, which emphasized the avoidance of tensions in NATO's southern flank, and public sentiment in favor of *Enosis,* which by 1954 had become so strong that it led the US embassy in Athens to assert that "no Greek government could stay in power if it ignored popular feeling and reversed its course." Eventually however, having failed to secure the union of Cyprus, all Greece could do was acquiesce to the island's independence in 1960, under the guarantee of Greece, Britain, and Turkey.

The newly independent country acquired a rigid "consociational" system that parceled authority to the two communities. This system quickly led to political paralysis and eventually broke down amid extensive ethnic violence and the emergence of armed Turkish Cypriot enclaves surrounded by Greek Cypriot militias. For most Cypriots and Greeks, independence had failed to resolve the matter. And so it was that when the new Athens military regime faced the challenge of an economic crisis in 1974, it made the fatal move of backing a nationalist coup against the government of Cyprus, which triggered a Turkish invasion, the division of the island, the permanent forced displacement of hundreds of thousands of people, and the downfall of the Athens regime. The Cyprus issue remains unsettled to this day, and the island is divided in two parts: the Republic of Cyprus, occupying the southern part and populated by Greek Cypriots; and the northern part, populated by Turkish Cypriots and settlers from Turkey who have set up their own, internationally not recognized state, the Republic of Northern Cyprus.[17]

What is the Aegean Sea Dispute?

Besides Cyprus, Greece and Turkey have had an enduring dispute over the Aegean Sea, which began in 1973. The Greek position on the issue is that the Aegean dispute started on November 1, 1973 when Turkey awarded exploration rights in twenty-seven maritime areas in the Aegean, concurrently attaching maps to the awards, which implied that half of the Aegean seabed was Turkish. Turkey, for its part, has claimed that the conflict, even in a latent form, had already started in the late 1960s when Greece awarded exploration rights in areas beyond Greek territorial waters. The dispute today encompasses a set of related issues, including the continental shelf, territorial sea, national airspace, demilitarization of the Eastern Aegean islands, tensions surrounding flight information regions and NATO operation control, and, more recently, status of several uninhabited islets. The conflict has lingered because of a deep mistrust between the two parties, fed by the mutually held belief that the other side is keen on challenging the status quo. For Turkey this takes the form of an attempt by Greece to transform the Aegean into a "Greek lake;" and for Greece, there is a fear that any change in the status quo in the Aegean would lead to the "enclavement" of Greek islands in the Eastern Aegean, that is their transformation into defenseless territories. Interestingly, the sensitive issue of the Muslim minority in Western Thrace has produced fewer sparks compared to the Cyprus and Aegean issues.[18]

After 1999, relations between Greece and Turkey improved, but the various points of contention between the two countries have yet to be solved. A full-fledged solution requires extensive bilateral talks with full support from the governments of both countries, as well as a paradigm shift in terms of how each country is perceived by the other one in order to decrease or eliminate mistrust. An important development in recent years has been the growth in interactions between Greeks and Turks, the result of rising travel from both directions. As people get to interact they often come to realize that they share several cultural traits, a development that could reduce mutual mistrust. Furthermore, a possible resumption of EU-Turkey accession talks could have a positive impact on Greco-Turkish relations.[19]

How was democracy restored?

The Cyprus coup had been a desperate attempt to bolster the declining fortunes of Greece's military regime, but it backfired monumentally, causing the collapse of the regime. The Turkish invasion of Cyprus caught Athens off guard leading to a decision of general mobilization that exposed the regime's total lack of military preparedness. In turn, this prompted the joint chiefs of staff to stage an internal coup, depose the regime, and immediately seek a political solution to the crisis by appealing to Konstantinos Karamanlis.

A dour and austere man hailing from Northern Greece, Karamanlis had been the leader of the right and a successful prime minister. Focused, austere, and reserved, he was motivated by an unflinching vision to modernize Greece. He had left Greece in 1963 after being defeated in the elections by George Papandreou. While living in self-imposed exile in Paris, he evolved toward more centrist and liberal positions. He was, therefore, able to appeal to both traditional conservatives and moderates. On the night of July 24, 1974, Karamanlis returned to Athens to preside over a transition government composed of a diverse group of prominent political figures.

The sudden, nonviolent manner through which the military regime had collapsed meant that the new democracy had to initially operate with a state apparatus still dominated by its appointees. To successfully handle the crisis, Karamanlis adopted a gradualist strategy aimed at maintaining the unity of the founding coalition that had come together in an extraordinary crisis situation, while placating a suddenly radicalized public opinion. The new government proceeded to legalize the Communist Party and chose to postpone the trial of the junta leaders until its new leaders had acquired a popular mandate. Karamanlis did get this mandate, with a landslide.

The party Karamanlis founded, New Democracy, triumphed in the parliamentary elections held on November 17, 1974. Soon after, in a referendum held on December 8, 1974, the majority of the electorate voted to abolish the monarchy, thus ditching an institution that had been associated with intense political conflict since 1915, before being tarnished irreparably by the partisan meddling of King Constantine during the 1960s. Armed with an impressive political mandate, Karamanlis could now abandon the gradualist approach in favor of more decisive action in controlling the military and security apparatus.

A transitional justice process was initiated and conducted in an exemplary fashion, setting an international precedent for human rights prosecutions of authoritarian leaders. It is now recognized that the Greek case was extraordinary in terms of how quickly and efficiently the process unfolded: hundreds of former officials were tried, including the regime leaders; several were sentenced (and some received severe sentences, including death, though immediately commuted to life); and the entire process was concluded in just eighteen months. In fact, the Greek case was the first time a government held its own officials accountable for past human rights violations. Overall, the democratization process was completed in a swift manner and foreshadowed future democratic transitions, pioneering what would later become known as the "third wave of democracy."[20]

The transition to democracy (known in Greece as *Metapolitefsi*) led to a sweeping reform of political institutions and encouraged the wholesale liberalization of social attitudes, heralding the most democratic and liberal era that Greece had ever experienced in its history. If 1967 had been an attempt to halt the gradual evolution of political institutions toward democracy and turn back the political clock, 1974 was in contrast a swift and abrupt dash into the future. In fact, the transition led to the establishment of political institutions that corresponded to the economic and social evolution that had taken place after 1950 and legitimized the social attitudes that had emerged during this time of rapid economic development. There was a general belief that Greece would now finally fulfill its original goal of becoming a truly modern European country by combining a dynamic and prosperous economy with stable and liberal democratic institutions.

Where did the new party system come from?

The most important change brought by the end of the dictatorship in 1974 was the establishment of a fully competitive democracy. A new constitution was drafted and passed, the most liberal in the country's history. A referendum abolished the monarchy, thus settling a fundamental institutional issue. The Communist Party was legalized, reversing the 1947 law that had banned it.

Although the democratic gains obtained after 1974 were unprecedented, the new party system emerged out of the pre-dictatorship one, which featured two dominant parties repre-senting the traditional political camps: the royalist camp at the right of center and the Republican camp at the left of center. The dominant parties were the National Radical Union (ERE), founded in 1956 by Karamanlis, who led it until 1964; and the Center Union (EK), founded in 1961 by Papandreou, also led by him until 1967. Karamanlis founded the New Democracy (ND) Party, which drew on ERE's traditions and electoral base, but with a modernized and forward-looking profile. After its electoral triumph in 1974, ND became a pillar of the new party system. Its rival, however, faced more difficulties. Papandreou had died in 1968 and his legacy was in dispute. On one side stood the Center Union–New Forces (EK-ND), the official caretaker, led by Papandreou's trusted lieutenants and the Republican old guard; on the other side stood a new party, the Panhellenic Socialist Movement (PASOK), led by Andreas Papandreou, George's son.

Andreas Papandreou had left Greece as a young man, before the onset of World War II. While still in Greece, he had dabbled in radical politics and was arrested by the Metaxas regime, but was able to leave the country for the United States after his arrest. There, he studied economics, became an American citizen, and served in the US Navy before embark-ing on a successful academic career that ultimately took him to the University of California. He returned to Greece in 1960, after Karamanlis asked him to set up and run an econom-ics research center, but quickly got involved in politics, on his father's side. His personal magnetism, academic creden-tials, liberal positions, and family links to the party leader boosted his political profile in Greece but created considerable animosity within the party. These intra-party squabbles were a key factor behind the split of the party in 1965 and the defec-tions of several high-profile members that followed as a result. The advent of the military regime radicalized him. He spent those years in Canada and Sweden, setting up a resistance movement that was more notable for its stringent, radical rhet-oric than its actions. In a matter of a few years, the formerly liberal US academic transformed himself into a postcolonial, anti-American, neo-Marxist firebrand, happy to condemn the Greek democratic transition as a sham, castigate European social democrats as sellouts to capitalism and the United States, and tout his affinity for Third World national liberation move-ments. It was on this ideological basis that he founded PASOK.[21]

The 1974 elections offered him his first chance, which he missed. EK-ND won out in the contest to represent the Republican camp, getting 20.42 percent of the vote compared to PASOK's 13.6 percent. Papandreou however, did not miss his second chance. Investing heavily in the creation of an exten-sive network of local branches, he turned PASOK into the first Greek noncommunist party to adopt the mass party model. He eventually outmaneuvered the Republican old guard, coming out ahead in the 1977 elections with 25.34 percent to his rivals' paltry 11.95 percent. This score meant that PASOK could now credibly claim to be the flag-bearer of the old Republican camp, a development that gave Papandreou the latitude to plan his master move: achieving victory in the 1981 elections.

How did the transition shape political culture?

In spite of the structural continuity with pre-1967 politics evinced by the party system, the content of post-transition politics was decisively new. Anti-Americanism reached lev-els never seen before, fed by justified grievances about US unconditional support of the military regime. The entire party system had moved toward the left, reflecting the pre-vailing political atmosphere of the time. It was as if Greek society wanted to make up for its long political immobility and instinctive conservatism.

Ideas that had been rejected as extreme just a few years back now entered the mainstream, and all kinds of radical notions became suddenly fashionable. The counterculture (or at least elements of it) was incorporated into the dominant culture; universities became hotbeds of Marxist politics with dozens of communist groups outbidding each other; and Andreas Papandreou emerged as a socialist leader with *Tiermondiste* (Third World-leaning) aspirations, projecting himself as a pioneer of the "third way" that was to be forged between overly moderate European social democracy and stalled Soviet communism. An emerging generation of highly educated youth, often the children of the people who defeated the communist insurgency during the 1940s, recast the leading communist figures of the civil war as inspiring and romantic revolutionary heroes. It was during that time that the sexual revolution reached Greece, bringing along with it the dream of a hedonistic lifestyle that upended the conservative, patriarchal culture of male honor and female reserve that had been dominant until then. Naturally, materialism and consumerism quickly followed suit.

Of course, all this ferment had a strong impact on religious values as well, though with a notable caveat. Religiosity (as measured by weekly attendance at Mass) took a dip, and secular perceptions regarding marriage, divorce, and abortion gained considerable ground to become majoritarian. Yet the Orthodox Church remained a powerful and influential institution as evidenced by its approval rate in public opinion surveys. The Church retained its ability to identify with the Greek nation and tap into a deeper cultural current, very much as the Catholic Church in Poland or Ireland is closely identified with these respective nations. The identification of Orthodox Church and Greek nation also explains why religion never emerged as a political cleavage in Greek politics.

Overall, changes that had unfolded more gradually in Western Europe and the United States took Greece by storm after 1974. What is perhaps more unusual is that in Greece the demand for both more personal freedom and more consumption became couched in a radical language whose centerpiece was the concept of progressivism. To be "progressive" meant to be modern. In contrast, concepts associated with the old state of affairs such as "law and order," came to be seen as regressive and undesirable. The shift from conservative to progressive values was sweeping and profound and had lasting consequences.

What was the political legacy of the cultural shift?

It is worth pointing to two lasting political legacies of this cultural shift: first, the emergence and institutionalization of a generalized practice of contentious action and "street politics"; and second, the development of a homegrown, far-left form of terrorism.

A notable feature of everyday politics in post-transition Greece is the high level of "contentious action," a widespread use of street protests and associated actions (strikes, university and high school occupations, highway blocks, etc.). These practices are ubiquitous and are both institutionalized and ritualized, and tend to follow a universally understood script. This feature of Greek politics came to global attention in the context of the anti-austerity protests of 2010–2012, which were much more intense than similar ones in other European countries experiencing comparable economic shocks. What many observers missed, however, was that although they were quite intense, Greek protests were not novel. Rather than being a simple product of the crisis, they drew from past practice. Highly disruptive protests were not uncommon and twice, in 1980 and in 1985, police action had resulted in the deaths of demonstrators. Indeed, the most destructive riots in Athens took place before the crisis began, in December 2008, following the deadly shooting of a teen-ager by a policeman.[22]

In terms of participation, the anti-austerity protests were essentially a continuation of previous trends rather than a new phenomenon. A survey of protesters in 2010 found that more than four out of five protesters were "regulars," having partici-pated in protests during the previous ten years. The role of street protests in the Greek political system requires some explanation. Rather than reflecting a Greek mythical spirit of resistance, as is often asserted, contenious action fulfills a symbolic role and a political function that are both related to the 1974 transition.

The symbolic role harks back to the student uprising in November 1973, a key pillar of the post-transition Republic. November 17 is a school holiday, celebrated every year and reaching its culmination in a mass demonstration that begins at the Polytechnic School and ends at the American embassy in Athens. The symbolism is unmistakable, and it helps turn contentious acts such as school occupations and street protests into ritual references to this original heroic deed. Indeed, it is often said with regards to school occupations that every gen-eration must have its own "student uprising," as an indispens-able rite of passage.

Mass protests fulfill a specific political function as well. They are part of a particular type of interest group politics— on which, more below. When interest group leaders fail to promote their agenda through the usual party channels, they resort to street pressure. In other words, mass protest is part of the bargaining process. The journalist Michael Lewis provides a stark description of the participants in a 2010 street protest that captures this dimension:

Thousands upon thousands of government employees take to the streets to protest the bill. Here is Greece's ver-sion of the Tea Party: tax collectors on the take, public school teachers who don't really teach, well-paid employees of bankrupt state railroads whose trains never run on time, state hospital workers bribed to buy overpriced supplies.... The Greek public-sector employees assemble themselves into units that resemble army platoons. In the middle of each unit are two or three rows of young men wielding truncheons disguised as flagpoles. Ski masks and gas masks dangle from their belts so that they can still fight after the inevitable tear gas."[23]

This last point takes us from spontaneous street violence to more organized forms of political violence, such as terrorism, another legacy of the transition.

What were the dynamics of terrorism in Greece?

A most enduring legacy of post-transition radicalism is far-left terrorism. Like Italy and Germany in the 1970s, Greece experienced sustained bouts of "revolutionary" terrorism that emerged out of the ferment surrounding the transition to democracy. Although lower in magnitude compared to either Italy or Germany, Greek terrorism proved much more elusive and persistent. This terrorist wave was launched in April 1975, when a newly formed terrorist group, *Epanastatikos Laikos Agonas* (Revolutionary Popular Struggle, or ELA), fire-bombed eight cars belonging to US servicemen. However, it was another organization, the Revolutionary Organization 17 November (17N), that became the most influential and lethal terrorist group among the almost two hundred and fifty groups that claimed responsibility for terrorist acts since the restoration of democracy in 1974. Both groups can be described as small, clandestine, urban guerilla organizations, ascribing to Marxist-Leninist ideology and aiming at the violent overthrow of the capitalist state, although 17N also adopted a strong nationalist profile under the guise of anti-imperialism.

17N was responsible for the assassination of twenty-two individuals between 1975 and 2002, many of them prominent politicians, judges, businessmen, and foreign diplomats. In contrast to similarly minded groups in Western Europe, such as the Red Brigades in Italy or the Red Army Faction in Germany, 17N did not gradually progress from low-level bombings to assassinations, but rather started with the high-profile assassination of CIA Athens station chief Richard Welch in December 1975. Furthermore, unlike these other groups, 17N did not expand from a loose network of smaller groupings sharing a similar ideology or a broader social movement, but was instead a small, tightly knit organization from the start that never really attempted to expand. The remarkable feature about 17N members is that they were linked by family ties: the structure of the group imitated a Greek extended family. It is this structure that explains the group's elusiveness and contributed to its mystique, feeding several conspiracy theories about the supposed ties between 17N with foreign secret services—on top of the Greek security services' incompetent handling of the problem. Furthermore, the two major parties, PASOK and New Democracy, failed to reach a consensus over how to define and thus combat terrorism, and used the issue as an expedient way to score political points against each other. Furthermore, the traumatic experience of the dictatorship and the presence of radical journalists in mainstream media made it hard to generate widespread support for a more forceful antiterrorist policy agenda and contributed to a laid-back, if not borderline supportive, public attitude.

Eventually, the demise of 17N came through a combination of policy change and plain luck. The détente in Greek-Turkish relations led to the upgrading of terrorism in the Greek security agenda, while the hosting of the 2004 Olympic Games in Athens made the Greek government much more receptive to American pressures to bring the members of 17N to justice, paving the way for closer cooperation between Greek and foreign intelligence services. 17N was finally dismantled in

June 2002 when a bomb exploded in the hands of a terrorist. Everyone was startled to discover that this mysterious and apparently omnipotent group, which operated with impunity for almost thirty years, was a band of rather mediocre brothers and cousins.[24]

The liquidation of 17N did not spell the end of terrorist activity in Greece. A new crop of groups has emerged, operating at a lower level of intensity, especially in the wake of the 2008 riots. Indeed, the link between highly ritualized and nonviolent protest on the one hand, and violent actions on the other hand, is the highly active Greek "anarchist" milieu which uses protests as a means for engaging in low-intensity violence (including firebombings, arson, and attacks against individuals) and provides a recruiting ground for those wishing to graduate into terrorist activity.[25]

How did Greece join the EEC and with what consequences?

The democratic transition made possible Greece's accession to the European Economic Community (EEC). Once the new regime was firmly in place, Greece launched the process that resulted in it joining the EEC in 1980. It was the first country of the periphery to do so, five years ahead of Spain and Portugal, thus foreshadowing the great expansion of the EU toward the East.

Greece sought to join the EEC for political rather than economic reasons. The architect of this project, Konstantinos Karamanlis, sought benefits such as stability, security, and democratic consolidation. From the EEC's perspective, the decision to admit Greece was also primarily motivated by political concerns: in particular, the stabilization of the new democracy was paramount, especially in a context where the Cold War was still on. Once more, Greece's accession was justified with references to its ancient legacy, a rhetorical move that was not devoid of political symbolism. As a European official put it, Greece's accession was a "fitting repayment by the Europe of today of the cultural and political debt that we all owe to a Greek heritage almost three thousand years old."

Beyond this rhetoric, it is clear that Greece's accession was also a critical development for the EEC itself. For one, the prospect of admitting Greece gave the EEC a new sense of the utility of enlargement. Moreover, it gave rise to an unprecedented set of new ideas about how to conceptualize, design, and optimize the enlargement process. Overall, Greece's accession constituted a key episode of European politics during the course of which the EEC discovered its power as a stabilizing factor in the context of what was then a Cold War crisis. In giving the green light to Greece's bid for membership, the EEC set out on a new path that would eventually transform it into a major international actor. Obviously, it is hard to overstate the extent to which membership in the EEC shaped Greece's self-perception and sense of security, despite the problems that arose from it. This was clearly a momentous event for Greece, as it moved the country much closer to the core of Western Europe than it ever had been in the past, thus fulfilling its ambitions.[26]

Despite the priority of political concerns, the most immediate effect of Greece's accession was economic, namely the slackening of protection enjoyed by Greece's industries. The result was a great expansion of the informal sector, which went from around 20 percent of GDP in the 1970s to 31 percent in 1988. Resources from sectors that in the past had enjoyed a considerable degree of protection from European competition were now channeled to sectors producing nontradable goods (i.e. goods that cannot be produced easily outside the country), which by definition were less prone to such external pressures—instead of being directed into an export-oriented industry that wasn't there in the first place. This development had important and mostly negative consequences, not least because it reduced government revenues. Economic activity shifted from the formal to the informal sector, slowing down the rate of technological diffusion, as production in the informal sector usually takes place in smaller and less sophisticated firms.[27]

The economic impact of Greece's accession to the EEC illustrates the logic of overreaching that has been visible throughout its historical path: in aiming too high, Greece paid a steep economic price. At the same time, without such overreaching it would have most likely failed to achieve a number of other, very positive outcomes, including its political stabilization.

What were the economic consequences of the transition to democracy?

The transition to democracy was both exhilarating and liberating. Nevertheless, it coincided with two negative economic shocks: the first was external and economic, and the second was domestic and political.

The economic slowdown occurred as a result of the first oil shock of 1973, which contributed to a drastic fall in investments and put an end to the period of postwar economic expansion. Additionally, it coincided with a reversal in immigration trends, with net migration rates becoming for the first time positive in the postwar period. This reversal of migratory flows reduced external remittances and put additional pressure on the economy.

Despite these adverse conditions, however, the New Democracy governments followed policies that attempted to contain inflation, leading to a deceleration of growth; they were therefore quite unpopular. Nevertheless, standards of living kept improving. For example, 22.6 percent of all the current Greek housing stock was built between 1971 and 1980, the most for a single decade. However, the situation worsened significantly after the second oil shock of 1979, which led to a sharp increase in inflation. This placed pressure on the government to tighten up its monetary policy and increase interest rates in order to prevent the vicious cycle of price and wage increases.[28]

The second effect was the explosion of expectations brought about by the liberalization of political institutions and the modernization of Greek society. In the past, consumption had been compressed. (It is telling that unit labor costs had declined by more than 30 percent during the 1967–1974 period relative to the EEC countries.) Now, the recently urbanized population, including the new middle class, began to agitate and demand better living standards including higher levels of consumption and social protection. These demands placed considerable pressure on the New Democracy governments and pushed them toward an expansionary fiscal policy, in turn exposing the fragility of the postwar developmentalist economic model. It now became very hard, if not completely impossible, to embark on a serious attempt to control inflation. As a result, New Democracy governments resorted to a policy mix that included protectionism, credit interventionism, and the wholesale nationalization of failing firms in order to temporarily soften the blow caused by the increase in the costs of production. Although these policies prevented an immediate collapse of the manufacturing sector, they led to the overburdening of state-controlled banks with bad loans; in turn, these banks were forced to continue lending to failing enterprises, only postponing the moment of reckoning through a painful readjustment of the manufacturing sector.[29]

These changes had visible effects on the size of the public sector. In the post–World War II period, the Greek public sector was modest and tightly run. It employed about 250,000 individuals, or 7.5 percent of the labor force, far below the Western European average. These numbers remained stable despite population growth until the transition to democracy: state employment hovered at around 261,000 in 1961 and 320,000 in 1971. By 1980, this number had gone up to 510,000, or 15 percent of the labor force, slightly lower than the OECD average, reflecting three distinct trends: the nationalization of many failing firms, the growth of the welfare state, and electoral pressures for a more expansionary fiscal policy. Likewise, public spending as a percent of GDP escalated from an average of 23.2 percent in 1961–1973 to 30 percent in 1980, still well below the Western European average.[30]

It was in this context of rapidly rising expectations that the Greek socialist party PASOK began its relentless march to power under the powerful slogan of "Change." PASOK's flamboyant and charismatic leader Andreas Papandreou, the complete antithesis to the austere Karamanlis, began to promise everything to almost everyone, whipping up a frenzy of expectations. Karamanlis left the government to take over the much more ceremonial presidency of the country in 1980. Under new leadership, ND faced the PASOK juggernaut in the October 1981 elections.

What was Greek socialism?

PASOK emerged as a new party within the traditional Republican camp in 1974, established its command over that camp in 1977, followed up with its 1981 electoral landslide (when it won 48 percent of the vote to New Democracy's 35.9 percent), and dominated Greek politics until the 2010 crisis. It won six elections and governed Greece for over twenty years.

It is no exaggeration to say that PASOK really put its stamp on Greek politics and society during the post-transition era. No other party was able to channel successfully the aspirations of Greek society and mold it to its own image as PASOK did. Its ascent to power was a milestone in Greek politics. This was the first time a socialist party assumed power in Greece and also the first time that a transfer of power from right to left was achieved smoothly and peacefully, indicating that Greek democracy had matured and consolidated. The meteoric rise of PASOK's fortunes from its foundation in September 1974 to its spectacular victory in October 1981, and its domination of Greek politics for the following thirty years, beg the question of its phenomenal success. How did it achieve this feat?[31]

The first thing to note is that PASOK did not start out as a typical, run-of-the-mill European socialist party. That is, it did not emerge during the nineteenth century from the working class and its trade unions. Up until its founding, the only left-wing party of significance in Greece had been the Communist Party, whose sectarian nature prevented it from projecting a mass appeal, with the partial exception of the peculiar occupation period. In contrast, PASOK's success rested in its ability to propose an attractive political package, expertly tailored to fit a society dominated by civil servants, small business owners, independent professionals, and small farmers—what could be described as a petty bourgeois social constellation, which Papandreou inventively labeled "nonprivileged" Greeks.

Through its phenomenal success, PASOK embodied (and attempted to transcend) three contradictions between modernity and tradition. They touch on issues of leadership, party, and policy that help make sense of its phenomenal success, but also its ultimate demise.

What were PASOK's three key contradictions?

The first contradiction concerns Papandreou's leadership: his image as a radical modernizer contradicted his profile as a traditional, paternalistic leader with an excess of populist charisma. Papandreou played up his US academic baggage, his professional economist background, his cosmopolitanism, and his credentials with various progressive world leaders. At the same time, however, he behaved as a paternalistic and traditional, almost tribal, leader who loved nothing more than to bask in the adoration of his supporters in spectacularly staged mass rallies, and whose political ascent resulted from his family links to a powerful political clan. Papandreou resembled a Third World populist leader more than a Western European social-democratic politician. Until the end, he remained either opposed to or deeply suspicious of democratic procedures within his own party, trusting instead a small coterie of close advisers. After a short period of internal strife, revolving around the political orientation of the party, Papandreou managed to concentrate personal power in his person to such an extent that the party became practically indistinguishable from his person. It is telling that when he lay incapacitated in a hospital bed during the last months of his life, the government was effectively paralyzed.[32]

The second contradiction has to do with the way PASOK operated as a political party: on one hand, PASOK became the first mass party in Greece with broad appeal. Although it absorbed a number of personalistic patronage networks associated with the old Center Union party, it was able to build an extensive national network based on both local and regional branches and a multitude of professional associations, with membership ranging into the thousands. Its emergence, therefore, constituted an organizational innovation in a landscape dominated by traditional parties of notables—that is, coalitions of semiautonomous politicians commanding local constituencies of personally loyal voters. And yet, instead of upending the tradition of clientelistic politics associated with these traditional parties, PASOK actually upgraded the practice of clientelism to levels unseen before, turning it into a means of rewarding party allegiance as opposed to personalistic ties. PASOK became a well-oiled political machine, albeit one that was overly dependent on both its leader's charisma and its ability to hand out jobs and favors.[33]

The last contradiction refers to PASOK's policy package. PASOK emerged as an aggressively radical party of the left with a sharp "anti-establishment" message, on occasion even outflanking the Communist Party. It scathingly critiqued European social democrats as sellouts; courted the national liberation movements of the Third World; and successfully appropriated political symbols that had been exclusively used by the Communists, including the wartime legacy of EAM and ELAS. While in opposition, it advocated policies that included the nationalization of major industries (a policy labeled "socialization") and the disengagement of Greece from both NATO and the European Community. Once in power, however, PASOK gradually tempered its agenda and adopted moderate policies. Political radicalism was abandoned in favor of a mix of developmentalism (and, initially, redistribution) with highly symbolic and generally popular reforms, such as the modernization of family law including the adoption of civil marriage and the promotion of gender equality or the legal recognition of EAM's resistance. Its moderate policies, however, were frequently accompanied by a virulent and polarizing discourse based on the premise of a radical and stark opposition between PASOK, as the standard-bearer of progressive politics, and New Democracy, accused of standing in for reactionary politics. Despite a policy agenda that gradually became highly pro-European, PASOK kept catering to (and feeding) the anti-Western tendencies of a substantial segment of the electorate, whose sense of insecurity and injustice added up to an "underdog" culture with historical roots in the country's thwarted nationalist ambitions and the legacy of the Civil War.[34]

In short, PASOK was a party led by a politician who could appear at once cosmopolitan and parochial, inclusive and tribal; it built an organization that was both bureaucratic and modern, but also driven by patronage; and it adopted a policy package that stressed a polarizing discourse with radical overtones, while supplying moderate policies. When balanced against each other, these contradictions made PASOK the most successful political party in Greece. It attracted a socially heterogeneous electorate of upwardly mobile but economically insecure voters whose fortunes were directly or indirectly tied to the public sector. When, however, this balancing was no longer possible, these contradictions came to look like a sham and caused the party to implode.[35]

How did PASOK shape Greece?

PASOK's domination of Greek politics, especially during its first turn in power (1981–1989), had a profound and lasting impact, an essential part of which can be traced back to five legislative acts: laws 1268 of 1982, 1285 of 1982, 1320 of 1983, 1505 of 1984, and 1586 of 1986. This is not to say that the party did not evolve over time. Papandreou's heirs, Kostas Simitis and then Andreas's son, George, anchored the party in a mainstream, left-of-center position. But they learned the hard way how hard it was to transcend his legacy.

On the positive side, PASOK's rise to power was a signal confirmation that the 1974 transition marked a deep, durable shift in the Greek political system. Greek democracy had arrived. The transition from New Democracy to PASOK was smooth and confounded many international observers who had expressed serious concerns based on PASOK's radical foreign policy agenda. Because PASOK had become the flag-bearer of those Greeks who felt politically excluded, its advent provided a much-needed sense of closure, inclusion, and renewal. This was signaled by one of the earliest and most symbolic legislative acts, Law 1285 of 1982, which stated that the individuals who had fought under the EAM/ELAS banner during Greece's occupation had indeed been members of the resistance rather than communist insurgents. This was accompanied by the provision of various benefits, including pensions and special access to public-sector jobs for their descendants. It was an important symbolic act, despite the fact that it degenerated into a thinly covered patronage policy that came to reward over 400,000 individuals, thus adding an enormous burden on the pension system. PASOK also introduced long-overdue reforms in family law and gender equality and invested in the upgrading of the welfare state that had been rudimentary up to then. Most importantly perhaps, PASOK's signal contribution is what it did not do. For all his radical swagger, Andreas Papandreou was a statesman who understood the importance of Greece's foreign alliances and, as a result, he immediately shelved his promises to take Greece out of NATO and the EEC. Greece's Western orientation was never questioned.[36]

On the negative side, however, a key legacy of PASOK was the infusion of civil society with a generous dose of populism, something that had a definite impact on prevailing social attitudes and norms. Greeks and non-Greeks alike tend to explain many of the country's shortcomings by reference to norms and culture. For example, tax evasion is "explained" as an outcome of a culture of cheating. Their tautological qualities aside, these kinds of arguments beg the question: How is this culture sustained over time? The answer points to incentives, which in turn emerge from institutions. PASOK shaped social norms through the new institutions it created. Because norms are notoriously sticky and tend to outlast the institutions that brought them into being, the 1980s still loom large in Greece despite the many changes that took place since, including the transformation of PASOK after 1995 and its potentially terminal decline after 2012. The impact of these institutional changes is particularly visible when it comes to three dimensions: administrative capacity, social attitudes, and the economy.

Why did administrative capacity decline?

The advent of PASOK had a definite and clear impact on the quality of the state's bureaucratic apparatus. To be sure, Greek public administration was never renowned for its efficiency. Recall how President Truman's special envoy in Greece, Paul Porter, described its workings in 1947. Yet, its performance did fluctuate over time. For example, the reforms introduced by the Trikoupis administration in the 1880s and especially the Venizelos administration in 1911 strengthened the political neutrality of civil servants vis-à-vis political parties, encouraged the professionalization of the civil service, and helped improve overall efficiency. Although a 1965 report found that the workings of public administration at the time were "complicated, slow moving, and inefficient," this was mainly the result of poor human capital and incentives, rather than corruption, partisanship, or clientelism. Of course, clientelistic and nepotistic practices were present before the 1980s, not to mention openly discriminatory rules; but for the most part, these practices manifested themselves on the sidelines of what was in principle a merit system, however imperfectly implemented. On top of it, the Greek public administration was a relatively small apparatus and hence its broader impact was circumscribed.[37]

The advent of PASOK produced a devastating legislative trifecta. First came Law 1320 of 1983, which abolished the posts of ministry general directors that were filled by career civil servants and replaced them with "special secretaries," who were party appointees; this law also eliminated competitive examinations, thus turning the hiring of civil servants into an ad hoc process, easy prey for patronage. Second was Law 1505 of 1984 introducing the so-called uniform wage structure, effectively disconnecting individual pay from performance in favor of an automatic seniority logic. Lastly, Law 1586 of 1986 established a "uniform" hierarchical structure, effectively disconnecting civil servant rank from expected levels of accountability.

These legislative innovations reinforced several harmful tendencies of the Greek bureaucracy: mismanagement, laxity, lack of accountability, worship of a highly formalistic and rigid legalism, prevalence of everyday informal practices that led to petty corruption, absence of sanctions for those caught breaking rules, and abuse of discretionary decision-making, a necessity in a context of rule inflation. Staff effectiveness was undermined as personnel evaluations required the agreement and signature of the employees being evaluated. Arbitrary perks and extensive and informal arrangements and practices exploded (including not showing up to work on Monday and Friday or days immediately preceding and following vacation periods). Apparently, there was even a special perk for all those who did not receive any other form of additional benefits!

The ensuing rise in partisanship and collapse of professionalization caused a marked decline in the quality of public administration and the nationalized firms. For example, a study describes how machinery aimed at equipping a petrochemical factory but never used for that purpose was bought for 41 billion drachmas in 1981 and sold as scrap metal for 105 million drachmas in 1988. A study of the National Bank of

Greece shows that whereas in 1981 almost 90 percent of the personnel had been hired through competitive examinations, by 1989 the number of employees had increased by 30 percent "mostly through the hiring of superfluous auxiliary or temporary personnel." By 1984 it was estimated that 89 percent of all card-carrying party members of PASOK had some professional connection with the public sector either through a permanent job, a temporary job, or a contract to do business with the it.[38]

The poor quality of Greek public administration received worldwide coverage when it was reported that the Greek Statistical Agency had grossly misreported basic economic indicators in 2009, including the size of the government deficit. In its 2011 report on this issue, an investigation committee of the European Commission pointed to a number of shortcomings in that agency that apply across the Greek state apparatus: inappropriate management, poor cooperation and lack of clear responsibilities between institutions and services, diffuse personal responsibilities, ambiguous empowerment of officials, absence of written instruction and documentation leaving the quality of the work subject to political pressures and electoral cycles, lack of accountability, and nontransparent or improperly documented bookkeeping. What is particularly striking is the fact that the performance of the Greek administration declined despite the availability of more resources and better human capital resulting from the incentives provided by the EU, including advanced training opportunities for staff, and of much better educated and remunerated personnel.[39]

What were some of the effects of maladministration?

It goes without saying that maladministration on such a scale had broad ramifications undermining the trust of citizens toward state institutions which were perceived as corrupt, ineffective, and dysfunctional. Indeed, a broad host of indicators shows that Greece scores below most of its European peers when it comes to citizen trust in institutions. Two implications of maladministration are worth highlighting: legal inefficiency and the decline of higher education.

Legal inefficiency has adverse effects on economic activity including private investment, foreign direct investment, entrepreneurship, export orientation, productivity growth, and income distribution, while encouraging corruption. This problem is captured by a variety of indicators. In 2010, Greece ranked 154th out of 183 economies in the overall de jure legal quality of the institutional framework protecting investors. On a 0–10 scale of a composite investor protection index (reflecting the extent of disclosure, easiness of shareholders' suits, and antitunneling provisions), Greece received a score of 3.3—significantly less than 5, which is the mean value across all countries in the world. Things are equally bad when it comes to de facto legal quality, on aspects as diverse as registering property, dealing with construction permits, and getting necessary administrative licenses to start a business—and this is reflected of course in the length of trial duration. It takes years to resolve even simple disputes, while it is not uncommon for important cases to linger in courts for years, and this applies to both civil and criminal cases. More specifically, it takes approximately 819 business days and 39 administrative procedures to resolve a simple case.[40]

Legal inefficiency also goes a long way toward explaining the absence of proper law enforcement. A recent example is a law passed in 2008 that banned smoking in public spaces, including restaurants and bars; it has never been enforced and the ban effectively lapsed. Another was the failure to collect payments for state housing loans, despite the fact that a law passed in 1986 was clearly providing for a process of payment collection. In fact, loan recipients were able to claim deductions for purposes of taxation, based on their presumed repayments.

Lack of enforcement is not only the result of legal ineffi-ciency; it is also the outcome of political decisions. An exam-ple is the case of forested land. Like other Mediterranean countries, Greece is prone to wildfires during its dry, hot, and windy summers. Arson contributes a significant (though unknown) fraction of wildfires each year, and arson by prospective property owners and developers is a common motivation behind many wildfires. It is estimated that over 400,000 homes have been built in areas that were previously classified as forests, while in certain suburbs of Athens up to 50 percent of large forested areas have surreptitiously had their designation changed to allow construction. Illegal con-struction is widespread and effectively legalized through regular amnesties. Given the absence of a detailed land reg-istry (less than 7 percent of the country has been properly mapped, despite significant financial aid from the European Union to do so), there is considerable uncertainty about prop-erty rights, a fact that gives local public officials broad discre-tion over the application of the various laws. Furthermore, there is evidence suggesting that the use of this discretion to favor private individuals not only results from idiosyncratic corruption but also varies systematically with election years, precisely when governments relax both the application and enforcement of legislation, thus resulting in a higher likeli-hood of wildfires.[41]

Lastly, consider higher education. One of the most impor-tant laws passed early by the first PASOK government (Law 1268 of 1982) was intended to modernize the antiquated sys-tem of Greek public higher education. The modernization it achieved, however, was of a clearly populist nature as it low-ered standards; distributed tenure across the board, including to teaching assistants and support staff; and, most ominously, introduced party machines in the governance of universi-ties—while retaining the centralized legal framework that keeps universities enclosed in a formalistic straitjacket that stipulates every little detail of their operation. Party interests were served primarily by the disproportionately large student representation instituted for various university bodies and elections, including in the appointment of rectors, deans, and departmental chairs. These elections were hijacked and appropriated by party-led youth organizations. In exchange for their work, party activists received various benefits such as high grades, degrees, and admission to graduate programs; in turn, political parties used universities as a recruiting ground for future leaders who became socialized in this particular milieu. These features help explain the system's consistently low performance, captured by various international ranking indicators but also through impact studies of university degrees, as well as the steady resistance to various reform attempts. It is not only inefficient, but also tremendously wasteful as successive governments have used universities as a public employment agency, expanding it into provincial towns lacking in infrastructure.[42]

What was the effect of populism on social norms and behavior?

At the heart of Greek culture lies a paradox that has been noticed by several observers. "The structure of the Greek economy is collectivist," one of them writes, "but the country, in spirit, is the opposite of a collective. Its real structure is every man for himself." But how does collectivism coexist with individualism?[43]

Greek society has always been highly suspicious of the state, which is seen as a hostile, extractive, and repressive entity. "Regulations, whenever they happened to interfere with individual and family self-interest, were obstacles to be overcome, not rules to be obeyed," McNeill observes. "The more formidable the regulation, the more energetic the effort to escape its incidence and the greater the occasion for bribery." As a result, society sought to deny the state resources both by withholding them (e.g., evading taxation) and appropriating them (e.g., taking over public land). This behavior made sense in times of scarcity and limited political representation, but it is much harder to explain (let alone justify) under conditions of democracy and relative plenty.

The rise of organized rent-seeking that took place under PASOK's watch during the 1980s goes a long way toward explaining the persistence of these behaviors. Although traditionally the state was seen as an institution of extraction, it could also deliver resources to individuals, provided it was properly manipulated—this being the logic of clientelism. As a result, most Greeks came to see the government as a source of particularistic goods. What changed after 1980 was the fact that there were increasingly more goods to distribute. Never before had so many people been hired by the state, with such salaries, pensions, and benefits—to the point where the average government job paid almost three times the salary of the average private-sector job. An egregious but not isolated example was the national railroad company, which had annual revenues of €100 million against an annual wage bill of €400 million, on top of €300 million in other expenses. This is how the average state railroad employee came to earn €65,000 a year.[44]

PASOK effectively justified and modernized rent-seeking. It justified it via a socialist-sounding discourse that stressed concepts such as redistribution and public goods. However, the absence of clear-cut class divisions common to industrial societies (e.g., capitalists and workers) led Andreas Papandreou to anoint the "people" as the beneficiary of redistribution. Since the "people" included almost everyone, this move rendered the idea of redistribution actually moot. Furthermore, the propagation of the idea that "anything is fair game," as long as it represents the legitimate demand of the people, meant that in practice it would be the groups with the highest blackmail potential that would most profit from such redistribution at the expense of weaker ones. Such groups included public-sector workers, particularly those in energy communications, transport, and garbage disposal.

This type of populism eventually also adopted by New Democracy, instilled a widespread sense of entitlement and came to both justify and disguise generalized rent-seeking. It became hegemonic in the sense of being accepted by most people as a self-evident and natural state of affairs. Instead of the traditionally socialist practice of high taxation and targeted redistribution, PASOK's populism promoted low taxation and quasi-universal, though unequal redistribution. Greece collected a very low percentage of direct taxes (7.7 percent of GDP compared to 12.2 percent in the Eurozone, in 2008), and the heavy reliance on indirect taxation accentuated the regressive character of the tax system. What is worse, the Greek version of the electoral business cycle took the form of successive governments' unwillingness to collect taxes during an election year. As a Greek finance minister put it, "In 2009, tax collection disintegrated, because it was an election year.... The first thing a government does in an election year is to pull the tax collectors off the streets." Both PASOK (and New Democracy afterward) became in Gerassimos Moschonas's pertinent words, less "tax and spend" parties and more "spend and don't tax" ones.[45]

This is how a (collectivist) expectation of broad state redistribution came to coexist with a universal (individualist) practice of withholding contributions. Obviously, such a combination is not sustainable for long.

How did PASOK shape the economy?

During its first stint in power (1981–1989), in what became known as the "populist decade," PASOK consolidated its dominant position within the Greek political system using a two-pronged strategy: an expansionary (and initially redistributive) fiscal policy coupled with growth of the public sector and related jobs.[46]

Having promised almost everything to everyone, PASOK was under considerable pressure to fulfill its mandate. After having been hit by the second oil crisis in 1979, the Greek economy was faring poorly. It was in this context that PASOK inaugurated an expansionary and redistributive fiscal policy, aimed at satisfying key segments of its electorate. This policy was designed to boost consumption and included a spectacular increase of minimum wages and salaries (by about 50 percent); additional wage increases on a progressive scale; an automatic wage indexation mechanism aimed at preventing the erosion of gains in real wages by galloping inflation; a provision that collective bargaining could result only in salary raises, not reductions; a substantial increase in the size of pensions; and, most importantly, a minimum universal pension scheme targeting farmers in particular. Public spending as a percent of GDP had already grown from an average of 23.2 percent in 1961–1973 to 35 percent in 1981, compared to an average of 45.6 percent for the EEC. By 1985 it reached 43 percent, and by 1990 it stabilized at around 50 percent. An important component of this growth was social policy spending, which went from 10 percent of GDP in 1980 to 16 percent in 1985—a necessity given the rudimentary state of the welfare state in Greece. This growth was partly absorbed by the rising cost of pensions and included the cost of other popular measures as well, such as better care of retired people, subsidized tourism, and most notably a National Health System. At the same time PASOK presided over an astonishing expansion of the state's size and scope. Recall that in 1980, the Greek state's payroll had reached 510,000. Public employment climbed to 682,000 in 1986 and 722,000 in 1991 (comprising about 20 percent of the labor force). This expansion resulted from a massive new round of nationalizations of failing private firms, the expansion of social services, and the use of public employment as a clientelistic strategy (see below).[47]

The remarkable thing is not so much how "big" the state became (in fact, its size was comparable to that of most

European states) but rather a number of other dimensions: the speed with which it grew, the fact that this period accounts for most of the growth of the public sector until the present, the persistently low quality of its output despite its growth, and its escalating cost—a function of the rise in both the number of employees and their remuneration and pensions. An additional problem was that although Greek society welcomed this growth (indeed pushed for it), it was ultimately unwilling to pay for it, as indicated by the extent of tax evasion.[48]

In the end, PASOK's fiscal and social policy proved incommensurate with Greece's effective tax base. What is more, the imbalance between the cost of the public sector and its tax base ultimately undermined PASOK's redistributive thrust, since the effective toleration of tax evasion by farmers and the self-employed shifted most of the tax burden on the shoulders of wage-earners. In other words, what the government gave with one hand through salary and pension raises, it took with the other, through an effectively selective taxation. This sleight of hand remained for a long time hidden by the growth of borrowing and the influx of EEC transfers. These transfers had been initiated by the EEC's regional policy framework and were meant to facilitate the convergence of the Greek economy with the more developed European North, starting from the mid-eighties. They grew in volume during the following two decades and eventually served in large part to finance these poor policy choices.[49]

Many of these policies proved popular among PASOK's heterogeneous electoral base so long as their contradictions were obscured: low-income wage-earners saw their revenues almost double, farmers saw their pensions multiply in value, and the self-employed could still tax-evade and thus did not have to foot the bill. Needless to say, the true cost of these policies would materialize in due time.

For all their popularity, PASOK's economic policies were unsustainable. During the first half of the 1980s, the country experienced a considerable loss of productivity. Absent a rise in productivity, the generous wage increases eroded the competiveness of Greek exports, thus causing Greece's trade deficit to rise. At the same time, the government's deficit exploded, jumping from 2.3 percent of GDP in 1980 to 14 percent in 1990. Absent an improvement of the state's taxation capacity, the necessary financing of these deficits could only come from borrowing, which jumped up from 28 percent of GDP in 1979 to 49 percent in 1984, before reaching a staggering 120 percent in 1990. In turn, this caused a rise in the debt servicing costs from 1.4 percent of GDP in 1980 to 9.4 percent in 1990, relegating the economy to a state of permanent recession. Inflation remained high (averaging about 18 percent annually) and a series of devaluations of the drachma produced meager results. The decline of economic competitiveness, along with high deficits, high real interest rates, persistent high inflation, and a noticeable hostility toward business, depressed investment (which fell to 19 percent of GDP), effectively driving away foreign investment. In turn, this led to low rates of capital accumulation with a predictable negative impact on growth. This amounted to the reversal during the 1980s of the industrialization gains that had been achieved during the 1960s and 1970s. Hundreds of firms went bust, while unemployment was only contained through the growth of the public sector and the government's decision to bail out many failing companies by bringing them under state control, a policy that may have been politically effective but was economically futile.[50]

While anemic economic growth was common across Europe during the 1980s, the explosion of public debt and most importantly its underlying mechanisms were specific to Greece. The effect of politics on economics was particularly visible through the political business cycle. The primary deficit as a percentage of GDP was much higher in election years during this period, compared to the previous one. Moreover, more than half of the increase in the total deficit as a percentage of GDP that took place during this period is accounted for by sharp increases in the primary deficit of election years. Overall, this was an unsustainable economic policy and it quickly led to an impasse.[51]

Faced with mounting problems, PASOK was forced to introduce austerity measures immediately after its triumphal reelection in the highly polarized 1985 elections (which it won with 45.8 percent of the vote versus New Democracy's 40.85 percent). These measures included a highly symbolic elimination of wage indexation and were supervised by finance minister Kostas Simitis. However, although they began to bear fruit, they were abandoned three years later: Simitis was fired when PASOK's hold on government was challenged by a combination of political fatigue and financial scandals. At this point, the government proceeded to spend its way toward a renewed mandate in the 1989 elections, thus effectively running the economy into the ground. This time, however, all this spending proved insufficient and PASOK lost with 39.1 percent to New Democracy's 44.3 percent. It was able, however, to keep a hold on its electorate while the electoral system in place prevented New Democracy from winning a parliamentary majority and, therefore, forming a stable government. A never-before-seen coalition government was formed between the right and the communist left, and new elections were called for November in the midst of serious economic trouble. New Democracy won those elections again, but despite a very high score (46.2 percent to PASOK's resurgent 40.67 percent), the electoral system again stood in the way of a parliamentary majority. A grand coalition government was formed, the economy stumbled more, and an unprecedented third round of elections was called for April 1990. This time, New Democracy reached 46.9 percent (to PASOK's 38.6 percent) and was able to obtain a very thin parliamentary majority. The economic situation now called for much more painful economic measures, which led to mass street opposition and strikes, orchestrated by none other than PASOK.

The country literally stared into the abyss. The American journalist Robert Kaplan describes the chaotic situation of that time starkly: "Terrorism continued. The economy was collapsing. To increase subsidies and create jobs for the PASOK faithful in the state bureaucracy, Papandreou had borrowed during the 1980s in the same way that Eastern European leaders had borrowed during the 1970s.... When I returned to my former home in 1990, Athens had become an urban disaster zone. Greek newspapers compared it to Cairo. The phone service was the worst in Western Europe.... I turned around. Cars belched heavily leaded exhaust fumes into the air. Mountains of black plastic garbage bags rose starkly off the gray concrete, uncollected for days due to a strike. The apartments opposite were lit by candlelight, as striking electricity workers had shut off the power. The workers had legitimate complaints, but their strikes were part of a larger scene of chaos and societal strife that were the undeniable refuse of Papandreou's rule." And yet, in a remarkable turnaround, Greece managed not only to avert disaster but also succeeded in kicking off an era of high growth and unprecedented prosperity.[52]

How did economic stagnation give way to economic boom?

PASOK's economic policies were a ticking bomb. Rampant inflation, soaring public debt, and a balance of payments crisis combined with political instability following PASOK's electoral defeat in 1989 to bring the country to the edge of collapse. However, not only Greece avoided collapse, it was able to engineer a remarkable, as well as unexpected, economic turnaround during the following twenty years. How was this achieved?

The New Democracy government under Konstantinos Mitsotakis did not last long. Its economic policies were unpopular and its parliamentary majority thin. So, when an up-and-coming conservative politician named Antonis Samaras defected from the party in 1993 because of a foreign policy disagreement over the former Yugoslav Republic of Macedonia, the government collapsed and new elections were called. PASOK, under the ailing Andreas Papandreou, won a resounding victory with 46.9 percent of the vote (to ND's 39.3 percent), inaugurating the second era of PASOK dominance that lasted until 2004.

The victory aside, it was now obvious that a return to the economic policies of the previous decade was no longer possible. In an irony of history it was PASOK that was called to fix the mess it had created during the previous decade. After Papandreou's death in 1996, the reformist Kostas Simitis took over PASOK's leadership and pushed PASOK away from its earlier policies.

In an ambitious move that resonated with similar past projects, Simitis made Greece's accession to the European Monetary Union (EMU) a national priority. He implemented a set of stabilization measures that brought deficits under control (achieving primary surpluses in 2000–2002) and tamed inflation (which went down from 14.4 percent in 1993 to 2.9 percent in 2004). For the first time, an ambitious privatization program took place along with an effort to liberalize capital flows and banking. The push toward a market-based credit administration system was caused by both external and internal factors. On the external front, Greece had to gradually liberalize its capital markets as part of its obligations toward the EEC. This strengthened the position of those favoring financial deregulation vis-à-vis the interest groups that had benefited from favorable terms of credit access. The latter included small manufacturing firms benefitting from preferential lending, exporters who aimed at retaining their export credit subsidies, and farmers who had also profited from cheap credit from the Agricultural Bank of Greece. Among the greatest beneficiaries of financial liberalization were the trade and banking sectors. The former benefitted from an increased access to credit, while the latter was able to recover from the accumulated portfolio burdens of the 1970s and 1980s (recall that state-controlled banks were required by the state to continue providing credit to failing enterprises during most of that period). To these measures one must also add the deregulation of telecommunications and certain product markets that had been heavily regulated; the growth of the shipping and tourism industries; the fiscal stimulus caused by the 2004 Olympic Games, which led to considerable investment in infrastructure; and the continued inflow of funds from the European Union, both from EU structural funds and the Common Agricultural Policy.[53]

These policies were boosted by the sudden and unexpected collapse of communist regimes in 1989 which proved a boon to the Greek economy. A massive influx of immigrant labor from Greece's northern neighbors (Albania in particular), and the opening of the Balkan markets that had been closed for decades to Greek firms, helped resuscitate the Greek economy. After twenty years, Greece was back on the road to growth. These positive results allowed successive governments under Simitis to set the country on the path to joining the EMU, which further stabilized the economy, especially after the drachma became part of the EMU in 1998. Investment started growing along with productivity. By the end of the 1990s, it looked like Greece was transformed from an ailing, closed economy to a dynamic postindustrial one, with services producing 70 percent of the GDP and employing 60 percent of the labor force.

When Greece adopted the common European currency in 2001, it unlocked access to inexpensive credit, which financed further infrastructure investment and boosted household consumption. Greece's borrowing costs dropped from 11.5 percent of GDP in the mid-1990s to 5 percent of GDP in the mid-2000s. Between 2001 and 2009, the country averaged an annual growth rate of 4.2 percent—the second highest in the Eurozone and twice the rate of the average member country.[54]

Of course, not everything was right. The current account balance kept worsening during this period, going from an average deficit of 12.5 percent of GDP during 1992–1996 to 16.8 percent during 2002–2006, much worse than the economies of Portugal and Spain. The public debt stabilized at around 100 percent of GDP instead of being reduced given the high growth environment, as dictated by sound economic policy. A particularly worrisome development was the decline in tax collection, which is even more startling in light of the meteoric rise in private consumption and overall prosperity. The deregulation of the banking sector turned it from an instrument of the government into a partner, introducing elements of corruption. Most ominously, no reforms took place in critical sectors like public administration, health care, and education. In short, the underlying institutional weaknesses persisted—perhaps they were even reinforced.[55]

Although Greece reached its highest GDP in history 2008, the collective psychological feeling that prevailed at the time of the 2004 Olympic Games in Athens is hard to surpass. The event was expensive, and organizing it was fraught with all sorts of problems, including massive schedule overruns. Most observers had expected that Greece would fail to pull the games off. Instead, they were a resounding success. During the beautiful summer days of 2004, most Greeks must have felt that their country had finally fulfilled the dreams of its founders. Unfortunately, this feeling would prove short-lived.

In sum, the post–Civil War era is notable for three major achievements. First, the economy took off in the 1950s, and Greece was able to escape poverty and join the economically developed nations of Europe. Second, it acquired the most liberal and inclusive democratic institutions of its history in 1974. Third, it was able to join the EEC in 1981 and the Eurozone in 2001, becoming an integral part of the core of Europe. In short, it appeared that Greece had been able to finally realize its perennial goals of economic-political modernization and integration into Western Europe that had been so central to its identity since its independence.

At the same time, however, all these projects placed Greek society under tremendous strain. The economic takeoff of 1950–1970 came at the cost of suppressing consumption through limitations to democracy and eventually autocracy. Conversely, the democratic institutions established in 1974 brought with them a virulent strain of populism that eroded the quality of institutions and undermined the country's economy. Lastly, the process of economic integration in Europe placed the Greek economy under performance pressure, while at the same time unwillingly funding and abetting the worst excesses of the Greek political system which further inhibited its capacity to change.

In other words, all three projects produced unprecedented achievements that were accompanied by significant disasters: the economic takeoff was followed by autocracy, the liberalization of political institutions engendered populism, and economic integration in Europe bequeathed the great crisis of 2009. However, the balance in the first two instances was mostly positive. Autocracy gave way to democracy and, in turn, populism failed to destroy most of the economic progress that had been achieved. As for the great crisis of 2009, to which I turn next, its final impact remains to be seen.

VI

THE GREAT CRISIS

How did Greece go from economic boom to bust?

Things in Greece looked ideal in 2008. By most indices of economic and human development, the country was in an enviable position. It was reaching the end of a decade that had been remarkable for its robust economic growth. An average real GDP growth rate of close to 4 percent had led to a per capita GDP of $32,100 (Purchasing Power Parity, PPP), bringing Greece into the exclusive club of the forty richest nations on earth. Perhaps more importantly, Greece ranked 26th globally on the Human Development Index (HDI), which combines indicators of life expectancy, educational attainment, and income. Growth translated into prosperity, reflected in a variety of indicators, such as very high rates of both primary and secondary home ownership (in 2013, 73 percent of the housing stock was occupied by owners versus 22 percent that were rentals, while 21 percent of the total housing stock was composed of secondary homes). Social modernization proceeded apace. Fertility rates dropped from 2.4 children in 1950 to 1.4 in 1990, and the share of urban population grew from 37 percent to 59 percent during the same period. By 2011, life expectancy reached 78.3 years for men and 83.1 years for women. In short, Greece was in the midst of unprecedented material prosperity, and its politics had acquired the predictable features of a two-party system strongly anchored at the center.[1]

Underneath the surface, however, things were far from perfect. Public opinion surveys indicated a growing malaise, expressing a combination of very low trust in most institutions and relatively low but persistent unemployment, especially among the country's youth. Social commentators were concerned by the spread of pervasive cynicism, crude materialism, and rising corruption. A few voices also raised red flags about enduring problems in the economy, which undermined the sustainability of the economic model that had produced all this spectacular growth. They were not heard, but they were right: the amazing expansion of the Greek economy had a very soft underbelly. It was based mainly on domestic consumption, fanned by a loose fiscal policy made possible by the influx of foreign capital following the liberalization of the financial sector and, more than anything else, a set of factors related to Greece's membership in the Eurozone.

It would be wrong to describe all of the Greek economy's growth as a bubble. Exports grew considerably during this period, although imports grew much faster. Portugal, facing similar incentives and eventually a similar bust, did not experience similar growth. Nevertheless, Greece's underlying weakness was visible in a variety of areas, including numerous obstacles to competition in key sectors of the economy such as energy and transportation; persistent difficulties in the ease of doing business; many barriers to entrepreneurship; the relatively poor quality of education as measured by standardized scores in science and mathematics; low levels of spending on research; and rampant corruption in the public sector.[2]

In many ways Greece presented a paradox: it was an advanced European economy with a per capita GDP that placed it among the wealthiest countries, but it also displayed some institutional features resembling those of the emerging economies of the developing world. Greece was a country populated by well-heeled households, featuring high individual consumption, good quality-of-life indicators, and reasonable levels of spending on infrastructure and public services, but also dysfunctional institutions and a lack of a sophisticated and competitive business sector. It looked a bit like a country rich in natural resources. So long as the Greek economy boomed, these problems could be ignored. But then the subprime crisis erupted in the United States, in 2008. Initially, the prevailing feeling was that the crisis would skip Greece. Indeed, Greek banks were not exposed to toxic assets from the United States. As a result, they were able to attract considerable deposit flows in the aftermath of the US crisis, peaking in June 2009. Then all hell broke loose.[3]

What triggered the crisis?

The trigger was Greece's inability to borrow in order to service its very high public debt, at the same time as its economic engine was slowing down. Greece's cost of borrowing began to rise in 2009. This cost is described by sovereign bond yield spreads between Greece and Germany, usually referring to ten-year bonds and measured in basis points (bps): the higher the bps, the higher the relative cost of borrowing. Simply put, spreads are the premium investors demand to buy Greek government debt rather than German benchmarks. Greek spreads had been minimal for many years following Greece's entry into the Eurozone, reflecting the generalized assumption among lenders that, by sharing the same currency, Greece was as creditworthy as Germany. Borrowing cheaply was one of the most valuable benefits enjoyed by Greece after it joined the European Monetary Union (EMU), on top of monetary stability.

The immediate cause of the rise in Greek spreads was the 2008 US subprime crisis, which caused a rise in risk aversion among investors and an accompanying credit crunch. It also prompted a revision of existing assumptions about lending, including the creditworthiness of states. Overly exposed debtors came in for much closer scrutiny. After underestimating risk for many years, markets were now moving to the opposite extreme, growing scared of large sovereign debt. Suddenly, the economic fundamentals of Greece were reexamined and doubts began to be expressed about the sustainability of its debt. The result was an explosion of Greek spreads from a low of 35 bps in early 2008 to 230 bps in December of that year, and a high of 300 bps in March 2009, though they came down to a more manageable 130 bps by September. By then, Greece retained a manageable cost of borrowing, but the wild fluctuation of spreads indicated very clearly that the situation could easily get out of hand. Nevertheless, Greek governments failed to address the problem.

In 2008 Kostas Karamanlis was the prime minister of Greece. The leader of the New Democracy Party, he was Konstantinos Karamanlis's nephew and had been prime minister since 2004. He had literally spent his way to reelection in 2007, which caused a subsequent collapse of tax revenues and an explosion of the deficit. This generated new pressure from the European Union (EU) for unpopular deficit reduction measures that Karamanlis was unwilling to take. Beleaguered by various scandals and facing a rapid deterioration of the economic situation, he came belatedly to realize the need for both political consensus between the two major parties and emergency economic measures to avert the looming crisis. His rival was George Papandreou, Andreas Papandreou's son, now the leader of PASOK. Instead of opting for consensus, Papandreou responded to Karamanlis by following the standard script of Greek politics that called for polarization and outbidding, failing to realize that times had changed. Karamanlis was forced to call early elections in October 2009, which made an already bad situation much, much worse.

Papandreou ran his election campaign on a Keynesian platform of demand stimulus, infamously proclaiming, "There is money!" He promised a €3 billion stimulus package, along with above-inflation wage and pension increases; higher taxes for the wealthy; and even a review of privatization of the notoriously spendthrift state-owned carrier Olympic Airlines and the Piraeus port operations, the only public enterprises that the Karamanlis government had managed to privatize. The campaign was successful and PASOK won handily with 43.9 percent of the vote, compared to New Democracy's meager 33.4 percent. Papandreou became prime minister and immediately implemented a "solidarity package" for low-income households. Journalistic reports from 2008 to 2009 describe a generalized sense of obliviousness and a failure to heed the danger.[4]

All hell broke loose when the new government announced a drastic revision of the government deficit for both 2008 and 2009. The size of the revision was enormous: the 2008 deficit was revised from 5 percent of GDP (the figure originally reported by Greece, published and validated by Eurostat in April 2009) to 7.7 percent of GDP. At the same time, the Greek government also revised the 2009 deficit forecast from 3.7 percent of GDP (the figure it had reported in the spring of that year) to a jaw-dropping 12.5 percent. Eventually the actual figure came to a staggering 15.6 percent—five times the Eurozone maximum of 3 percent. The European Commission's official report on this issue published the following year scathingly noted, "Revisions of this magnitude in the estimated past government deficit ratios have been extremely rare in other EU Member States, but have taken place for Greece on several occasions."[5]

These revisions caused enormous consternation and commotion in both the EU and, more importantly, the financial markets, which reacted by sending Greek spreads into the stratosphere: they reached 380 bps in January 2010. At the same time, credit rating agencies downgraded Greece's creditworthiness. The government's emergency announcement of a stability program to achieve fiscal consolidation in December was too little and came too late, failing to assuage the markets. A consensus began to form that Greece's public debt of 120 percent of GDP was unsustainable. The first months of 2010 saw constant vacillations from both the Greek government and the European Union about the course of action to be adopted, making a bad situation worse. The principles, timing, conditions, and modalities of assistance to Greece were all matters for continuous and often inconclusive discussion, and there were contradictory declarations by leaders of the EU and Germany in particular. When in May 2010 the spreads reached 1,280 bps, exactly when Greece needed large amortizations of its debt, the Greek government found itself unable to raise the capital required to service its debt. Faced with the prospect of a catastrophic sovereign default, the government requested financial assistance from the IMF and the Eurozone countries on April 27, 2010.[6]

Greece's inability to service its debt was the trigger, but the causes went deeper. It is possible to parse these causes into three parts: European/institutional, domestic/economic, and domestic/political.

What were the European institutional causes of the crisis?

How was Greece able to borrow at the same low rates as Germany given what should have been then (and were in retrospect) pretty obvious weaknesses of its economy? The answer points to flaws in the design of the common European currency.

At the end of the 1980s, the European Economic Community decided to become an economic and monetary union, a decision formalized in 1992 with the Treaty on European Union, signed in the Dutch town of Maastricht. The signatory countries accepted sharing of a currency and a central bank, thus abdicating their monetary sovereignty. At the same time, however, they retained their fiscal sovereignty, that is, their ability to draw their budgets. The mismatch between a common currency and separate fiscal policies had several shortcomings. For instance, each member country had an incentive to free-ride on the credibility of the common currency by running a budget deficit if others did not, thereby undermining it.

Obviously, the framers of the treaty were aware of these shortcomings but lacked the political power required for the colossal political step of the abolition of fiscal sovereignty—essentially the replacement of national sovereignty by a political union. Thus, the treaty specified common guidelines about fiscal policy, including, among other factors, specific limits on inflation rates by reference to an agreed average, limits on budget deficits (not to exceed 3 percent of GDP), and limits on gross government debt (not to exceed 60 percent of GDP). These criteria were reinforced in the 1997 Stability and Growth Pact. However, enforcement of these guidelines remained discretionary and limited by procedural red tape, various exemptions, and long deadlines. In fact, leading member states, such as France and Germany, were the first to flout these guidelines. Furthermore, there was no institutionalized contingency plan about how to deal with fiscal crises of member states, should such crises erupt. There was actually no explicit legal obligation to support Eurozone members with financial problems (both by the EU or another state), including no privileged access to financial institutions and no support from the European Central Bank (ECB); assistance was to be extended on a discretionary basis only.

This set of regulations led to contradictory outcomes: on the one hand, states were not effectively prevented from engaging in fiscal laxity, but on the other hand they no longer had instruments to deal with its consequences, since central banks and national currencies had been abolished and the concomitant possibility of currency devaluation had vanished. Likewise, the lack of a banking union meant that the crisis could spread from the government to the banking system and back, creating a vicious cycle.[7]

Clearly, this was a recipe for potential disaster, but the treaty framers were willing to assume the risk as a way to indirectly achieve the unification of Europe. This is exactly how Chancellor Helmut Kohl put it in 1991, at the completion of the Maastricht accords on political, economic, and monetary union: "One thing is certain. When this Europe in 1997 or 1999 has a common currency from Copenhagen to Madrid and from The Hague to Rome, when more than 350 million people live in a common space without border controls, then no bureaucrat in Europe is going to be able to stop the process of political unification."[8]

It was precisely this type of claim that helped financial markets believe that the EU would not let countries of the Eurozone default on their debts. As long as this was believed, whatever clauses in the debt contracts might say, Greece and others could borrow very cheaply—and they did. Put differently, the assumption that no country would be allowed to default (mirrored in the fact that the European Central Bank and regulators treated national government bonds the same, irrespective of the country of origin), along with the assumption that all European economies would converge, meant a collapse in borrowing costs in the periphery and a convergence in spreads. In turn, this fueled massive consumption booms in the South, as evidenced in current account deficits. In Greece that deficit went to finance the public-sector budget deficit, while in Ireland and Spain it financed private-sector deficits, particularly in real estate. Put differently, policies restricting domestic demand in countries like Germany produced excess savings that fueled debt booms in countries like Greece, Ireland, or Spain. Hence current account deficits in the South mirrored current account surpluses in the North of the Eurozone. "Success" in the North and "failure" in the South were symmetric processes, flip sides of the same coin.

Seen from this perspective, the Greek crisis was the canary in the coalmine of a much bigger problem. This was not, in other words, a problem of lazy or cheating Greeks, as initially framed (although this does not mean that Greece was free of responsibility, as we will see below), but a systemic crisis on a European scale. The European Monetary Union was just not viable as designed, and the crisis was not merely a case of violation of rules, but of flawed rules in the first place. The huge imbalances between creditors and debtors had to be addressed through either exit from the euro or some kind of policy package that mixed transfers and internal devaluation. In turn, this package had to be part of a broader institutional reform addressing issues of economic union, banking union, and political union at once.

What were the domestic economic causes of the crisis?

The flaws in the architecture of the European Monetary Union meant that a crisis was bound to erupt. But why did it erupt first in Greece of all places, and why did it take the initial form of a public debt crisis? This is where the domestic element enters.

Greece's Achilles heel was its persistently high public debt. Indeed, Greece had failed to take advantage of the economy's growth in order to shrink its debt. As a result, the country's debt hovered consistently over 100 percent of GDP and was steadily mounting in spite of Greece's GDP growth, going from 103 percent of GDP in 2000 to 115 percent in 2009. Worse, a significant portion of this debt was net external debt, which grew from 45 percent of GDP in 2000 to 100 percent in 2009. The extent to which Greece's debt burden was mainly external is evident from the fact that in March 2010 two-thirds of the total government debt was owned by foreign banks and other foreign entities. In fact, a measure of a country's insolvency can be seen in net interest payments, that is, the share of GDP required annually to service its net external debt. In 2009, Greece had to spend 3.2 percent of its GDP on it, more than any other Eurozone country.

The Greek debt was not just an outgrowth of spending, however. As we saw, successive Greek governments had adopted a fiscal policy that combined mounting spending with a drop in revenues. In 2007, for instance, the government spent 45 percent of the GDP while collecting less than 40 percent from taxation. Greece was consistently underperforming when it came to the collection of direct taxes, a problem manifested in the proliferation of tax exemptions targeted to specific groups and the exemption from taxation of entire social groups.[9]

This is where the infamous tax evasion issue comes in. Tax cheating in Greece came into worldwide focus in the wake of the crisis. Michael Lewis described a conversation he had with an employee of the tax collection agency: "He just took it for granted that I knew that the only Greeks who paid their taxes were the ones who could not avoid doing so—the salaried employees of corporations, who had their taxes withheld from their paychecks. The vast economy of self-employed workers— everyone from doctors to the guys who ran the kiosks that sold the *International Herald Tribune*—cheated (one big reason why Greece has the highest percentage of self-employed workers of any European country). 'It's become a cultural trait,' he said." Lewis went on to describe the scale of Greek tax cheating as incredible in scope and breathtaking overall. For example, many professionals declared incomes that placed them consistently below the taxation threshold.

The empirical evidence backs up the anecdotal observations. Economies with large numbers of self-employed individuals are prone to tax evasion, and Greece is one of them. Its percentage of self-employed individuals is at 35.1 percent, compared to the Organization for Economic Cooperation and Development (OECD) average of 15.8 (in 2007), and it has a corresponding low share of wages as a percent of GDP (35.2 percent vs. 48.5 percent for Germany in 2007). In 2010 the declared income of salaried individuals and pensioners amounted to 70.2 percent of total declared income, and they paid 55.5 percent of the total collected income tax. In contrast, nonsalaried individuals' declared income was 16.8 percent of total declared income, and their part of the total collected income taxes was just 15.8 percent. A recent study using novel and reliable individual-level data estimated the lower bound of tax evasion in Greece for 2009 at €28 billion of unreported income, amounting to forgone government revenues reaching as high as 31 percent of the 2009 government deficit. On average, the true income of the self-employed is estimated to be 1.92 times larger than their reported income. As expected, tax evasion is particularly prevalent among the self-employed professions, including doctors, engineers, private tutors, accountants, financial service agents, and lawyers. And there are plenty in these professions, with one lawyer for every 250 persons in Greece compared to one for 593 in Germany; a notary for every 3.446 persons in Greece compared to one for every 7,287 in Italy; and one pharmacy for every 950 people in Greece compared to the European average of one for every 4,000. Yet another study found that the distribution of tax evasion across income groups in Greece is U-shaped in that it over-represents the lower and higher income brackets. For instance, it is estimated that full collection and elimination of the farmers' tax exemption would raise income tax collection by 33 percent while reducing inequality considerably.[10]

Unlike the very real tax evasion issue, other negative stereotypes about Greece that surfaced early on, particularly the claim about "lazy Greeks," do not correspond to reality. The OECD figures show that Greeks work the longest hours in Europe, although their productivity is not correspondingly high. Lastly, while everyone's attention was fixated on the public debt and government deficit, Greece's current account (or trade) deficit was being overlooked. As we saw, this was a reflection of the systemic European problem. The Greek economy faced a considerable inflation differential as part of the Eurozone and a loss of competitiveness relative to both OECD and Eurozone states, thus feeding a growing trade deficit. The combination of high economic growth, deteriorating competitiveness, and persistent fiscal imbalances worsened the external balance of the Greek economy. The current account deficit reached 13 percent of GDP in 2008 from a close-to-balance position in the mid-1990s. Lastly, Greece was also incapable of attracting significant levels of foreign direct investment inflows.[11]

Both the growing government deficit and debt and (especially) the trade deficit problems went unaddressed, hidden below the general euphoria. Political parties and the media failed to bring these issues to public attention; never did a public debate take place, and the public remained in the dark. For all their reformist drive, the Simitis administrations were held hostage by the PASOK political machine, which constrained reforms. The most egregious example was the attempt in 2001 to reform the inefficient pension system, which was defeated by street action and the threat of an internal party revolt. As for the Karamanlis administrations that succeeded Simitis they were content to not rock the boat and kept spending (and not taxing) with abandon. On one hand, the "political cost" of halting unsustainable policies and reforming the economy to make it more competitive was steep. On the other hand, the debt problem could easily be bypassed since the country had access to cheap borrowing. But although Greece's access to cheap borrowing resulted from EMU flaws, its failure to address the fundamental problems of the economy was a result of its very own political institutions.

What were the domestic political causes of the crisis?

Public deficits exploded and were subsequently impossible to pare down because their direct beneficiaries had political clout that allowed them first to obtain their preferred policies and then to block reforms that went against their interests. This clout is the direct result of the way interest group politics were shaped by PASOK in the 1980s. Put differently, political institutions go a long way toward explaining the toxic combination of high spending and low revenues.

To begin with, Greek public debt fueled private consumption. A 2008 survey found that the world's biggest fans of designer goods hailed from Greece, where almost half of all consumers claimed to buy designer brands themselves and nearly three-quarters claimed to know a label-chaser. The Greeks, this report went, had proven to be voracious apparel consumers. They were able to do so because the Greek state spent liberally. Public enterprises were overstaffed, poorly managed, saddled with huge payroll costs, and running colossal deficits. Thousands were hired, typically through opaque procedures. For example, a single ministerial decree (No. 164 of 2004, also known as the "Pavlopoulos decree," named after the New Democracy government minister who issued it) shifted at once the contracts of thousands of public workers from limited to indefinite duration, essentially giving them life tenure. Public-sector salaries rose faster than private-sector ones, fueling an unprecedented wave of private consumption, which in 2009 overshot the EU average by 12 percent despite the fact that average incomes in Greece were 5 percent below the EU average and labor productivity was 20 percent below.[12]

Why was the state so liberal in spending and so miserly at collecting—and why was it unable to fix this imbalance in the face of a lethal risk? The answer points to the institutions mediating relations between state and society, namely political parties. Parties developed an informal social contract with society, whereby votes were exchanged for private goods. Traditionally this was done through clientelism, the exchange of votes for favors between individual voters and politicians. PASOK came to power in 1981 by promising to abolish this practice but, instead, expanded and upgraded it. The provision of benefits was now processed primarily through party-affiliated organizations rather than individual politicians in a much more bureaucratic way; it required loyalty to the party rather than to some individual political broker. The amount and quality of goods exchanged for votes improved vastly. The newly nationalized firms offered hundreds of well-paying and cushy jobs, while the influx of substantial transfers from the European Economic Community's regional policy framework went in large part to finance PASOK's patronage machine. Indeed, PASOK's political success from this operation was so spectacular that it was soon imitated by New Democracy, which also proceeded to build a mass party and engaged in similar patronage practices when in power. This trend was reflected in a remarkable increase in party membership during the 1980s that was not only unprecedented in Greek history but also unusual in the European context. As a result, it is very hard to find a state agency not deeply infused with political patronage.[13]

Of particular interest is how this social contract was carried out. As part of its so-called democratization drive, PASOK pioneered the creation of party-affiliated organizations that colonized every aspect of social activity, from high schools to neighborhood associations, including trade unions and all kinds of professional groupings. It then used these organizations to acquire control of these associations. The use of proportional representation, in particular, allowed the transformation of associational elections into mini general elections that reproduced and reinforced the polarization prevailing at the national level. For example, the yearly elections for university student governments became hotly contested and widely followed contests among student affiliates of the political parties. This was an effective way for parties to recruit members, mobilize society, and get their message through—and indeed, the leaders of unions and other associations tended to use their positions as a springboard for high-profile political careers, often ending up as MPs and government ministers.[14]

In light of this, it is tempting to describe the Greek political system as one of total party domination over a weak civil society, a temptation that many observers succumb to. Yet, this is hardly an instance of political parties just lording it over civil society. Instead, this system provides a vehicle through which various social groups (i.e., civil society) are able to gain considerable leverage over state resources by being present and active inside the parties. This process results in the penetration of government, and by extension the state, by interest groups that are able to directly obtain group-specific goods or indirectly extract group-specific rents, either through favorable legislation or by blocking universalistic reforms that threaten their privileges. What they are able to gain through this process varies considerably and ranges from sinecures in the public sector to life employment, privileged pensions, protection from market downturns, investment subsidies, and even large profits from government contracts. The gradual weakening of party machines after the 1990s has reinforced their power, and their leaders have gradually gained additional clout. Incidentally, this type of interest group politics suggests that Greece is a much stronger and less atomized civil society than typically assumed.[15]

Of course, interest group politics and rent seeking are ubiquitous across the world. What makes Greece perhaps less common is the centrality of this process in policymaking as well as its democratization, as it pertains to a large number of interest groups rather than being restricted to a few powerful players. Groups that profit from it run the gamut of society, from large professional associations on one end all the way to a narrow business elite of economic oligarchs on the other. As a result, rents are widely distributed. For example, an estimated one hundred and ninety-nine special consumption and transaction taxes have been instituted to fund twenty-four pension and healthcare funds of various professions, including lawyers, doctors, civil engineers, journalists, military personnel, hotel owners, and shipping employees. The lawyers' fund, for instance, is financed by a tax on property transactions amounting to 1.3 percent of the value of each transaction, the engineers' fund has benefited from a 1 percent charge on the value of public works, the doctors' fund gets a 6.5 percent charge on all transactions involving medications, and journalists have extracted a special 21.5 percent tax on advertising expenditures to finance their pension and health care fund. These taxes have contributed to generous pensions and other benefits, including health care, well above what simple salary contributions could have achieved. Furthermore, these groups have been protected from competition by numerous regulations.[16]

Some of these benefits are won through informal channels entailing opaque processes related to the drafting of the content of government budgets and special ministerial decrees. The top tax-evading groups had at least the sympathetic ear of 221 MPs out of the 300. Out of 300 MPs in 2009, there were 70 lawyers, 40 doctors, 43 engineers, 28 education professionals, and 40 finance professionals. When the small party of the Democratic Left joined the coalition government in 2012–2013, its own choice as justice minister was the former president of the Athens Lawyers' Association, who immediately used his position to benefit that group. However, the ability that these groups have at blocking reforms is achieved in a more systematic way through party-affiliated professional organizations.[17]

Once interest group politics are factored into the policy-making process, several otherwise puzzling features of the Greek social landscape begin to make sense. A few examples: Greece's social protection expenditure matches the EU average but results in much inferior outcomes; the performance of Greece's educational system is one of the worst in Europe despite the lowest student-teacher ratio; Greeks who send their children to public schools simply assume they will need to hire private tutors—who are often their children's public school teachers—to make up for deficient class instruction; until the crisis Greece's welfare system delivered very generous pensions (covering 96 percent of average salaries, starting at 58 years of age and costing 13.5 percent of GDP, compared to 61 percent at 63 years, and 10 percent of GDP for OECD countries) in the absence of corresponding contributions; there are many more physicians per capita than the OECD average (6.1 versus 3.1 per 1,000); spending on pharmaceuticals is very high, but the health care system performs poorly; public enterprises have managed to escape from popular ire despite scandalous payroll costs, poor management, and humongous deficits; and mass media operate without proper licenses but derive a large part of their income from state-owned companies' ads.[18]

Interest group politics is sometimes informally described as "corruption." In 2013, Transparency International ranked Greece in the 80th position globally on perceptions of corruption, at the very bottom of the EU. In the first EU summit he attended in 2009, after being sworn in as prime minister, George Papandreou famously acknowledged to a stunned audience the widespread presence of systemic corruption in Greece. What is remarkable is the general toleration of such practices among the citizenry. Michael Lewis described how surprised he was by the complete lack of interest in what was obviously shocking material about corruption that he kept encountering during his travels in Greece. This toleration can be understood when placed in the context of interest group politics that benefit large segments of the population.[19]

The implications are dire since this system hinders competition; increases red tape and administrative burdens; and, by establishing a regime of opacity in administrative and legal processes, effectively undermines the democratic process. Interest group politics are also connected with the emergence and persistence of a "dualist" political economy, a common problem across countries of the European South. This type of political economy is one based on a sharp divide between "insiders" and "outsiders," reflected in a variety of dimensions, from labor market access and regulation to welfare, health, and pension coverage and tax collection enforcement. For example, insiders such as public-sector employees enjoy strong protections against market upheavals (e.g., civil servants have life tenure) and have above-average salaries, pensions, and benefits, though they tend to be fully taxed. Likewise, many self-employed professions (doctors, lawyers, and even farmers) are also insiders, protected from market pressure through special legislation (e.g., high barriers to entry in these professions) and highly subsidized pension funds, and they can easily evade taxation. In contrast, employees of small private enterprises are often outsiders, enjoying few rights and protections, and are often employed informally. At the bottom, one finds immigrant workers and the unemployed youth (although the latter may indirectly benefit from the insiders' privileges through family connections).[20]

In sum, it is interest group politics institutionalized by PASOK during the 1980s, rather than supposedly powerful and unchanging cultural attributes that explains how the debt and deficit ballooned and why it was so hard to bring them under control afterward.

What was the Memorandum of Economic and Financial Policies?

Because Greece was a member of the Eurozone, a sovereign default amounted to an exit from the common currency. This prospect entailed a destructive and potentially global destabilizing shock, since the euro's credibility was premised on the lack of an exit option for member states. At the same time, Greece's sovereign debt crisis was also quickly morphing into a banking crisis because many European banks owned Greek government bonds that would turn toxic in the event of a Greek default. In short, this was a crisis whose significance extended well beyond Greece.

Taking the potential of global contagion and panic into account, the EU decided to act in order to avert what many thought could turn into a Lehman Brothers moment. Lacking the appropriate institutions to deal with this problem, the EU improvised a tripartite structure (which became known as the "Troika"), comprised of the European Commission, the European Central Bank, and the IMF. The inclusion of the IMF was both unusual and controversial and was justified on two grounds: first, due to the EU's lack of expertise in handling this type of crisis; and second, as a means of signaling strict conditionality, both to avoid the moral hazard associated with a no-strings-attached rescue and as a way to punish the irresponsible behavior of Greek governments.

This was the first-ever IMF program directed at a member of the euro area, and it stretched its own rules almost to their limits because, even with the implementation of the agreed policies, the economic uncertainties were so significant that the IMF staff was unable to vouch whether there was a high probability that Greece's public debt was sustainable. Indeed, the IMF had to amend its own rules (by appealing to the high risk of international spillover effects) so as to be able to move ahead.[21]

On May 2, 2010, a financial agreement was signed between Greece, the European Commission, the ECB, and the IMF on a package of economic and financial policies described in a "Memorandum of Economic and Financial Policies," popularly known as the "Memorandum." The program provided for financial assistance to Greece totaling €110 billion, disbursed over three years and split between the Eurozone countries (€80 billion) and the IMF (€30). The aim was to restore fiscal balance and competiveness while protecting the financial sector. The program set forth a mix of "front-loaded" fiscal consolidation, internal devaluation (currency devaluation being impossible, all adjustment in relative prices had to be through reductions in wages, benefits, and costs), and structural reforms. It also included measures such as reductions in pensions and public-sector wages, increases in the value-added tax, higher assessments on real estate, emergency assessments, and a number of measures to improve tax administration. With respect to improving competitiveness, the program included a reduction in minimum wages, the divestiture of state assets, the opening of so-called closed professions, and policies aiming at boosting entrepreneurship through the reduction of red tape. The program eschewed upfront debt restructuring, (i.e., a debt write-down) mainly at the insistence of creditor countries whose banks owned Greek government bonds, which could have caused the crisis to spread into their banking systems. The program optimistically projected a return to growth by 2012.[22]

Despite general apprehension, the program took off on good footing. At the very least, certainty appeared to have taken the place of indecision and ambivalence. The macro-economic evolution in 2010 was roughly in line with program forecasts, and the first IMF evaluations were positive. The Greek government appeared to be fully on board, and public opinion followed suit. Surveys showed that over 50 percent of respondents were willing to go along with the measures rather than see the country default. And indeed, Greece bit the bullet and achieved a yearly fiscal adjustment in 2010 of 6 percent of GDP, which was the greatest ever attempted. This adjustment amounted to a deficit reduction of more than €14 billion.

By early 2011, however, it became clear that things were not developing as anticipated. This was due to a number of factors: the rapid pace of fiscal contraction, the credit crunch, the growing political uncertainty, and the poor state of the European economy. Furthermore, the program failed to prevent the contagion. As the weaknesses of the euro architecture were laid bare, markets began to panic, causing a chain reaction that led to the rise of spreads for other countries. Against a background of heightened market concern, collapsing domestic demand, and further decline in GDP, investment in Greece collapsed and exports stagnated. The program went off-track and, as a result, the Greek debt burden became more unsustainable than ever. At this point, it became clear that all early assumptions about the Greek economy's ability to adjust and the capacity of the Greek political-administrative system to implement the program's measures had been unrealistic. The fall 2011 IMF report was devastating: most measures were way off. Structural reforms had stalled, while both expectations and investment had collapsed. The Greek economy was in free fall, in a state of depression rather than simple recession.[23]

The realization that the financial rescue of Greece was failing created serious problems within the EU, as member states (with Germany at the top) were unwilling to foot the bill for an additional package, and the new EU institution tasked with this job was not in place yet. Uncertainty returned and this inflamed the financial markets further, leading to the spread of the crisis. Now Ireland and Portugal had to be rescued, while the much larger economies of Spain and Italy moved into the danger zone of escalating spreads and, thus, of a potential inability to service their debt.

At last, the inadequacy of the Greek program was acknowledged in March 2011. A second rescue package was officially announced in July 2011, extended in October, and ultimately implemented in February 2012. This one totaled €164.5 billion, bringing the total bailout to an unprecedented €274.5 billion. By way of comparison, the Irish rescue package in December 2010 had cost €85 billion and the Portuguese one in May 2011 was €78 billion. This time, the package included a landmark debt-restructuring deal with the vast majority of Greece's private-sector lenders, which became known as the PSI (Private Sector Involvement). After a complex negotiation process, the Greek government announced in March 2012 that the holders of 82.4 percent of the €177.3 billion of debt that was issued under Greek law had agreed to swap their bonds for new ones, worth as much as 52 percent less—the largest such deal in history. In effect, private-sector bondholders agreed to forgive close to €100 billion.[24]

What did the adjustment program achieve?

Under the best conditions, the adjustment program would have been very painful. As it played out, conditions were far from optimal. In fact, the exact opposite was the case: Greece was hit by a perfect economic storm. The Greek economy experienced a series of distinct but interrelated shocks that combined to send it into a vicious downward spiral, effectively causing its collapse. To put it simply, both the IMF and the EU bet on optimistic assumptions that failed to materialize.[25]

The shock to the Greek economy was colossal. Four years down the road, personal incomes had been reduced by a third, nearly one Greek in three was unemployed (unemployment reached 27 percent compared to the IMF projection of 15 percent, including youth unemployment of around 60 percent), and the economy had shrunk by a quarter (nearly 25 percent since 2008, against an initial IMF projection of a 5.5 percent contraction up to 2012). The Greek recession was similar in magnitude to the US Great Depression of 1929–1933. Domestic demand collapsed, capital fled the country (Greek banks lost €1.5 billion worth of deposits in the week that followed the program's announcement alone), a severe credit crunch hit the business sector and paralyzed all economic activity, the banking system effectively imploded, and intense uncertainty about the country's currency future caused investment to decline by 46 percent. Overall, Greece dropped from 40th to 56th place in the world in terms of per capita GDP in just four years. The pain was not shared evenly across society as plans to downsize the number of civil servants never really materialized and the private sector ended up generating all the job losses.

The program also failed to address the problem that triggered the crisis in the first place—Greece's debt. In fact, the severe lending policy imposed on Greece, which creditors believed was necessary from a moral hazard perspective, undermined its debt sustainability targets. The size of the public debt as a proportion of the country's GDP overshot program projections by a dramatic margin, reaching 170 percent of GDP in 2013 and projected to go up to 189 percent in 2015 (compared to 130 percent at the onset of the crisis). In turn, the realization that debt continued to be unsustainable reinforced the uncertainty about Greece's prospects, thus undermining its economy.

In short, this economic storm led to the economic collapse of the country, further stoking the fear of an inevitable Greek sovereign default. This prospect came to be known as "Grexit," since a sovereign default only made sense if Greece abandoned the euro, an outcome that could destroy the credibility of the common European currency.

What went wrong?

The Greek adjustment program was unprecedented—and the least successful of all the adjustment programs implemented in 2010–2011. These programs attempted to solve an economic problem that had not surfaced since the end of World War II, namely the attempt by financially open and mature countries to adjust within a monetary union, that is, by internal rather than currency devaluation. The institutional setup of assistance combining a tripartite structure, along with the creation of successive European financing institutions dedicated to tackling this type of problem, was equally unprecedented. Predictably, this exceptional situation encouraged rushed decision-making. The friction between debtor and creditor nations reflected important political fissures within the European Union and injected considerable animosity into the entire process.[26]

Greece was asked to undertake an extraordinary fiscal adjustment while simultaneously reorganizing its entire economy, reforming its administrative apparatus, and revising its underlying social contract. All this was supposed to happen in an international context characterized by great economic and political uncertainty; an emerging supranational entity, the EU, unclear about its future direction; and financial markets prone to panic. The requirements associated with these goals were not only extreme, but also often contradictory to each other. For example, a reorganization of a country's economy requires massive credit and liquidity, which were being sucked out of the country by the process of fiscal adjustment.

More specifically, two types of program failures stand out: first, failures caused by the fact that appropriate measures were either incompletely implemented or not implemented at all; and second, failures that resulted from measures that were successfully implemented but proved harmful.

Let us begin with incomplete implementation or nonimplementation failure. Reviews of the program have pointed to the lack of ownership of the program by Greek elites and the population at large, the shortcomings of the Greek political system (particularly interest group politics), and the low capacity of Greece's administrative machinery, which was made worse by across-the-board salary reductions that lowered morale and led to the degradation of existing expertise. Structural reforms were poorly implemented or enforced (e.g., tax collection), announced repeatedly but not implemented (e.g., the opening of closed professions), or effectively blocked (e.g., the exemption of the pension and health funds of lawyers, doctors, engineers, and journalists from the common pension and health fund). Furthermore, the privatization process proved disappointing, and the effort to rationalize the administrative apparatus faced enormous obstacles, including bureaucratic inertia. The Troika overestimated Greece's capacity to implement structural reforms and discovered that enacting legislation did not always amount to effective implementation and enforcement.[27]

More generally, politics interfered with the implementation of the program in a major way. A series of political upheavals affected the country's willingness and ability to implement agreed-on measures, and negotiations with the Troika were regularly interrupted. The extended election period in 2012 effectively put on hold the implementation of reforms and the privatization process, while fiscal institutional reforms came to a halt. As a result, several performance criteria, indicative targets, and structural benchmarks were not observed. Time was required to restart reforms, bring the program back on track, and reach understandings with the authorities and Greece's European partners on measures to place debt on a sustainable trajectory. These delays had significant repercussions.[28]

Overall, strenuous opposition from vested interests, the unwillingness of political elites to sacrifice their power base, and the prevailing state of general disorganization undermined the implementation of structural reforms. In turn, the perception that the program was failing quickly became a self-fulfilling prophecy.

The second type of failure consists of unanticipated negative effects of successfully implemented measures. Fiscal consolidation, in particular, had much more severe effects on the state of the economy than originally anticipated. In 2010 Greece was already in recession, and the imposition of a shock therapy consisting of a 10 percent GDP reduction on its leveraged and uncompetitive private economy was going to be a risky venture, to say the least. As it turned out, private demand failed to replace public demand, especially once banks effectively shut down credit. Without liquidity, even sound businesses failed. In addition, contagion effects in the Eurozone, the poor performance of the global economy in 2011, and adverse political developments in Greece amplified the fiscal shock beyond anything anticipated.[29]

Why did it go wrong?

What were the causes of failure? In addition to errors in program design and calibration, the planners failed to fully appreciate the structure of the Greek economy and its rigidities. They appear to have underestimated the source of its lack of competitiveness, the impact of the labyrinthine legal and regulatory framework, and the willingness of politicians to go along with the reforms. They also underestimated the impact of international economic and political developments. Greece's current account (or trade balance) deficit provides an example of how the program missed its target. The planners pushed for considerable wage reductions (unit labor costs in Greece fell by 22 percent) as a way to make Greek exports more competitive. On the surface, this measure appeared successful: the current account moved into surplus territory. On closer examination, however, this was achieved by a compression of imports rather than a rise in exports. In fact, Greek exports actually dropped, in contrast to what happened in Ireland and Portugal. This is a serious problem, because if the pattern persists into the future, it would mean that when Greece's GDP begins to grow the current account deficit will also increase again. The export growth failure is due to at least three factors, all of which were overlooked by program planners: Eurozone macroeconomics, the negative feedback loop of the program, and the structure of the Greek economy.

First, the emphasis on internal devaluation in the debtor countries of the Eurozone as a way to correct their current account deficit was premised on the assumption that each member country was an autonomous entity rather than a member of a currency union along with its major trade partners; that is, the planners failed to take into account the fact that if all Eurozone countries enter simultaneously into a crisis, the demand for goods will collapse. By pressuring debtors to internally devalue, while failing to pressure creditors to concurrently expand and inflate, the EU opted for an asymmetric policy response to the broader crisis, thus producing deflation and mass unemployment.

Second, planners did not correctly anticipate the program's negative feedback loop. Export growth requires credit access. However, the banking sector, which was relatively healthy when the crisis began, was not in a position to extend credit even to sound businesses. In fact, it was able to survive only because of extraordinary support from the ECB. Banks underwent repeated recapitalizations and a messy consolidation in response to several blows: a massive flight of bank deposits caused by political uncertainty (in part due to program failures); huge losses following the debt write-down due to their enormous exposure to Greek government bonds (€40 billion compared to their core capital of €20 billion); and a steady rise in nonperforming loans, as businesses went bust and households were unable to service mortgages—one-third of total loans and mortgages to be precise, exceeding €65 billion in 2014. Without access to liquidity, businesses were unable to survive, let alone grow their exports.

Third, the planners missed a key feature of the Greek economy, the composition of its business sector, and particularly the size distribution of its firms. Greece has the lowest average size of firms in the EU (in the nonfinancial business economy), the lowest proportion of employment in firms of over 250 employees, and the third-lowest proportion of value added produced by large firms. Firms employing up to nine people account for 58 percent of all business, 46 percent of all employment, and 32 percent of all value added (as compared to 14 percent and 7 percent, respectively, for the EU average). These microfirms tend to lack good management, standardized production processes, and appropriate fixed assets that can be readily deployed to increase output when labor costs go down. In other words, the solution to the problem of competitiveness in Greece is not just a matter of giving better incentives to existing firms, as the planners believed, but rather providing better incentives for the creation of new firms.[30]

Needless to say, the adjustment program came in for severe criticism from multiple perspectives of wildly variable quality. Critics argued that the program could have been more flexible, better designed to take into account the specific features of the Greek economy, less front-loaded with an earlier debt write-down and a different policy mix, and with less emphasis on fiscal consolidation or "austerity." In retrospect, the consensus is that the error was the decision to forgo an upfront debt restructuring, a decision due to political considerations by both the Greek and EU governments—and one premised on the danger of contagion due to exposure by banks and pension funds to Greek government bonds. In the end, the contagion was not avoided and the benefits of an upfront debt write-down were lost. The European response was also criticized for being, at best, procrastinating, hesitant, slow, and messy and displaying a noticeable lack of solidarity. Depending on their political predilection critics focused on different areas, with the pain caused by internal devaluation generally topping the list. The most devastating critique is that the program itself had become part of the problem through the fiscal shock it inflicted on the Greek economy. Critics pointed out that austerity inevitably creates a downward spiral by depressing demand, reducing tax revenues even further, and making the debt burden even harder to control. Indeed, the collapse of Greece's GDP grew the size of the debt to a level where it was seen as being unsustainable.[31]

And yet, for all their significance, it would be wrong to highlight only the program's failures. The balance does contain some pretty significant achievements that tend to be overlooked. Clearly, the most important one is that the rescue averted a catastrophic bankruptcy with terrible consequences for the country, while ensuring its solvency. Moreover, the program met its fiscal consolidation goals and achieved a large reduction in the fiscal deficit through increases in taxes and reduction of public-sector wages, pensions, and benefits. In 2014 Greece achieved a primary surplus, a remarkable achievement that few thought possible. "Greece had never run a significant budget surplus in its entire history," an observer noted confidently in 2011. "To imagine it could do so in the middle of an inevitably severe recession was complete madness." Yet in the course of just five years (2009–2014), Greece managed to turn its primary budget balance from a deficit of 10.6 percent of GDP to a surplus of 1.5 percent, a difference amounting to more than 20 billion euros a year. In October 2013 the IMF noted that Greece had achieved the largest fiscal adjustment in modern history, running the highest cyclically adjusted surplus in Europe and the second-largest cyclically adjusted primary surplus in the world. Greece's public sector shrank considerably, losing close to 150,000 employees, primarily due to attrition and retirements, between 2010 and 2014. Spending came under control and some of the worst excesses of the past were corrected. For example, a census of public pensions uncovered a stunning 200,000 bogus disability and old age pensioners that bled the budget, including 3,423 cases of individuals who had been dead before they began to receive their pensions. The estimated savings are €1.3 million monthly. Ninety-three special taxes financing specific pension funds were slated for elimination. Likewise, a drive to improve the efficiency of healthcare spending resulted in effective cost-control measures. And, as we saw, unit labor costs went down and a large number of structural reforms were implemented, addressing some of the worst distortions of the Greek economy.[32]

It is also worth emphasizing that things are perhaps less gloomy on the debt front than they may seem. The conditional promise made to Greece in November 2012 by the Eurogroup—to consider further measures so as to ensure a debt-to-GDP ratio substantially lower than 110 percent by 2022—has opened up the possibility of a further debt write-down, this time an official sector debt restructuring (OSI). This could be done through further lowering of debt interest costs and further extending official loan maturities. In fact, the existing structure, duration, composition, and financing of the Greek debt are quite unique at this point. The three official creditors of Greece (IMF, EU, ECB) own over three-quarters of its outstanding sovereign debt, with no payments on existing EU loans due whatsoever before 2023, and extremely low interest rates on very long duration loans. This makes the annual debt service cost much lower than one would expect from the high debt-to-GDP ratios, rendering traditional measures of debt sustainability misleading.

To sum up: in an ideal world, the program would have been better designed, more flexible, better adapted to the particularities of the Greek economy, and more generous. And the response from Europe would have been more coherent. At the same time, one must also recognize that this was an unprecedented and highly complex crisis unfolding on multiple levels simultaneously, in a context characterized by a slackening world economy, panicking financial markets, and massive uncertainty as to the future of both Greece and the euro. On top of it, the political constraints were exceedingly narrow. There was simply no appetite among the European electorates for policies that could be seen as subsidizing "irresponsible" Greeks. And while the program was painful, the size of the Greek problem was huge. We have seen how the structural problems of the Greek economy resulted from decades of poor political and economic choices and growing maladministration.

Lastly, it is worth underlining that some of the most popular alternatives advocated by critics of the program were likely to be as painful, if not more, and without much potential long-term benefit. Stimulating demand in Greece, as the austerity critics demanded, had been tried on the eve of the crisis by both the Karamanlis and Papandreou governments, and ended up contributing to the explosion of both the current account deficit and debt. Flush with money, Greek consumers had either flocked to imported goods or ended up subsidizing inefficient and uncompetitive businesses geared exclusively toward domestic consumption. As for the sovereign default and Gr exit option, its cost dwarfed that of the adjustment program.[33]

Was Grexit a sound option?

As the crisis peaked, the main alternative to the adjustment program turned out to be not a better calibrated or more generous adjustment program but rather the so-called Grexit option. Up to 2012, most analysts converged in thinking that Greece stood no realistic chance of avoiding an outright default and that the crisis's endgame entailed a Greek exit from the Eurozone.

When Bloomberg polled a random sample of its subscribers in June 2010, it found that 73 percent thought that a Greek default was likely. The influential economist Nouriel Roubini, who had predicted the 2008 US crisis (thus becoming aptly nicknamed "Dr. Doom" for his apocalyptic predictions), declared forcefully in 2010 that a Greek default was a foregone conclusion. "Whichever way you sliced the numbers, they just kept pointing toward default," summarized another analyst. "Despite all the official denials, it looks as if a Greek default is unavoidable at some point. It might happen in 2011 or 2012. The country might even manage to hang on until 2013," pontificated yet another one. Summarizing the prevailing opinion, one observer concluded in 2011 that "There is little evidence that Greek society was in any shape to accept austerity on that scale." In fact, social unrest was seen as the most likely mechanism that would push the country toward the precipice, along the lines of what had occurred in Argentina in 2001. The most intrepid pundits even fantasized about social revolutions and authoritarian counterrevolutions.[34]

Grexit was not only predicted, it was also advocated by many pundits on both the right and left of the political spectrum, who argued that the Greek people could not possibly bear the pain required by the adjustment; that the Greek economy did not belong to the Eurozone anyway; and that the only way for Greece to move ahead was to default on its enormous debt, reacquire its own currency, and proceed to devalue it.

The mounting anticipation of Grexit contributed to the escalation of uncertainty and the growing woes of the Greek economy, causing a massive capital flight from Greece. No economy can survive persistent devaluation fears and, in fact, the endgame did take place in the summer of 2012, in the form of elections that were for all intents and purposes a referendum about the future of the country and its currency. Indeed, we know now that the EU and the IMF were preparing for this eventuality. They had set up a secret group tasked with planning a possible Greek default and collapse. Their blueprint, known as "Plan Z," included a detailed script about how to reconstruct Greece's economic and financial infrastructure if it were to leave the euro.[35]

Its massive technical and practical problems aside (just the overnight printing of new banknotes is an enormous undertaking), a Greek exit from the Eurozone accompanied by a depreciation of the new drachma would have resulted in a massive increase of the Greek debt as a percentage of the GDP, since it would have to be repaid in euros. This would have made a default necessary. However, its cost would be borne by Greek creditors who owned deposit accounts in Greek banks or Greek government bonds—and they would have been likely to react forcefully to such a loss, exactly as they did in Argentina, in 2001. This outcome would have also caused an enormous redistribution of wealth in favor of net debtors and against net creditors, that is, primarily those Greeks who had not sent their money abroad. Many analysts think that currency devaluation is psychologically more acceptable than internal devaluation. In the Greek case, however, a steep devaluation would have produced an equally steep increase in the price of both foreign and imported goods and services, as well as domestic and exportable ones, without a corresponding rise in wages. The ensuing social tensions would have forced the government to offer wage increases that could have been satisfied only through the inflationary printing of banknotes.

More generally, devaluation had consistently proven to be a stunted instrument of economic policy in Greece's recent past, with very limited results—a reflection of the structure of its business sector. In the short term, it would have amounted to a true humanitarian catastrophe, as the country, lacking a credible currency and access to international credit, would have had difficulty meeting its needs in energy and food. It is also questionable whether Greece would have enjoyed the type of immediate economic boost usually associated with devaluation given that its most valuable export is tourism, an economic activity that is highly dependent on both (imported) energy and social stability. Unlike Argentina, which experienced growth after defaulting in 2001, Greece did not export commodities.

In sum, Grexit would have likely ushered in an inflationary economy with an unstable and weak currency, limited access to credit, extensive capital controls, and considerable shortages, run by politicians with few incentives to change their ways given their access to money printing presses. Additionally, this outcome would have been politically and internationally costly, depriving Greece of its position in Europe at a time of high regional instability—in a dangerous neighborhood. All of which goes to explain why public opinion surveys kept recording large majorities in favor of Greece's continuing membership in the Eurozone despite the hardship.

What was the political fallout of the crisis?

Inevitably, economic collapse carries with it significant political implications. The political fallout of the crisis was contained until the summer of 2011. Despite widespread anti-austerity protests (resulting in three deaths in Athens, in May 2010, when a bank was firebombed by demonstrators who remain at large to this day), PASOK was able to perform satisfactorily in the 2010 regional and municipal elections, and public opinion surveys suggested that it was able to hold on to its base.

Things began to change in 2011 when the economic situation deteriorated and the failure of the program's initial projections became clear to everyone. The summer of 2011 witnessed widespread protests in Athens that were used as a recruitment ground by both the far right and the far left. Street protests during that period were accompanied by extensive rioting. Although caused by only a few hundred self-styled anarchists, they produced spectacular images that were beamed live across the world, contributing to a sense of impending doom.

Having been elected on a mandate to spend, Papandreou found himself inside a completely new world that exceeded what he could ever have imagined. Initial paralysis gave way to deep ambivalence vis-à-vis a program that had not been anticipated, nor was it consistent with the party's programmatic and ideological values, however watered down they had become over the years. The New Democracy opposition, whose pronounced maladministration had contributed to the explosion of the deficit, went all out against the program, promising less onerous, yet unrealistic alternatives.

By the summer of 2011, the program came to be widely perceived in Greece as an utter failure, even a deliberate punishment inflicted on the nation by foreign powers, especially Germany. Many went so far as to reverse causality and argue that it was the program that had caused the crisis rather than the other way around. There was widespread resentment about the country's status of limited sovereignty, expressed in frequent references to the Nazi occupation of Greece during World War II, a rhetoric fanned by the inflammatory stereotypes about lazy and cheating Greeks coming out of the popular German media.

In the end, the dominant narrative about the crisis was informed by the rhetorical tropes of the populist ideology that had triumphed during the 1980s. The old anti-American and anti-imperialist discourses were easily recycled into an anti-capitalist and anti-German narrative. Media analysis became suffused with "charlatan economics" and conspiracy theories that mixed extreme nationalism with simplistic Marxism. The result of the program's massive credibility collapse was the loss of legitimacy suffered by its supporters, including most "orthodox" economists, advocates of reform, and PASOK itself, since the program had been adopted under its watch. The very foundations of the post-transition party system began to crumble.[36]

When, in late October 2011, it became clear that a second rescue package would be needed, Papandreou felt trapped. Popular opposition grew and street protests were amplified; the withdrawal of popular support from PASOK became palpable. In attempting to gamble hopelessly for resurrection, Papandreou came up with the poorly hatched idea of calling a referendum about the program. However, when he dropped his idea at the European summit in Cannes, apparently without any prior discussion, he caused a commotion. Forced by the leaders of Germany and France to reframe it as a referendum on Greece's Eurozone membership, he was faced with an internal party revolt (as well as general outrage) and was forced to step down.

A new, grand coalition, the PASOK-ND government, was then formed under former ECB banker Lucas Papademos. His main task was to get the second rescue package approved by the parliament and to manage the debt write-down deal, both thankless albeit necessary tasks if Greece was to stay in the Eurozone. The package was eventually approved on February 12, 2012 amid extensive riots and widespread arson in downtown Athens. Massive defections took place from the two big parties: forty-three PASOK and ND MPs rebelled by voting against their leaders and were immediately ejected, while a dozen more resigned—an unprecedented development in the highly disciplined, post-transition Greek party politics. The Papademos government survived the vote, but the blow to both parties was massive. At the same time, constant bickering between the parties bogged down the reform process. Political instability and generalized fears that Greece was headed toward default further aggravated the state of the economy. It is in this volatile context that New Democracy leader Antonis Samaras forced new elections that were called for May 6, 2012.

A former New Democracy whiz kid, and a college roommate of George Papandreou at Amherst College, Samaras quit the party after a foreign policy controversy over the Macedonian issue and subsequently instigated the fall of the Mitsotakis government in 1993. After founding his own party and failing to make a noticeable dent in the New Democracy electorate, he spent several years outside politics, only to be brought back into ND by Karamanlis. Following New Democracy's defeat in 2009 and Karamanlis's resignation, he ran for the party leadership and, to general surprise, he won.

Samaras had built his political profile in opposition to the adjustment program. He had voted against the first rescue package and had opposed the terms of the bailout. No wonder then that his turnaround in February 2011 undermined his credibility and caused a split in his party. By now, both PASOK and ND, the pillars of the Greek party system, were widely despised as representing the corrupt and ineffective Athens political establishment that led the country to ruin. Voters also felt betrayed by the collapse of the post-transition social contract, whereby their votes for PASOK and ND had brought them jobs, favors, and an enviable standard of life. Several new parties emerged to capture this generalized discontent; they were spread across the entire political spectrum, yet shared a vocal opposition to both the program and the political establishment. The May elections had turned into a free-for-all.[37]

Indeed, the elections offered voters the opportunity to express their discontent by sanctioning the two dominant parties and signaled the beginning of a major electoral realignment. New Democracy emerged as the strongest party, but with barely 18.9 percent, this was clearly a defeat. PASOK's 13.2 percent was not just a defeat but a humiliating rout. The two parties lost control of the game, as their combined vote fell to 32 percent from 77.4 percent in 2009 (the year of their worst common performance since 1977). A substantial portion of the electorate picked vocal critics of the program, ranging from the far-left unreformed communists (8 percent) to the far-right neo-Nazis of the Golden Dawn party (7 percent). Prior to the crisis, Golden Dawn was a politically insignificant and marginal group of thugs that took advantage of the immigration crisis and rise in crime to establish itself in several Athens neighborhoods. Its newfound organizational presence gave it visibility, and when the crisis erupted it was able to capitalize on it, articulating an extreme nationalist and populist discourse against the adjustment program and promising to "clean up the stench." The rise of this violent, extremist group was a direct threat to the country's democratic institutions.

The free-for-all dimension of this election was also manifest in the 19 percent of the vote that went to parties that received less than 3 percent each (the electoral threshold for electing a single MP); the abstention rate, which reached a record-breaking high of nearly 35 percent; and the score obtained by the Coalition of the Radical Left (SYRIZA), which tripled its electoral share from 4.6 to 16.8 percent and, overtaking PASOK, entered parliament as the second-largest party. Most importantly, SYRIZA managed to emerge as the champion of the discontented. This hodgepodge coalition of former communists and various far-left groups, led by thirty-seven-year-old former student activist Alexis Tsipras, had never polled above 5.4 percent until then. By peddling a combination of proud defiance and hope, and blending a populist and nationalist rhetoric harkening back to Andreas Papandreou, Tsipras succeeded in attracting not only a substantial portion of former PASOK voters but also MPs and cadres from its once-mighty political machine and affiliated trade unions.[38]

The two formerly dominant parties fell two seats short of being able to form a coalition government in parliament. A caretaker government was installed and new elections were called for June 17, amid enormous uncertainty, economic paralysis, and a mass bank-deposit flight. Since the beginning of the crisis, Greek banks had faced a so-called bank jog that had seen their deposits fall from €245 billion to less than €174 billion on the eve of the 2012 elections. In May 2012 alone, the banks lost €9 billion worth of deposits. According to Greek officials, about a third of that money was pulled out of the country entirely, another third was spent to maintain rapidly falling living standards, and a final third was squirreled away in mattresses and pillowcases for fear that euros could be turned into drachmas if they were kept in banks. The bank jog accelerated to become a true bank run on the eve of the critical June elections. Just two days before the elections, on June 15, Greeks withdrew more than €3 billion from their bank accounts, about 1.5 percent of the country's entire economic output. To prevent the Greek economy from a full-fledged collapse in the run-up to elections, the ECB pumped into the

Greek economy an astounding €28.5 billion in new banknotes primarily through the mechanism of Emergency Liquidity Assistance (ELA). The amount of cash in circulation in Greece more than doubled, reaching €48 billion just before the June 2012 elections, up from €19.3 billion in early 2009. With political paralysis at the top, the broken bureaucratic machinery of the Greek state almost came to a standstill. Greece teetered on the brink of the abyss while the world held its breath.[39]

The June elections were tense and polarized. They turned, in fact, into a referendum on Greece's place in the Eurozone. SYRIZA had proclaimed that if it won it would unilaterally withdraw Greece from the program. No matter what its actual intentions were, its electoral victory would have triggered a wave of sheer panic that would have likely ended with Greece exiting the Eurozone. In the end, both New Democracy and SYRIZA increased their vote shares by over 10 percent (to 29.7 and 26.9 percent, respectively). But ND came in first and, thanks to a parliamentary seat bonus provided by the electoral system, it was able to form a coalition government along with the fatally wounded PASOK (now polling just 12.28 percent) and the small Democratic Left party, an outcome that was widely seen as a victory for Greece's pro-euro forces.

Why did Greece choose the way it did?

What explains the electoral outcome of June 2012? The severity of the Grexit alternative helps shed light on why two widely anticipated outcomes failed to materialize.

For one, when the moment for the crucial decision came up in June 2012, the Greek electorate chose to remain in the Eurozone, against most predictions to the contrary. In a polarized and referendum-like context, it voted in the pro-euro parties. Furthermore, order did not break down, notwithstanding pervasive and apocalyptic predictions that it would. Despite the spectacle, the riots that took place between 2010 and 2012, gracing countless television screens and magazine covers around the world, were the highly staged, limited, and easily contained work of a few hundred rioters, not the manifestation of a genuine social explosion.

For all the real hardship and blistering rhetoric about a "foreign occupation," a majority of Greeks understood (or at least intuited) that Eurozone membership provided a guarantee of political stability and prosperity.

Onward to where?

By the end of 2012, it appeared that Greece had proved the Grexit forecasts wrong. The outcome of the elections stabilized the political situation domestically, while the EU followed suit by making a clear decision to keep Greece in the Eurozone. In July, the president of the European Central Bank, Mario Draghi, ended the wild turbulence of the financial markets with his now famous "whatever it takes" declaration: he essentially promised that the ECB would stand as a lender of last resort through Outright Monetary Transactions (OMT), a program under which the bank purchases secondary sovereign bond market bonds issued by Eurozone member states, and also featuring the lowering of interest rates, mass liquidity provisions, and various other support programs. In November, Eurozone ministers reached an agreement on the Greek debt that provided much better terms, including extension of maturities, interest deferral, and lower interest rates. By the end of the year, €12.2 billion worth of deposits returned to the Greek banks. Since then, government bond yields and spreads in the vulnerable economies have gradually dropped to almost precrisis levels, uncertainty about the future of the euro has receded, and the macroeconomic outlook has improved. Greece was even able to return to the markets and sell bonds in April 2014, an outcome no one would have bet on two years before. Most importantly, Greece returned to growth in the fall of 2014 after six years of recession. GDP rose in the third quarter by 1.7 percent compared to a year earlier, a figure equivalent to a 0.7 percent quarter-on-quarter rate of growth, seasonally adjusted.[40]

The Greek people surprised the naysayers by displaying remarkable resilience to economic pain. Summarizing the situation in early 2013, a journalist pointed out that "the parade of economists and investors led by Nouriel Roubini predicting Greece's ejection from the eurozone failed to appreciate the resolve of European policy makers to protect their union and the amount of pain Greeks are willing to stomach. 'People underestimated these factors,' Nouriel Roubini pointed out twelve months after predicting Greece's exit in remarks to the 2012 World Economic Forum's annual meeting in Davos, Switzerland."[41]

Although the economic situation in Greece continues to be challenging, there is no doubt that the Greece of June 2014 is different from the Greece of June 2012, let alone from the Greece of 2008. Nevertheless, despite the very real progress, challenges remain formidable. The debt issue still looms large, liquidity is returning to the economy at a slow rate, growth is likely to be low, and the unemployment rate, which has begun to decline, remains enormous. While the critical issue of bank recapitalization appears to be resolved, the problem of nonperforming loans has yet to be addressed (as of this writing), with nonserviced loans having reached 31.9 percent. Greece's domestic political situation remains potentially unstable with the governing coalition in a weak spot and the opposition unclear about its intentions, while the global macroeconomic outlook is lukewarm. Lastly, there is no question that the truly challenging work of rebuilding the Greek economy on a more productive foundation lays ahead.

Looking to the future, it is possible to discern three broad paths for Greece. The country could still suffer a catastrophic collapse, most likely as a result of a default resulting from a political crisis. Second, it could survive within the Eurozone, but stagnate if it shuns necessary structural reforms or if Germany and the "North" insist on deflating and refuse to consider the idea of conditional transfers. Lastly, Greece could shift its economy toward a new productive model and take advantage of what Europe has to offer, particularly if the Eurozone decides to change direction. What is clear is that if Greece remains in the Eurozone, it won't be able to run the kind of oversize deficits it did in the past, since no one would finance them anymore. The presence of this financial strait-jacket, along with the experience of the crisis, argues against a rerun of some of the most toxic practices of the Greek political system, at least in the medium run.

To sum up, Greece's euro adventure condenses some of the key features that had surfaced during its history. It began with an ambitious political project based on the grand vision to tether Greece to the European core, both politically and economically, despite the country's well-known weaknesses. Although elite-driven, this project eventually inspired the population at large. However, the changes took place faster than Greece's institutions, both political and economic, could handle. The result was the great crisis of 2009. As in the past, this crisis was not purely Greek, and it brought to the surface the much broader issue of the imperfections of the European Union. The Greek crisis acquired international significance because it forced Europe to face up to its fundamental problems of monetary, fiscal, banking, and political union. And because of its international significance, Greece was rescued, in a highly imperfect way, and was spared a catastrophic collapse and exit from the Eurozone that would have likely erased all the gains brought by Greece's European project.

VII

FUTURE

What are the seven boom-bust-bailout cycles of Greek history?

Looking back at the historical trajectory of modern Greece, it is possible to discern a succession of seven major boom, bust, and bailout cycles. All began with highly ambitious projects that often struck contemporary observers as unfeasible, if not outright ridiculous, but nevertheless inspired enough people and thus were launched.

The first project came at the dusk of the eighteenth century and dawn of the nineteenth century: the organization of an insurrection aimed at creating a new independent country in a geographic area that included lands where a celebrated ancient civilization had left its universally admired mark. The second one, begun immediately after independence was achieved, was institutional: the construction of a modern European state, along with a cohesive nation and an inclusive parliamentary democracy, in what was a primitive corner of the Ottoman Empire. The third project followed on the footsteps of the second one in the last part of the nineteenth century: the creation, on top of the new institutions, of a competitive economy with a modern infrastructure in a country with difficult terrain, no natural resources, and a disadvantageous geographic location. The fourth project was the territorial expansion of Greece, during the opening of the twentieth century, in a bid to turn it into the regional superpower of Southeastern Europe. The fifth project, following World War II and the Greek Civil War, amounted to a great economic leap out of chronic poverty, so as to turn Greece into a modern economy and society within the capitalist world. The sixth project was the establishment and consolidation, during the closing decades of the twentieth century, of a fully inclusive liberal and democratic political order. Lastly, the seventh project was the bid toward full economic integration within the most advanced economies of Europe, during the opening of the twenty-first century.

These seven projects shared a common goal: transcending the twin constraints of history and geography. Underlying them was a fiercely held belief that Greece would become a "normal" Western European country. These projects varied in terms of success, but shared a key underlying similarity: all seven of them looked close to impossible when they were launched. Who would have thought in 1820 that an independent modern Greek state would emerge out of the Ottoman Empire, or in the mid-1840s that a functioning state and economy would be built there, or that Greece would turn out to be the most successful state of Southeastern Europe? Who would have thought in the late 1940s that Greece would emerge out of poverty and achieve an undreamed-of prosperity? Likewise, few thought in the early 1970s that Greece would become a stable, inclusive, liberal democracy. And for that matter, how many people believe today that Greece can become a successful economy within the Eurozone?

The ambition of these projects required a considerable degree of self-confidence, hinting at the nature of the political actors that articulated them in the first place and undertook their execution. They were often members of a diaspora or had a noticeable extroverted and cosmopolitan outlook. Furthermore, they all shared the same core belief about Greece's mission, namely to build a nation with a European identity and a state with a European outlook.

In short, theirs was nothing less than a dogged pursuit of modernity. And this is true for all of them, from the European-trained intellectuals and merchants who first launched the project of modern Greece, to ambitious statesmen such as Harilaos Trikoupis, Eleftherios Venizelos, Konstantinos Karamanlis, or Kostas Simitis—and also, in more convoluted and circuitous ways, political leaders like Ioannis Kolettis, Ioannis Metaxas, George Papandreou and his son Andreas.

Of course, aspiring to modernity is hardly a feature unique to Greece. The historical success of Western Europe (and of many countries that were settled by Europeans) engendered similar aspirations in almost every non-European nation. The political and economic project that came to be known as modernization took on massive proportions in the aftermath of World War II and the great wave of decolonization. Modernization continues to inspire to this day, even though the term has lost its cachet having been replaced by "development," "democratization," or "growth," among many others. Greece is rather unusual, however, in that it embarked on the modernization drive very early: it is one of the earliest late modernizers. Seen from this perspective, the trials and tribulations it underwent while importing and implanting Western institutions prefigured in many ways the new, brave postcolonial world that emerged out of World War II.

Despite the strength and vigor with which all seven projects were articulated and pursued, they were all primarily part of an elite vision with little initial traction in their contemporary social world. Like others in the developing world, the great mass of people in Greece, initially at least, were either indifferent to this vision or hostile to it. They did not share or even understand these grand projects, which were often disruptive of traditional practices and demanded exceptional sacrifices. Typically, the costs were immediate but the benefits future and uncertain. Even when these projects were eventually embraced by the population, they overtaxed its capacity beyond what was often reasonable to expect. As a result, they met with considerable pushback, limiting the capacity of elites to deliver what they had envisioned.

It was thus that outsize ambition bred equally outsize disaster. Consider the setbacks. The War of Independence was militarily defeated by both internecine war and successful counterinsurgency. The administrative machinery of the newly independent state was so weak that its monopoly on violence was immediately challenged by local strongmen and assorted brigands. The Greek state's humiliating defeat in the war of 1897 against the Ottomans showed the world its real military capacity. The late-nineteenth-century push toward economic modernization had a similar fate, ending in international receivership after a massive sovereign default. The "Great Idea" to replace the Ottoman Empire as the regional superpower, met its tragic end in mass population displacement, accompanied by civil conflict and military coups. The postwar developmental takeoff was almost nipped in the bud by a communist insurgency; tainted by exclusionary politics, the postwar political regime ended with a military autocracy. The post-transition democratic institutions were undermined by populist rent-seeking, abetted by a growing stream of EEC transfers and, later, a deluge of cheap loans. And, closer to us, the world has been witnessing with disbelief during the past few years the ghastly consequences of the country's failure to adapt its institutions to the demands of the common European currency.

The history of modernization is littered with failures and disasters and these were momentous calamities. Disasters are costly and painful, but in the end the question comes down to the balance sheet. Do gains exceed losses or is it the other way around? Were these projects worth pursuing or were they in vain?

William McNeill writes about Greece's postwar leap that "for nearly all of the people involved, whatever has been lost or thrust to the margins of life, while sometimes regretted, does not begin to counterbalance the gains." It is possible to generalize McNeill's assessment to all seven projects. Consider the record: despite its military defeat in the War of Independence, Greece emerged as an independent state—the first one in the Balkans. The initial state-building efforts may have looked pathetically inadequate, leading to nothing more than a Potemkin Village–style state machinery, but they did lay the foundations for the emergence of a functioning state, a cohesive nation, and a surprisingly inclusive parliamentary democracy. The ambitious economic modernization effort undertaken during the late nineteenth century may have been based on massive foreign borrowing, but it bequeathed significant infrastructural improvements that set the stage for the extensive reorganization and territorial expansion that took place during the early twentieth century. Greece's Anatolian adventure, a classic example of misguided territorial overreach if ever there was one, ended in disaster and human tragedy, but it also rejuvenated the country through the infusion of a large, dynamic, hard-working refugee population, while redirecting its energy toward domestic economic development. It also put a definitive end to irredentist adventurism and led to the implementation of an unusually comprehensive and egalitarian land reform. The Civil War caused terrible bloodshed and material destruction but, alone among all its Balkan neighbors, Greece avoided the calamity that was communism. The advent of the Cold War contributed to the formation and maintenance of an exclusionary political regime, but it also kick-started Greece's remarkable leap out of economic backwardness and poverty. The democratization and liberalization of the country's political institutions following the collapse of the military regime may have paved the way for the emergence of appalling rent-seeking institutions, but they also guaranteed the emergence of stable democratic politics along with unprecedented freedom and inclusion for all. It was the democratic transition that also paved the way for Greece's accession to the European Community. In turn, Greece's participation in the process of European integration and the adoption of the common European currency exacerbated the distortions of Greece's political institutions and economic structure, leading to the 2009 crisis. However, it was the European integration process that also ushered in an era of unprecedented prosperity and promise.[1]

We still do not know what the final outcome of the most recent disaster, the 2009 crisis, will be. At the time of this writing, however, we do know that predictions of a catastrophic collapse of the country did not materialize. By remaining tethered to the Eurozone, Greece is effectively taking a huge bet: namely, that its self-imposed monetary and fiscal straitjacket will act as a powerful incentive for reforming its political institutions and economy.

Overall then, what differentiates the Greek experience from many modernization experiments in the postcolonial world is a largely positive balance sheet. Time and again, Greece has managed to punch way above its weight. Again, Greece is not alone in having negotiated successfully the difficult path toward freedom and prosperity: think of Japan or South Korea, for instance. But the set of successful cases remains small and the path to modernity is strewn with disappointments and terrible setbacks.

What explains this consistently positive balance sheet? Obviously, the ambition of the initial goals was a necessary condition. Without the ambition, the country would not have embarked on these projects or would not have pursued them with the same determination. At the same time, ambition was hardly a sufficient condition: it led to disasters that could have ended in permanent setbacks. How was the worst avoided? In most instances, the leading factor was a decisive foreign intervention in favor of Greece. In the words of Michael Llewellyn Smith, "The contrast between the greatness of Greece's ambitions and the poverty of her resources put a special premium on outside support."[2]

Again, consider the record. As soon as the Greek rebellion petered out, Greece was rescued by the Great Powers, who succeeded in imposing their will in favor of a new independent Greek state on the reluctant Ottomans. The establishment of the institutions of the new state was assisted by foreign missions, and foreign policy disasters were often mitigated by favorable foreign interventions. The foreign financial control imposed in the late 1890s following Greece's military defeat and sovereign default helped avert a more catastrophic collapse. Foreign humanitarian assistance proved essential in helping the country absorb the shock of the Anatolian disaster in 1922. Greece might not have escaped a communist takeover or geographic dismemberment along the lines of Germany, Korea, or Vietnam without the 1944 British intervention in Athens or massive US foreign assistance after 1947. The EEC's support was critical to ensure the smoothness of the 1974 transition to democracy, as well as the stability and endurance of the new democratic institutions. Lastly, without the massive bailout of 2010, Greece would have faced a catastrophic default along with exit from the Eurozone.

What explains these crucial and generally favorable foreign interventions? The ability of Greece to generate foreign interventions in its favor separates the Greek experience from that of the other Balkan states. Several authors have underlined the Western distaste for involvement in the Balkans, which was rooted in the perception of their supposedly fundamental un-European character. It was this apartness of the Balkans from European civilization that was "the chief reason for Western aloofness and indifference to the area itself and to any action or involvement in it." In contrast, Greece's ancient legacy always marked it as a special case among the Europeans. But of course, it makes little sense to look for benevolence from self-interested powers seeking to maximize their interests.[3]

Consider the following striking fact: most of Greece's projects and subsequent travails received considerable global attention, way out of proportion with its size, resources, or strategic importance. The Greek rebellion against the Ottoman Empire captured the hearts of both liberals (who saw it as a noble struggle for freedom) and romantics (who were enthralled by the reappearance of Greece on the world stage). A Greek defeat struck them as a great tragedy that had to be averted. The creation of the Greek state was seen as an attempt to bring European civilization to a backward corner of Europe and a Greek defeat would have amounted to a Western European setback. The Anatolian disaster was a huge humanitarian catastrophe that had to be redressed, and the Greek Civil War had the potential to cause a domino effect. Likewise, a successful transition to democracy in 1974 was seen as signaling the end of military regimes in noncommunist Europe and, of course, the 2009 crisis was a global financial event on top of being the critical juncture for the future of the Eurozone and the European Union.

Global attention often corresponded to a perception that the stakes were high, hence the spur of foreign intervention. To this we must add the ability of Greek leaders to pick the right foreign allies (Greece was almost always on the winning side of major wars); the legacy of ancient Greece (prime symbolic capital); and the resilience of the Greek people, who consistently surprised most observers. Writing at the peak of the 2009 crisis, an analyst argued, "There was nothing in the country's history, economy, or political system to suggest it was willing to endure the kind of grinding austerity for a generation or more that would be necessary to make its industry competitive with Germany and France within a currency union." In fact, the opposite is true.[4]

That these foreign interventions were ultimately favorable to Greece should not detract from the fact that they were often perceived negatively in Greece. Either because they were accompanied by painful immediate effects or because they were humiliating, they naturally caused a sense of wounded pride among Greeks. Many Greeks expressed negative feelings vis-à-vis Great Britain during the nineteenth century, vis-à-vis the United States in the second half of the twentieth century, and vis-à-vis Germany following the 2009 crisis.

Indeed, the sense of being a puppet in the hand of powerful forces in the international arena has become a deeply rooted part of Greek identity. Hence, the widely held perception that Greek history is characterized by a unique spirit of resistance is a reflection less of actual reality and more an expression of wounded pride. In addition to the emotional cost, these interventions have bred a sense of moral hazard and recklessness, for if outsiders will step in to correct Greek mistakes, then it makes sense to take big risks and not to invest in sound institutions. In turn, this has likely reinforced the ambition of Greek elites and has fed these successive boom-bust-bailout cycles.

How does Greece's past inform its present and future?

The great crisis of 2009 is the latest of these boom-bust-bailout cycles. Greece's decision to join the EMU was a classic case of overreaching. There is no doubt that this decision was based on an overestimation of Greece's real capacity. Moving into a group of countries with much more developed economies and higher-quality institutions was hard and risky. Most Europeans suspected as much. In fact, the same skepticism had emerged within the EEC three decades before, when Greece had applied for admission. The European Commission had issued a lukewarm "Opinion on the Greek Application," which was submitted to the Council of Ministers in January 1976. It made the case for the postponement of Greece's entry because of economic backwardness, political instability, and turbulent relations with Turkey. In an unprecedented act, however, the Council of Ministers unanimously rejected the Commission's opinion two weeks after it had been submitted. At a press conference at the end of the council meeting, the prime minister of Luxembourg, Gaston Thorn, pointed out, "For the nine delegations there could be no trial period or political considerations attached to Greece's accession." He did not deny that a number of economic problems would have to be solved, but, he said, "answers would be found during the negotiations." The EEC overlooked these objections because it decided that it had a democratic obligation to support Greece in its move away from autocracy and, in the context of the Cold War, a vested strategic interest in preventing Greece's economic and political collapse.[5]

In applying to join the EEC in the 1970s and the Eurozone in the 1990s, Greece aimed high—perhaps impossibly high. Yet, few would doubt today that despite all the problems, joining the EEC was enormously positive for Greece. As it were, it wasn't a bad decision for the EEC either. By welcoming in a relatively poor, recently democratized country, the EEC signaled for the first time that it was much more than a regional association of nine wealthy West European countries, their mere "common market." In fact, admitting Greece into the EEC was the first move toward the creation of a pan-European political union, paving the way for an unprecedented political experiment that called for the creation of a major economic and political union capable of acting as an anchor of democratization, prosperity, and peace. The European decision-makers of the time were right. In spite of the challenges it has faced, the impact of the EU on the European continent has been extraordinary, most visibly in its ability to smooth the messy aftermath of the fall of communism.[6]

Will a similar assessment about Greece's joining the euro emerge twenty years from now? The jury is still out about the outcome of the 2009 crisis. Although it makes little sense to project the past into the future, it is nevertheless important to point out that the past points to a pattern that allows us to both better understand Greece's present predicament as well as to reach a more informed assessment about its future trajectory.

NOTES

Chapter 1

1. Maria Todorova, *Imagining the Balkans* (New York: Oxford University Press, 1997), v.

2. William H. McNeill, *The Metamorphosis of Modern Greece since World War II* (Chicago: University of Chicago Press, 1978), 247.

3. Jean Pisani-Ferry, André Sapir, and Guntram Wolff, "EU-IMF Assistance to Euro-Area Countries: An Early Assessment," *Bruegel* Blueprint Series No 19 (2013): 45; Peter Spiegel, "How the Euro Was Saved," *Financial Times*, May 12, 2014.

4. Konstantinos Tsoukalas, *Morfes synecheias kai asynecheias. Apo tin istoriki ethnegersia stin oikoumeniki dysforia* (Athens: Themelio, 2013), 37–38; Dimosthenis Kurtovik, *Elliniko hangover* (Athens: Nefeli, 2005), 26.

5. "European Luminaries Reflect on Euro: 'Seventeen Countries Were Far Too Many,'" *Spiegel Online International*, September 11, 2012, http://www.spiegel.de/international/europe/spiegel-interview-with-helmut-schmidt-and-valery-giscard-d-estaing-a-855127.html; Z. Duckett Ferriman quoted in Todorova, *Imagining the Balkans*, 16; Annie S. Peck, "Greece and Modern Athens," *Journal of the American Geographical Society of New York* 25 (1893): 511.

6. Peter Aspden, "Testament and Truths," *Financial Times*, March 17–18, 2012; Roger Cohen, "The Great Greek Illusion," *New York Times*, June 20, 2011.

7. Patrick Leigh Fermor, *Roumeli: Travels in Northern Greece* (London: Murray, 1966); Michael Herzfeld, *Ours Once More: Folklore, Ideology, and the Making of Modern Greece* (New York: Pella, 1986, 18–20); Konstantinos Tsoukalas, "The Irony of Symbolic Reciprocities— The Greek Meaning of 'Europe' as a Historical Inversion of the European Meaning of 'Greece,'" in Mikael af Malmborg and Bo Strath, eds., *The Meaning of Europe: Variety and Contention within and among Nations* (New York: Berg, 2002), 42–43.

8. Nikos G. Svoronos, *Histoire de la Grèce moderne* (Paris: Presses Universitaires de France, 1953); references are from the Themelio, Athens, 1975 Greek ed., 12; 155.

9. Mark Mazower, "Democracy's Cradle, Rocking the World," *New York Times*, June 29, 2011, A27

10. Samuel Huntington, *The Clash of Civilizations and the Remaking of World Order* (New York: Simon & Schuster, 1996), 162; Giorgos Dertilis, *Istoria tou Ellinikou Kratous, 1830–1920*, 5th ed. (Athens: Estia, 2009), 75; Economist Intelligence Unit, "Birth Right," 2014, http://www.economist.com/blogs/graphicdetail/2013/01/daily-chart?fsrc=scn/tw/te/bl/ed/birthright; Social Progress Index, 2014, http://www.socialprogressimperative.org/en/data/spi/countries/GRC.

11. Nicos Mouzelis, *Modern Greece, Facets of Underdevelopment* (London: Macmillan, 1978).

Chapter 2

1. Averil Cameron, *Byzantine Matters* (Princeton: Princeton University Press, 2014), 46–67.

2. Paschalis Kitromilides, "'Imagined Communities' and the Origins of the National Question in the Balkans," *European History Quarterly* 19 (1989): 149–94.

3. Christine M. Philliou, *Biography of an Empire: Governing Ottomans in an Age of Revolution* (Berkeley: University of California Press, 2011).

4. Thomas Gallant, *Social History of Modern Greece* (New York: Cambridge University Press, 2011), 7; Richard Clogg, *A Concise History of Greece*, 3rd ed. (Cambridge: Cambridge University Press, 2013), 26; Paschalis Kitromilides, *Enlightenment and Revolution: The Making of Modern Greece* (Cambridge, Mass.: Harvard University Press, 2013).

5. Paschalis Kitromilides, *The Enlightenment as Social Criticism: Iosipos Moisiodax and Greek Culture in the Eighteenth Century* (Princeton: Princeton University Press, 1992).

6. Kitromilides, *Enlightenment as Social Criticism*; Kostas Kostis, "*Ta kakomathimena paidia tis istorias*," *I diamorfosi tou neoellinikou kratous, 18os–21os aionas* (Athens: Polis, 2013), 107–8.

7. Gallant, *Social History of Modern Greece*, 9; Roderick Beaton, "Introduction," in Roderick Beaton and David Ricks, eds., *The Making of Modern Greece: Nationalism, Romanticism, and the Uses of the Past (1797–1896)* (Farnham: Ashgate, 2009), 1–15; Richard Stites, *The Four Horsemen: Riding to Liberty in Post-Napoleonic Europe* (Oxford: Oxford University Press, 2013); Davide Rodogno, *Against Massacre: Humanitarian Interventions in the Ottoman Empire, 1815–1914* (Princeton: Princeton University Press, 2012); Gary Bass, *Freedom's Battle: The Origins of Humanitarian Intervention* (New York: Alfred Knopf, 2008).

8. Elli Skopetea, *To "Protypo vasileio" kai i megali idea (1830–1880)* (Athens: Politypo, 1988), 25; Kitromilides, "'Imagined Communities'"; Kitromilides, *Enlightenment as Social Criticism*, 183.

9. George Frangos, "The Philiki Etairia: A Premature National Coalition," in Richard Clogg, ed., *The Struggle for Greek Independence* (London: Macmillan, 1973), 93–94; Kostis, "*Ta kakomathimena paidia tis istorias*," 67; 109.

10. Apostolos Vacalopoulos, *The Greek Nation, 1453–1669* (New Brunswick, N.J.: Rutgers University Press, 1976), 211; Douglas Dakin, *The Greek Struggle for Independence: 1821–1833* (London: Batsford, 1973), 18; John Koliopoulos, *Brigands with a Cause: Brigandage and Irredentism in Modern Greece, 1821–1912* (Oxford: Clarendon Press, 1987), 45.

11. Frangos, "The Philiki Etairia"; Kostis, *"Ta kakomathimena paidia tis istorias,"* 125–26; 175–78.

12. K. E. Fleming, *The Muslim Bonaparte: Diplomacy and Orientalism in Ali Pasha's Greece* (Princeton: Princeton University Press, 1999).

13. Clogg, *Concise History of Greece,* 39–40.

14. Beaton, "Introduction," 3; William St. Clair, *That Greece Might Still be Free: The Philhellenes in the War of Independence* (Oxford: Oxford University Press, 1972), 15; Douglas Dakin, *The Greek Struggle for Independence,* 149; Skopetea, *To "Protypo Vasileio,"* 211.

15. St. Clair, *That Greece Might Still be Free,* 14; Skopetea, *To "Protypo Vasileio,"* 30; Kostis, *"Ta kakomathimena paidia tis istorias,"* 151.

16. David Brewer, *The Flame of Freedom: The Greek War of Independence, 1821–1833* (London: John Murray, 2001), 139; St. Clair, *That Greece Might Still be Free,* 66; Rodogno, *Against Massacre.*

17. Rodogno, *Against Massacre*; Alexis Dimaras, "The Other British Philhellenes," in Richard Clogg, ed., *The Struggle for Greek Independence: Essays to Mark the 150th Anniversary of the Greek War of Independence* (London: Macmillan, 1973), 200–23; Marios Hatzopoulos, "From Resurrection to Insurrection: 'Sacred' Myths, Motifs, and Symbols in the Greek War of Independence," in Roderick Beaton and David Ricks, eds., *The Making of Modern Greece: Nationalism, Romanticism, and the Uses of the Past (1797–1896)* (Farnham: Ashgate, 2009), 81–94; Kostis, *"Ta kakomathimena paidia tis istorias,"* 163.

18. Bass, *Freedom's Battle,* 73, 114, 142, 151; Rodogno, *Against Massacre,* 54, 88–89.

19. Christopher M. Woodhouse, *The Philhellenes* (London: Hodder and Stoughton, 1969), 37–38; Dimaras, "Other British Philhellenes"; Skopetea, *To "Protypo Vasileio,"* 167.

Chapter 3

1. Skopetea, *"To Protypo vasileio"*; Kostis, *"Ta kakomathimena paidia tis istorias,"* 142.

2. Skopetea, *To "Protypo vasileio,"* 171.

3. John Anthony Petropulos, *Politics and Statecraft in the Kingdom of Greece, 1833–43* (Princeton: Princeton University Press, 1968), 213–14; Keith Legg, *Politics in Modern Greece* (Stanford: Stanford University Press, 1969), 54, 104; Skopetea, *To "Protypo Vasileio,"* 41–51.

4. Kostis, *Ta kakomathimena paidia tis istorias,* 208–10.

5. Dertilis, *Istoria tou Ellinikou Kratous, 1830–1920,* 218; Kostis, *Ta kakomathimena paidia tis istorias,* 196–97, 248.

6. Clogg, *Concise History of Greece,* 49.

7. Konstantinos Tsoucalas, *Exartisi kai anaparagogi: O koinonikos rolos ton ekpedeftikon michanismon stin Ellada (1830–1922)* (Athens: Themelio, 1975); Andreas Kazamias, "Modernity, State-Formation, Nation Building, and Education in Greece," in Robert Cowen and Andreas Kazamias, eds., *International Handbook of Comparative Education* (London: Springer, 2009), 239–56; Apostolis Papakostas, "Why Is There No Clientelism in Scandinavia? A Comparison of the Swedish and Greek Sequences of Development," in Simona Piattoni, ed., *Clientelism, Interests, and Democratic Representation: The European Experience in Historical and Comparative Perspective* (Cambridge: Cambridge University Press, 2001), 31–53.

8. Koliopoulos, *Brigands with a Cause.*

9. The jubilee ceremonies of 1871 enshrined symbolically the transformation of Orthodoxy into secular Greek national identity (Gallant, *Social History of Modern Greece,* 71).

10. Skopetea, *To "Protypo vasileio,"* 21, 40, 69.

11. Theodore George Tatsios, *The Megali Idea and the Greek-Turkish War of 1897* (New York: Columbia University Press, 1984), 19; Paschalis Kitromilides, "On the Intellectual Content of Greek Nationalism: Paparrigopoulos, Byzantium and the Great Idea," in David Ricks and Paul Magdalino, eds., *Byzantium and the Modern Greek Identity* (Aldershot: Ashgate, 1998), 260; Thanos Veremis, *The Military in Greek Politics: From Independence to Democracy* (London: Hurst & Company, 1997), 41; Thanos Veremis, "From the National State to the Stateless Nation 1821–1910," *European History Quarterly* 19, no. 2 (1989): 135–48; Victor Roudometof, "The Social Origins of Balkan Politics: Nationalism, Underdevelopment and the Nation-State in Greece, Serbia and Bulgaria, 1880–1920," *Mediterranean Quarterly* 11, no. 3 (2000): 144–63; Paschalis Kitromilides, "'Imagined Communities' and the Origins of the National Question in the Balkans," *European History Quarterly* 19, no. 2 (1989), 149–94; Skopetea, *To "Protypo vasileio"*; Giorgos Dertilis, "I Istoria den epanalamvanetai kai den didaskei: Oikonomikes kriseis kai kratos stin Ellada." Paper presented at ELIAMEP, Athens, Greece, 2010.

12. Kitromilides, "'Imagined Communities'."

13. Philliou, *Biography of an Empire*, xxv, 170–76.

14. Douglas Dakin, *The Unification of Greece, 1770–1923* (New York: St. Martin's Press, 1972), 84; Tatsios, *The Megali Idea and the Greek-Turkish War of 1897*, 112.

15. Basil G. Gounaris, *To Makedoniko Zitima apo ton 19o os ton 21o aiona* (Athens: Alexandreia, 2010).

16. Mark Mazower, *The Balkans: A Short History* (New York: Modern Library, 2002), 39.

17. Basil G. Gounaris, "Social Cleavages and National 'Awakening' in Ottoman Macedonia," *East European Quarterly* 29, no. 4 (1995): 409–27.

18. Gounaris, *To Makedoniko Zitima*, 39; Gounaris, "Social Cleavages and National 'Awakening' "; Anastasia N. Karakasidou, *Fields of Wheat, Hills of Blood: Passages to Nationhood in Greek Macedonia, 1870–1990* (Chicago: University of Chicago Press, 1997); Ipek K. Yosmaoglu, *Blood Ties: Religion, Violence and the Politics of Nationhood in Ottoman Macedonia, 1878–1908* (Ithaca: Cornell University Press, 2013); Keith Brown, *Loyal unto Death: Trust and Terror in Revolutionary Macedonia* (Bloomington: Indiana University Press, 2013).

19. Carles Boix, *Democracy and Redistribution* (New York: Cambridge University Press, 2003); Daron Acemoglu and James E. Robinson, *Economic Origins of Dictatorship and Democracy* (New York: Cambridge University Press, 2009).

20. Adam Przeworski, "Conquered or Granted? A History of Suffrage Extensions," *British Journal of Political Science* 39, no. 2 (2009): 291–312; Dakin, *The Unification of Greece*, 76; Dertilis, *Istoria tou Ellinikou Kratous*, 75; Nicos K. Alivizatos, *To Syntagma kai oi exthroi tou sti Neoelliniki Istoria, 1800–2010* (Athens: Polis, 2011), 92–95.

21. Konstantinos Tsoucalas, "On the Problem of Political Clientelism in Greece in the Nineteenth Century," *Journal of Hellenic Diaspora* 5, no 2 (1978): 5–17; Papakostas, "Why Is There No Clientelism in Scandinavia?"; Kostis, *"Ta kakomathimena paidia tis istorias,"* 272.

22. Georgios Sotirelis, *Syntagma kai Ekloges stin Ellada 1864–1909* (Athens: Themelio, 1991), 43, 390–98, 406; Romilly Jenkins, *The Dilessi Murders: Greek Brigands and English Hostages* (London: Longmans, 1961).

23. Marietta Economopoulou, "Parties and Politics in Greece (1844–1855)," PhD diss., University of Oxford, 1984, 3, 268; Dakin, *The Unification of Greece*, 79; Alivizatos, *To Syntagma kai*

oi exthroi tou; Papakostas, "Why Is There No Clientelism in Scandinavia?" 47.

24. Damianakos, *Charilaos Trikoupes and the Modernization of Greece, 1874–1894*, Ph.D. diss., New York University, 1977, 108–18; Keith Legg and John Roberts, *Modern Greece: A Civilization on the Periphery* (Boulder, Col.: Westview Press, 1997), 31.

25. Socrates Petmezas, *I Elliniki agrotiki oikonomia kata ton 19o aiona: i perifereiaki diastasi* (Iraklio: Crete University Press, 2003); Socrates Petmezas, "Agriculture and Economic Growth in Greece," working paper, University of Crete, 2003; Kostas Vergopoulos, *Agrotiko zitima stin Ellada: to provlima tis koinonikis ensomatosis tis georgias* (Athens: Exantas, 1975); Giorgos Dertilis, *Atelesphoroi i telesphoroi: foroi kai exousia sto neoelliniko kratos* (Athens: Alexandreia, 1993); William McGrew, *Land and Revolution in Modern Greece, 1800–1881* (Kent, Ohio: Kent State University Press, 1985), 23; Kostis, *"Ta kakomathimena paidia tis istorias,"* 301–23.

26. George Th. Mavrogordatos, "The 1923 Exchange of Populations: An Ongoing Debate," paper presented at the Gennadius Library, 2013, 7.

27. David Hannell, "Lord Palmerston and the 'Don Pacifico Affair' of 1850: The Ionian Connection," *European History Quarterly* 19, no. 4 (1989): 495.

28. Jenkins, *The Dilessi Murders.*

29. Theodore George Tatsios, *The Megali Idea and the Greek-Turkish War of 1897*, 112–15.

30. McGrew, *Land and Revolution in Modern Greece*, 7–11, 36–37.

31. Ibid., 121, 134, 162.

32. Ibid., 153, 219–21; Ioanna Pepelasis-Minoglu, "Political Factors Shaping the Role of Foreign Finance: The Case of Greece, 1832–1932," in John Hariss, Janet Hunter, and Colin M. Lewis, eds., *The New Institutional Economics and Third World Development* (London: Routledge, 1995), 263; John Lampe and Marvin Jackson,

Balkan Economic History, 1550–1950: From Imperial Borderlands to Developing Nations (Bloomington: Indiana University Press, 1992), 235.

33. Tsoucalas, *Exartisi kai anaparagogi*, 148–49, 233; Alexis Fragiadis, *Elliniki Ikonomia: Apo ton agona tis anexartisias stin ikonomiki ke nomismatiki enosi tis Eyropis* (Athens: Nefeli, 2007), 90.

34. McGrew, *Land and Revolution in Modern Greece*, 97; Carmen Reinhart and Kenneth Rogoff, *This Time Is Different: Eight Centuries of Financial Folly* (Princeton: Princeton University Press, 2011).

35. Dertilis, *Istoria tou Ellinikou Kratous*, 195–205; John Levandis, *The Greek Foreign Debt and the Great Powers 1821–1898* (New York: Columbia University Press, 1944), 49–53.

36. Levandis, *Greek Foreign Debt*, 73, 90; Sophia Lazaretou, "Government Spending, Monetary Policies and Exchange Rate Regime Switches: The Drachma in the Gold Standard Period," *Explorations in Economic History* 32, no. 1 (1995): 33; Michalis Psalidopoulos and Adamantios Syrmaloglou, "Economists in the Greek Parliament (1862–1910): The Men and Their Views on Fiscal and Monetary Policy," in Massimo M. Augello and Marco Enrico Luigi Guidi, eds., *Parliament in the Liberal Age (1848–1920)* (London: Ashgate, 2005), 231; Dertilis, "I Istoria den epanalamvanetai kai den didaskei: Oikonomikes kriseis."

37. John S. Koliopoulos and Thanos Veremis, *Modern Greece: A History since 1821* (Chichester: Wiley-Blackwell, 2010), 62; Dimitris Pournaras, *Charilaos Trikoupis: i zoi kai to ergon tou* (Athens: Historike Bibliotheke, 1950), 77–78; Alexander Damianakos, *Charilaos Trikoupes*, 289–93; Dertilis, *Istoria tou Ellinikou Kratous*, 72.

38. Kostis, "Ta kakomathimena paidia tis istorias," 491; Damianakos, *Charilaos Trikoupes*, 271–81; Lazaretou, "Government Spending,

Monetary Policies and Exchange Rate Regime Switches"; Legg and Roberts, *Modern Greece*, 31–32.

39. Giorgos Dertilis, *Koinonikos metaschimatismos kai stratiotiki epemvasi, 1880–1909* (Athens: Exantas, 1977), 177–87; Victor Papacosma, *The Military in Greek Politics: The 1909 Coup d' Etat* (Kent, Ohio: Kent State University Press, 1977); Dakin, *The Unification of Greece*, 181; Kostis, *"Ta kakomathimena paidia tis istorias,"* 504.

40. Mark Mazower, "The Messiah and the Bourgeoisie: Venizelos and Politics in Greece, 1909–1922," *Historical Journal* 35, no. 4 (1992): 885–905.

41. Michael Llewellyn Smith, *Ionian Vision: Greece in Asia Minor 1919–1922* (London: Hurst, 1998), xiii.

42. Kostis, *"Ta kakomathimena paidia tis istorias."*

Chapter 4

1. George Leon, *Greece and the Great Powers, 1914–1917* (Thessaloniki: Institute for Balkan Studies, 1970); George Leontaritis, *Greece and First World War: From Neutrality to Intervention, 1917–1918* (Boulder, Col.: East European Monographs, 1990); Kostis, *"Ta kakomathimena paidia tis istorias,"* 558–61; Llewellyn Smith, *Ionian Vision*.

2. George Th. Mavrogordatos, *Stillborn Republic: Social Coalitions and Party Strategies in Greece, 1922–1936* (Berkeley: University of California Press, 1983); Kostis, *"Ta kakomathimena paidia tis istorias."*

3. Mavrogordatos, *Stillborn Republic*, 284–86; Koliopoulos and Veremis *Modern Greece*, 81.

4. Alexandros Pallis, *Greece's Anatolian Venture and After* (London: Methuen, 1937), 44.

5. Koliopoulos and Veremis, *Modern Greece*, 87–88; Pallis, *Greece's Anatolian Venture*, 74, 112–139, 229–230; Dakin, *The Unification of Greece*, 225; Mavrogordatos, *Stillborn Republic*; Clogg, *A Concise History of Greece*, 95.

6. Dimitris Pentzopoulos, *The Balkan Exchange of Minorities and Its Impact upon Greece* (Paris: Mouton, 1962); Elisabeth Kontogiorgi, *Population Exchange in Greek Macedonia* (Oxford: Oxford University Press, 2006); Dakin, *The Unification of Greece*, 243.

7. Kontogiorgi, *Population Exchange in Greek Macedonia*, 65.

8. Pallis, *Greece's Anatolian Venture and After*, 169; George Th. Mavrogordatos, "The 1923 Exchange of Populations: An Ongoing Debate," paper presented at the Gennadius Library, January 15, 2013.

9. Mavrogordatos, "The 1923 Exchange of Populations," 6; George Th. Mavrogordatos, "To anepanalipto epitevgma," *Deltio Kentrou Mikrasiatikon Spoudon* 9, no. 9 (1992): 9–12; Bruce Clark, *Twice a Stranger: The Mass Expulsions That Forged Modern Greece and Turkey* (Cambridge, Mass.: Harvard University Press, 2009).

10. Pentzopoulos, *The Balkan Exchange of Minorities*, 59, 137, 149; John S. Koliopoulos, *Plundered Loyalties: World War II and Civil War in Greek West Macedonia* (New York: New York University Press, 1999); Thanos Veremis, "1922: Political Continuations and Realignments in the Greek State," in Renee Hirschon, ed., *Crossing the Aegean: An Appraisal of the 1923 Compulsory Population Exchange Between Greece and Turkey* (New York: Berhahn Books, 2003), 60–62; Kontogiorgi, *Population Exchange in Greek Macedonia*, 75–76; Mavrogordatos, "The 1923 Exchange of Populations," 6; Dimitra Giannuli, "Greeks or 'Strangers at Home': The Experience of Ottoman Greek Refugees during Their Exodus to Greece, 1922–1923," *Journal of Modern Greek Studies* 13, no. 2 (1995): 271–87.

11. Renée Hirschon, *Heirs of the Greek Catastrophe: The Social Life of Asia Minor Refugees in Piraeus* (Oxford: Clarendon Press, 1989).

12. Mavrogordatos, *Stillborn Republic*.

13. Thanos Veremis, "Some Observations on the Greek Military in the Inter-War Period, 1918–1935," *Armed Forces and Society* 4, no. 3 (1978): 527–41; Mavrogordatos, *Stillborn Republic*, 305; Papacosma (1977: 180–84).

14. Kostis, *"Ta kakomathimena paidia tis istorias,"* 623–33.

15. Mark Mazower, *Greece and the Interwar Economic Crisis* (Oxford: Oxford University Press, 1991), 13–18, 237.

16. David H. Close, *The Origins of the Greek Civil War* (London: Longman, 1995), 25.

17. Davide Rodogno, *Fascism's European Empire* (Cambridge: Cambridge University Press, 2006).

18. Stathis N. Kalyvas, *The Logic of Violence in Civil War* (New York: Cambridge University Press, 2006).

19. Violetta Hionidou, *Famine and Death in Occupied Greece, 1941–1944* (Cambridge: Cambridge University Press, 2006); Mark Mazower, *Inside Hitler's Greece: The Experience of Occupation, 1941–44* (New Haven: Yale University Press, 1993).

20. Christopher Montague Woodhouse, *Apple of Discord: A Survey of Recent Greek Politics in Their International Setting* (London: Hutchinson, 1948); Mazower, *Inside Hitler's Greece.*

21. John L. Hondros, "Greece and the German Occupation," in David H. Close, ed., *The Greek Civil War, 1943–1950: Studies in Polarization* (London and New York: Routledge, 1993), 32–55; Stathis N. Kalyvas, "Armed Collaboration in Greece, 1941–1944," *European Review of History* 15, no. 2 (2008): 129–42.

22. Stathis N. Kalyvas, "Red Terror: Leftist Violence during the Occupation," in Mark Mazower, ed., *After the War Was Over: Reconstructing Family, State, and Nation in Greece, 1944–1960* (Princeton: Princeton University Press, 2000), 142–83; Kalyvas, "Armed Collaboration in Greece."

23. Mark Mazower, *Salonica City of Ghosts: Christians, Muslims and Jews 1430–1950* (New York: Knopf, 2005); Kostis, *"Ta kakomathimena paidia tis istorias,"* 663–664.

24. Nikos Marantzidis, "The Greek Civil War (1944–1949) and the International Communist System," *Journal of Cold War Studies* 15, no. 4 (2013): 25–54.

25. John O. Iatrides, *Revolt in Athens: The Greek Communist Second Round, 1944–1945* (Princeton: Princeton University Press, 1972); Close, *The Origins of the Greek Civil War.*

26. Marantzidis, "The Greek Civil War."

27. John O. Iatrides, "Revolution or Self-Defense? Communist Goals, Strategy, and Tactics in the Greek Civil War," *Journal of Cold War Studies* 7, no. 3 (2005): 3–33; Marantzidis, "The Greek Civil War."

28. Nikos Marantzidis, *Dimokratikos Stratos Elladas (1946–1949)* (Athens: Alexandria, 2010).

29. Nikos Marantzidis, *Yasasin Millet: Zito to Ethnos. Prosfygia, katochi kai emfylios: Ethnotiki taftotita kai politiki symperifora stous tourkofonous elinorthodoxous tou dytikou kosmou* (Irakleio: Panepistimiakes Ekdoseis Kritis, 2001).

Chapter 5

1. Stavros Thomadakis, *Kratos kai anaptixi stin Ellada: ena exeliktiko didimo* (Athens: Alexandria, 2011), 162–63; Panos Kazakos, *Apo ton ateli ecsynchronismo stin krisi* (Athens: Patakis, 2011), 42.

2. Paul A. Porter, "Wanted: A Miracle in Greece," *Collier's*, September 20, 1947, 14:106–8.

3. McNeill, *The Metamorphosis of Modern Greece*; David H. Close, *Greece since 1945* (London: Longman, 2002).

4. Barry Eichengreen, Marc Uzan, Nicholas Crafts, and Martin Hellwig, "The Marshall Plan: Economic Effects and Implications for Eastern Europe and the Former USSR," *Economic Policy* 7, no. 14 (1992): 13–75; Konstantina Botsiou, "New Policies, Old Politics: American Concepts of Reform in Marshall Plan Greece," *Journal of Modern Greek Studies* 27, no. 2 (2009): 209–40; Jon Kofas, *Intervention and Underdevelopment: Greece during the Cold War* (University Park: Pennsylvania State University Press, 1989), 126; Giorgos Mirkos, *Dogma Truman kai to schedio Marshall stin Ellada* (Athens: Livanis, 2004), 73–75; Apostolos Vetsopoulos, "Efforts for the Development and Stabilization of the Economy during

the Period of the Marshall Plan," *Journal of Modern Greek Studies* 27, no. 2 (2009): 275–302; McNeill, *The Metamorphosis of Modern Greece*, 93.

5. McNeill, The Metamorphosis of Modern Greece, 95.

6. Ibid., 91; 104.

7. Manolis Galenianos, "Explaining the Stagnation of the Greek Economy in 1980–95," unpublished paper, 2000, 4–6.

8. Alexis Fragiadis, *Elliniki Ikonomia: Apo ton agona tis anexartisias stin ikonomiki ke nomismatiki enosi tis Europis* (Athens: Nefeli, 2007); McNeill, *The Metamorphosis of Modern Greece*; Galenianos, "Explaining the Stagnation of the Greek Economy"; George Pagoulatos, *Greece's New Political Economy: State, Finance and Growth from Postwar to EMU* (New York: Palgrave, 2003).

9. Fragiadis, *Elliniki Ikonomia*, 172; Pagoulatos, *Greece's New Political Economy*, 58–59, 70, 221.

10. Theodore Couloumbis, "Ellinoamerikanikes sheseis kai epivoli diktatorias: Mia epaktimisi," in Alkis Rigos, Seraphim Seferiades, and Evanthis Hadjivassiliou, eds., *I Syntomi Dekaetia tou '60* (Athens: Kastaniotis, 2008), 79; Stan Draenos, *Andreas Papandreou: The Making of a Greek Democrat and Political Maverick* (London: I. B. Tauris, 2012).

11. Konstantina Maragkou, "The Foreign Factor and the Greek Colonels' Coming to Power on 21 April 1967," *Southeast European and Black Sea Studies* 6, no. 4 (2006): 427–43; Alexis Papahelas, *O viasmos tis ellinikis dimokratias. O Amerikanikos paragon, 1947–1967* (Athens: Estia, 2009); Nicos Mouzelis, *Modern Greece: Facets of Underdevelopment* (London: Macmillan, 1978), 127; Thanos Veremis, "The Military," in Kevin Featherstone and Dimitrios Katsoudas, eds., *Political Change in Greece: Before and After the Colonels* (London: Croom Helm, 1987), 220; Evanthis Hadjivassiliou, "Autapates, dilimmata kai i apotyxia tis politikis:

O stratos stin poreia pros ti diktatoria," in Manolis Vassilakis, ed., *Apo ton Anendoto ste Diktatoria* (Athens: Papazisis, 2009), 422, 442.

12. Charles W. Yost, "Fact and Fantasy," *Christian Science Monitor*, July 6, 1972, 18.

13. Alexis Heraclides, *I Ellada kai o ex anatolon kindynos* (Athens: Polis, 2001).

14. Heraclides, *I Ellada*; Alexis Heraclides, *Aspondoi geitones. Ellada-Tourkia, i dienexi tou Aigaiou* (Athens: Sideris, 2007).

15. Ioannis Stefanidis, *Isle of Discord: Nationalism, Imperialism and the Making of the Cyprus Problem* (New York: New York University Press, 1999).

16. Monteagle Stearns, *Entangled Allies: US Policy toward Greece, Turkey, and Cyprus* (New York: Council of Foreign Relations Press, 1992), 26–27; Evanthis Hadjivassiliou, *Strateigikes tou Kypriakou: I dekaetia tou 1950* (Athens: Patakis, 2005); Theodore Couloumbis, *The United States, Greece and Turkey: The Troubled Triangle* (New York: Praeger, 1983).

17. Tozun Bahcheli, *Greek-Turkish Relations since 1955* (Boulder, Col.: Westview Press, 1990), 37; Stefanidis, *Isle of Discord*, 276, 54.

18. Heraclides, *I Ellada*; Heraclides, *Aspondoi geitones*.

19. Heraclides, *I Ellada*, 226–40.

20. Nikiforos Diamandouros, "Transition to, and Consolidation of, Democratic Politics in Greece, 1974–1983: A Tentative Assessment," *West European Politics* 7, no. 2 (1984): 50–71; Samuel Huntington, *The Third Wave: Democratization in the Late Twentieth Century* (Norman: University of Oklahoma Press, 1991); Yannis Voulgaris, *I Ellada apo tin Metapolitefsi stin Pagkosmiopoiisi* (Athens: Polis, 2008), 68; Kathryn Sikkink, *The Justice Cascade: How Human Rights Prosecutions Are Changing World Politics* (New York: Norton, 2011).

21. George Th. Mavrogordatos, "Rise of the Green Sun: The Greek Election of 1981," Occasional Papers No. 1 (London: Center of Contemporary Greek Studies, King's College, 1983); Draenos, *Andreas Papandreou*.

22. Aikaterini Andronikidou and Iosif Kovras, "Cultures of Rioting and Anti-systemic Politics in Southern Europe," *West European Politics* 35, no. 4 (2012): 707–25; Stathis N. Kalyvas, "Why Athens Is Burning?" *New York Times*, November 11, 2008.

23. Wolfgang Rüdiger and Georgios Kariotis, "Who Protests in Greece? Mass Opposition to Austerity," *British Journal of Political Science* (June 2013): 1–27. Perhaps the most vivid and insightful critical description of the Greek crisis is provided in Michael Lewis, *Boomerang: Travels in the New Third World* (New York: Norton, 2011), 79–80.

24. Georgios Kariotis, "Securitization of Greek Terrorism and Arrest of the 'Revolutionary Organization November 17,'" *Cooperation and Conflict* 42, no. 3 (2007): 271–93; George Kassimeris, "Greece: Twenty Years of Political Terrorism," *Terrorism and Political Violence* 7, no. 2 (1995): 74–92.

25. Kalyvas, "Polarization in Greek Politics."

26. Clogg, *A Concise History of Greece*, 2; Eirini Karamouzi, "Greece's Path to EEC Membership, 1974–1979: The View from Brussels," PhD diss., Department of International History, London School of Economics, 2011, 233–36.

27. Thomadakis, *Kratos kai anaptixi stin Ellada*, 145–47.

28. ELSTAT data, http://m.euro2day.gr/1250650/article.aspx.

29. Pagoulatos, *Greece's New Political Economy*, 88–89, 102–103.

30. Chrisafis Iordanoglou, *Kratos kai omades symferonton. Mia kritiki tis paradedegmenis sofias* (Athens: Polis, 2013), 30–37, 70–73.

31. Voulgaris, *I Ellada apo tin Metapolitefsi stin Pagkosmiopoiisi*, 89. PASOK received 48.07 percent of the popular vote (up from

25.34 percent in the 1977 elections) and 172 seats in the 1981 elections.

32. Angelos Elephantis, "PASOK and the Elections of the 1977: The Rise of the Populist Movement," in Howard R. Penniman, ed., *Greece at the Polls: The National Elections of 1974 and 1977* (Washington, D.C.: American Enterprise Institute for Public Policy Research, 1981), 110.

33. In 1976, PASOK boasted 1,021 organizational units (regional/ local organizations and cells) compared to 284 for New Democracy. See John Loulis, "New Democracy: The New Face of Conservatism," in Penniman, *Greece at the Polls*, 72; George Th. Mavrogordatos, "From Traditional Clientelism to Machine Politics: The Impact of PASOK Populism in Greece," *South European Society and Politics* 2, no. 3 (1997): 1–26; Mavrogordatos, "Rise of the Green Sun"; Takis Pappas, *Making Party Democracy in Greece* (New York: Macmillan, 1999).

34. Stathis N. Kalyvas, "Polarization in Greek Politics: PASOK's First Four Years, 1981–1985," *Journal of the Hellenic Diaspora* 23, no. 1 (1997): 83–104; Nikiphoros Diamandouros, "Politics and Culture in Greece, 1974–1991: An Interpretation," in Richard Clogg, ed., *Greece: 1981–89: The Populist Decade* (New York: St. Martin Press, 1993), 4.

35. Gerassimos Moschonas, "The Path of Modernization: PASOK and European Integration," *Journal of Southern Europe and the Balkans* 3, no. 1 (2001): 11–24; Yannis Voulgaris, *I Ellada tis Metapolitefsis* (Athens: Themelio, 2002); Takis Pappas, *Charismatiko komma: PASOK, Papandreou, exousia* (Athens: Patakis, 2008).

36. Giorgos Antoniou and Eleni Paschaloudi, " 'To apsogo prosopo tis istorias tholonei': I anagnorisi tis eamikis antistasis kai to politico sistima (1945–1995)," in Vasilis Gounaris, ed., *Iroes ton Ellinon. Oi Kapetanioi, ta palikaria kai i anagnorisi ton ethnikon agonon, 19os–20os aionas* (Athens: Idryma tis Voulis ton Ellinon, 2014).

37. Georges Langrod, "Reorganisation of Public Administration in Greece," OECD publications, No. 17795, 38, 54, 1965; Mavrogordatos, "From Traditional Clientelism to Machine Politics."

38. Iordanoglou, *Kratos kai omades symferonton*; Mavrogordatos, "From Traditional Clientelism to Machine Politics"; Dimitri Sotiropoulos, *Kratos kai metarrythmisi sti sygxroni Notia Evropi* (Athens: Potamos, 2007); Calliope Spanou, "On the Regulatory Capacity of the Greek State: A Tentative Approach Based on a Case-Study," *International Review of Administrative Sciences* 62, no. 2 (1996): 219–37; Mavrogordatos, "From Traditional Clientelism to Machine Politics"; Dimitris Stergiou, *Ayti einai i Ellada* (Athens: Ellinika Grammata, 2000), 318, 157, 372, 338–39.

39. Dimitri Sotiropoulos, *Populism and Bureaucracy: The Case of Greece under PASOK, 1981–1989* (Notre Dame: University of Notre Dame Press, 1996), 112; Iordanoglou, *Kratos kai omades symferonton*, 24–29. The annual reports of the General Inspector of Public Administration (www.gedd.gr) make for some dire reading.

40. Elias Papaioannou, "The Injustice of the Justice System," 2011, http://greekeconomistsforreform.com/public-sector-productivity/the-injustice-of-the-justice-system.

41. Spyros Skouras and Nicos Christodoulakis, "Electoral Misgovernance Cycles: Evidence from Wildfires and Tax Evasion in Greece and Elsewhere," unpublished paper, Athens University of Economics and Business, Department of International and European Economic Studies, 2010; Suzanne Daley, "Who Owns This Land? In Greece, Who Knows?" *New York Times*, May 26, 2013; Papaioannou, "The Injustice of the Justice System."

42. George Th. Mavrogordatos, "Styx and Stones," *Times Higher Education*, May 24, 2012.

43. Lewis, *Boomerang*, 44, 55.

44. McNeill, *The Metamorphosis of Modern Greece*, 95.

45. Takis Pappas, "Why Greece Failed," *Journal of Democracy* 24, no. 2 (2013): 31–45; Gerassimos Moschonas, "To Navagio tis Ellinikis oikonomias kai to PASOK. Oi politikes piges tis krisis tou chreous," unpublished manuscript, 2011, 65; Lewis, *Boomerang*, 49, 44; George, Th. Mavrogordatos, "Civil Society under Populism," in Richard Clogg, ed., *Greece: 1981–89: The Populist Decade* (New York: St. Martin Press, 1993), 61, 63; Manos Matsaganis and Aristos Doxiadis, "National Populism and Xenophobia in Greece," *Counterpoint* 2012; Skouras and Christodoulakis, "Electoral Misgovernance Cycles"; Thomadakis, *Kratos kai anaptixi stin Ellada*, 67.

46. Clogg, *A Concise History of Greece*.

47. Iordanoglou, *Kratos kai omades symferonton*, 72–77; Pappas, "Why Greece Failed."

48. Payroll costs of the public sector grew from 8.3 percent of GDP in 1974 to 9.4 percent in 1980, 11.4 percent in 1985, and 12.5 in 1990. They went down in 1995 (10.2), but up again in 2000 (10.6), 2005 (11.6), and 2009 (13.4) (Iordanoglou 2013: 53–54, 65–66). Public employment stabilized during the 1990s and rose again in the 2000s, reaching 21 percent as opposed to an OECD average of 22 percent. By 2010, the Greek state had 768,000 on its payroll, exceeding for the first time the OECD average (Iordanoglou, *Kratos kai omades symferonton*, 35–66).

49. Moschonas, "To Navagio tis Ellinikis oikonomias," 18; Iordanoglou, *Kratos kai omades symferonton*, 72–77; Mavrogordatos, "From Traditional Clientelism to Machine Politics."

50. Euklid Tsakalotos, "The Political Economy of Social Democratic Economic Policies: The PASOK Experiment in Greece," in A. Glyn, ed., *Social Democracy in Neoliberal Times: The Left and Economic Policy since 1980* (Oxford: Oxford University Press, 2001), 155; Yannis Voulgaris, *I Ellada tis Metapolitefsis* (Athens: Themelio, 2002), 161; Galenianos, "Explaining the Stagnation of the Greek

Economy." By 1983, 19 out of the 50 largest Greek firms were under state control. The total number of public enterprises reached 200 (Legg and Roberts, *Politics in Modern Greece*, 89).

51. Real GDP grew at an annual rate of 1.5 percent during 1981–1985 and 1.8 percent during 1986–1990, while total deficit as a percentage of GDP climbed from 3.6 percent in 1980 to 11 percent in 1988. By 1988, 40 percent of the revenues were dedicated to public debt service (Thomadakis, *Kratos kai anaptixi stin Ellada*, 42, 127, 137–39, 193).

52. Robert Kaplan, *Balkan Ghosts: A Journey through History* (New York: Picador, 2005), 277–79.

53. Pagoulatos, *Greece's New Political Economy*, 112–13, 151–57, 160; Kazakos, *Apo ton ateli ecsynchronismo*, 65–66; European Commission, "The Economic Adjustment Programme for Greece," Occasional Paper 61, May 2010, 7.

54. Moschonas, "To Navagio tis Ellinikis oikonomias"; Kazakos, *Apo ton ateli ecsynchronismo*; Pagoulatos, *Greece's New Political Economy*.

55. Stathis N. Kalyvas, Giorgos Pagoulatos, and Haridimos Tsoukas, eds., *From Stagnation to Forced Adjustment: Reforms in Greece, 1974–2010* (Oxford: Oxford University Press, 2013); Tasos Giannitsis, *I Ellada stin krisi* (Athens: Polis, 2013); Pagoulatos, *Greece's New Political Economy*, 220; Moschonas, "To Navagio tis Ellinikis oikonomias."

Chapter 6

1. ELSTAT data, http://m.euro2day.gr/1250650/article.aspx.

2. European Commission, "The Economic Adjustment Programme for Greece—Third Review," February 2011, http://crisisobs.gr/en/repository/?ct=98&st=104. Among OECD countries Greece scored fifth from the bottom in both mathematics and science in 2009. In 2009, the country ranked 96th among 181 countries in terms of regulatory burdens and business environment (World Bank Business Report, 2009, http://www.doingbusiness.org/

reports/global-reports/doing-business-2009/). In 2008 it ranked 67th out of 134 countries in the Global Competitiveness Index (GCI) published by the World Economic Forum (WEF) and 100th out of 178 countries in terms of ease of "Doing Business" measured by the World Bank. It had the lowest ranking of all 34 OECD members; and it ranked 34th and 38th out of 58 countries in two earlier indices used by the WEF, surpassing only one or two OECD members (Costas Arkolakis, Aristos Doxiadis, and Manolis Galenianos, "The Challenge of Trade Adjustment in Greece," unpublished paper, 2014).

3. Dionysis Chionis, *Elliniki krisi. I peripeteia tou chreous* (Athens: Papasotiriou, 2014), 25.

4. Yannis Pretenderis, *O Psychros emfylios. Ta prosopopa kai ta gegonota pou dielysan mia chora* (Athens: Patakis, 2012).

5. European Commission, "The Economic Adjustment Programme for Greece—Third Review," 3.

6. Pisani-Ferry, Sapir, and Wolff, "EU-IMF Assistance to Euro-Area Countries."

7. Article 122 of the TFEU specified that such support was permitted if the country "is in difficulties or is seriously threatened with severe difficulties caused by natural disasters or exceptional occurrences beyond its control."

8. Clive Crook, "Germany Must Decide What the European Union Is For," *Bloomberg News*, February 15, 2012.

9. George Alogoskoufis, "Macroeconomics and Politics in the Accumulation of Greece's Debt: An Econometric Investigation, 1975–2009," London School of Economics, GreeSE Paper No. 68, 2013; Moschonas, "To Navagio tis Ellinikis oikonomias"; Jorge Dis Diaz, "External Debt Statistics of the Euro Area," paper presented at the IFC Conference on "Initiatives to Address Data Gaps Revealed by the Financial Crisis," Bank for International Settlements, Basel, Switzerland, August 25–26, 2010; Costas

Azariadis, Yannis Ioannides, and Christopher A. Pissarides, "Development Is the Only Solution: 17 Proposals for a New Development Strategy," *Athens Review of Books*, May 2011.

10. Aristos Doxiadis, *To Aorato Rigma. Thesmoi kai symperifores stin Elliniki Oikonomia* (Athens: Ikaros, 2013); Nikolaos Artavanis, Adair Morse, and Margarita Tsoutsoura, "Tax Evasion across Industries: Soft Credit Evidence from Greece," Chicago Booth Paper No. 12-25, 2012; Lewis, *Boomerang*, 49–53; Pappas, "Why Greece Failed"; Manos Matsaganis and Maria Flevotomou, "Distributional Implications of Tax Evasion in Greece," GreeSE Paper No. 31, 2010, Hellenic Observatory Papers on Greece and Southeast Europe, London School of Economics.

11. Charlotte McDonald, "Are Greeks the Hardest Workers in Europe?" BBC News, February 25, 2012; Arkolakis et al., "The Challenge of Trade Adjustment in Greece," European Commission, "The Economic Adjustment Programme for Greece, " Occasional Paper 61, May 2010, http://ec.europa.eu/economy_finance/publications/occasional_paper/2010/pdf/ocp61_en.pdf, 7.

12. European Commission, "The Economic Adjustment Programme for Greece—Third Review," 17; "Consumers and Designer Brands: A Global Nielsen Report," April 2008, 2.

13. Takis Pappas and Zina Assimakopoulou, "Party Patronage in Greece: Political Entrepreneurship in a Party Patronage Democracy," in Petr Kopecký, Peter Mair, and Maria Spirova, eds., *Party Patronage and Party Government in European Democracies* (Oxford: Oxford University Press, 2012), 144, 147, 159; Dimitris Sotiropoulos, "Two Faces of Politicization of the Civil Service: The Case of Contemporary Greece," in Guy Peters and Jon Pierre, eds., *Politicization of the Civil Service in Comparative Perspective: The*

Quest for Control (London: Routledge, 2004), 268; Mavrogordatos, "From Traditional Clientelism to Machine Politics."

14. George Th. Mavrogordatos, *Omades piesis kai dimokratia*, 3rd ed. (Athens: Patakis, 2005).

15. Iordanoglou, *Kratos kai omades symferonton* and Mavrogordatos, *Omades piesis kai dimokratia* provide an extensive and subtle analysis of this process.

16. Manos Matsaganis, "The Welfare State and the Crisis: The Case of Greece," *Journal of European Social Policy* 21, no. 5 (2011): 501–13; Michael Mitsopoulos and Theodore Pelagidis, "Vikings in Greece: Kleptocratic Interest Groups in a Closed, Rent-Seeking Economy," *Cato Journal* 29, no. 3 (2009): 399–416; Stephen Grey and Dina Kyriakidou, "A Nexus of Media, Business and Politics Lies behind the Country's Crisis, Say Critics," Reuters, December 17, 2012.

17. Pavlos Eleftheriadis, "The Structure of Greek Oligarchy," unpublished paper, 2013; Artavanis et al., "Tax Evasion across Industries."

18. Doxiadis, *To Aorato Rigma*; Iordanoglou, *Kratos kai omades symferonton*, 78–111; Mitsopoulos and Pelagidis, "Vikings in Greece"; Eleftheriadis, "Structure of Greek Oligarchy."

19. Iannis Konstandinidis and Georgios Xezonakis, "Sources of Tolerance for Corrupted Politicians in Greece: The Role of Trade Offs and Individual Benefits," *Crime, Law, and Social Change* 60 (2013): 549–63; Mitsopoulos and Pelagidis, "Vikings in Greece"; Kazakos, *Apo ton ateli ecsynchronismo*, 112; Lewis, *Boomerang*, 54.

20. Matsaganis, "The Welfare State and the Crisis"; Iordanoglou, *Kratos kai omades symferonton*; Mavrogordatos, *Omades piesis kai dimokratia*; Mavrogordatos, "From Traditional Clientelism to Machine Politics"; Doxiadis, *To Aorato Rigma*.

21. International Monetary Fund, "Greece: Ex Post Evaluation of Exceptional Access under the 2010 Stand-By Arrangement," June 10, 2013.

22. International Monetary Fund, "Greece: Staff Report on Request for Stand-By Arrangement," IMF Country Report No. 10/110, May 2010.

23. Pisani-Ferry at al., "EU-IMF Assistance to Euro-Area Countries," 45–51.

24. European Commission, "The Second Economic Adjustment Programme for Greece—First Review," December 2012, 58.

25. Pisani-Ferry et al., "EU-IMF Assistance to Euro-Area Countries."

26. Pisani-Ferry et al., "EU-IMF Assistance to Euro-Area Countries," 7–12.

27. Pisani-Ferry et al., "EU-IMF Assistance to Euro-Area Countries," 44.

28. Pisani-Ferry et al., "EU-IMF Assistance to Euro-Area Countries"; International Monetary Fund (IMF), "IMF Country Report No. 13/20," January 2013.

29. Pisani-Ferry et al., "EU-IMF Assistance to Euro-Area Countries."

30. Arkolakis et al, "The Challenge of Trade Adjustment in Greece"; Doxiadis, *To Aorato Rigma*.

31. Paul de Grauwe and Yuemei Ji, "The Legacy of Austerity in the Eurozone," CEPS Commentary, 2013; Nikos Chrysoloras, "Greece's Successful Death" (Athens: Eliamep Policy Paper No. 16, 2013); Matthew Lynn, *Bust: Greece, the Euro, and the Sovereign Debt Crisis* (Hoboken, N.J.: Bloomberg Press, 2011).

32. Lynn, *Bust*, 200; International Monetary Fund, "World Economic Outlook," October 2013; *Kathimerini*, September 16, 2014.

33. European Commission (2012); IMF (2013); Pisani-Ferry et al., "EU-IMF Assistance to Euro-Area Countries."

34. Simon Kennedy, "How Roubini Got It Wrong on a Greece Eurozone Exit," *Bloomberg News*, January 21, 2013, http://business. financialpost.com/2013/01/21/how-roubini-got-it-wrong-on-a-

greece-eurozone-exit/; Opinions cited by Lynn, *Bust*, 211–220; Stathis Kouvelakis, "The Greek Cauldron," *New Left Review* 72 (2011): 31–32.

35. Spiegel, "How the Euro Was Saved."

36. Georgios Karyotis and Wolfgang Rüdig, "Blame and Punishment? The Electoral Politics of Extreme Austerity in Greece," *Political Studies*, forthcoming; Doxiadis and Matsaganis, "National Populism and Xenophobia," 47–52; Pisani-Ferry et al., "EU-IMF Assistance to Euro-Area Countries"; Moschonas, "To Navagio tis Ellinikis oikonomias," 68–69.

37. Stathis N. Kalyvas, "Greece Votes Itself in the Foot: The Rise of the Coalition of the Radical Left and the Demise of Europe," *Foreign Affairs*, June 12, 2012.

38. Elias Dinas, Vassiliki Georgiadou, Iannis Konstantinidis, and Lamprini Rori, "From Dusk to Dawn: Local Party Organization and Party Success of Right-Wing Extremism," *Party Politics*, forthcoming; Doxiadis and Matsaganis, "National Populism and Xenophobia"; Kalyvas, "Greece Votes Itself in the Foot."

39. Bank of Greece, *To Chroniko is megalis krisis. I Trapeza tis Ellados, 2008–2013* (Athens: n.p., 2014); Peter Spiegel, "Inside Europe's Plan Z," *Financial Times*, May 14, 2014.

40. "Within our mandate, the ECB is ready to do whatever it takes to preserve the euro. And, believe me, it will be enough." Speech by Mario Draghi, President of the European Central Bank, at the Global Investment Conference in London, July 26, 2012, https://www.ecb.europa.eu/press/key/date/2012/html/sp120726.en.html.

41. Kennedy, "How Roubini Got It Wrong"; Chrysoloras, "Greece's Successful Death."

Chapter 7

1. McNeill, *The Metamorphosis of Modern Greece*, 247. For a similar point, see also Kurtovik, *Elliniko hangover*, 41.

2. Llewellyn Smith, *Ionian Vision*, xiv.

3. Ivo Banac, "Misreading the Balkans," *Foreign Policy* 93 (1993): 181; Todorova, *Imagining the Balkans*, 185.

4. Lynn, *Bust*, 220.

5. Karamouzi, "Greece's Path," 81–82.

6. Ibid.

SUGGESTIONS FOR FURTHER READING

Below is a small selection of books in English that are accessible to readers seeking to learn more about specific periods and topics of modern Greek history.

For a succinct introduction to modern Greek history, see Richard Clogg, *A Concise History of Greece*, 3rd ed. (Cambridge: Cambridge University Press, 2013); and John S. Koliopoulos and Thanos M. Veremis, *Modern Greece: A History since 1821* (Chichester: Wiley-Blackwell, 2009). A broader regional perspective is provided by Mark Mazower, *The Balkans: A Short History* (New York: Modern Library, 2000).

On the Greek Enlightenment and War of Independence, see Paschalis Kitromilides, *Enlightenment and Revolution: The Making of Modern Greece* (Cambridge, Mass.: Harvard University Press, 2013); David Brewer, *The Flame of Freedom: The Greek War of Independence, 1821–1833* (London: John Murray, 2001); and Gary Bass, *Freedom's Battle: The Origins of Humanitarian Intervention* (New York: Alfred Knopf, 2008).

On the politics of state building and nation building in the new Greek state, see John Anthony Petropulos, *Politics and Statecraft in the Kingdom of Greece, 1833–43* (Princeton: Princeton University Press, 1968); John S. Koliopoulos, *Brigands with a Cause: Brigandage and Irredentism in Modern Greece, 1821–1912* (Oxford: Clarendon Press, 1987); and Victor Papacosma, *The Military in Greek Politics: The 1909 Coup d' Etat* (Kent, Ohio: Kent State University Press, 1977).

On the Anatolian disaster and population exchange, see Michael Llewellyn Smith, *Ionian Vision: Greece in Asia Minor 1919–1922* (London: Hurst, 1998); and Bruce Clark, *Twice a Stranger: The Mass Expulsions That Forged Modern Greece and Turkey* (Cambridge, Mass.: Harvard University Press, 2009). Two novels that draw on this event in a highly readable and insightful way are Jeffrey Eugenides, *Middlesex* (New York: Farrar, Straus & Giroux, 2002); and Louis de Bernières, *Birds without Wings* (New York: Knopf, 2004). Interwar politics are analyzed masterfully in George Th. Mavrogordatos, *Stillborn Republic: Social Coalitions and Party Strategies in Greece, 1922–1936* (Berkeley: University of California Press, 1983).

For the occupation and Civil War see Mark Mazower, *Inside Hitler's Greece: The Experience of Occupation, 1941–44* (New Haven: Yale University Press, 1993); Christopher Montague Woodhouse, *Apple of Discord: A Survey of Recent Greek Politics in Their International Setting* (London: Hutchinson, 1948); and David H. Close, *The Origins of the Greek Civil War* (London: Longman, 1993). A combination of personal memoir and journalistic investigation, Nicolas Gage's *Eleni* (New York: Random House, 1983) provides a richly textured description of the Civil War in a mountain village.

On postwar politics, see Evanthis Hatzivasiliou, *Greece and the Cold War: Frontline State, 1952–1967* (London: Routledge, 2006); David Close, *Greece since 1945: Politics, Economy, and Society* (Harlow: Pearson, 2002); and especially William H. McNeill, *The Metamorphosis of Modern Greece since World War II* (Chicago: University of Chicago Press, 1978). On terrorism see John Brady Kiesling, *Greek Urban Warriors. Resistance & Terrorism 1967-2012* (Athens: Lycabettus Press, 2014).

On the most recent developments, see Stathis N. Kalyvas, Giorgos Pagoulatos, and Haridimos Tsoukas, eds., *From Stagnation to Forced Adjustment: Reforms in Greece, 1974–2010* (Oxford: Oxford University Press, 2013); Takis S. Pappas, *Populism and Crisis Politics in Greece* (New York: Palgrave Macmillan, 2014); Yannis Palaiologos, *The 13th Labour of Hercules. Inside the Greek Crisis* (London: Portobello Books); and John Peet and Anton LaGuardia, *Unhappy Union: How the Euro Crisis—and Europe—Can Be Fixed* (London: Economist Books, 2014).

INDEX